SYMPHONY OF SCRIPTURES

AN INTERTEXTUAL STUDY OF ACTS 10:1–15:35

SYMPHONY OF SCRIPTURES

AN INTERTEXTUAL STUDY OF ACTS 10:1–15:35

Zsolt Barta

GLOSSAHOUSE DISSERTATION SERIES VOLUME 7
GDS 7

GlossaHouse
Wilmore, KY
GH
www.glossahouse.com

SYMPHONY OF SCRIPTURES:

AN INTERTEXTUAL STUDY OF ACTS 10:1–15:35

GlossaHouse, LLC
110 Callis Circle
Wilmore, KY 40309
www.GlossaHouse.com

Barta, Zsolt, 1978-

Symphony of Scriptures: An Intertextual Study of Acts 10:1–15:35
Zsolt Barta. – Wilmore, KY : GlossaHouse, ©2018.
xii, 249 pages 22.86 cm. — (GlossaHouse dissertation series; volume 7)

A revision of the author's dissertation (doctoral), Eötvös Loránd University, Faculty of Humanities, 2016.

Includes bibliographical references and indexes.

1. Bible. Acts, X, 15-XV, 35 --Criticism, interpretation, etc. I. Title. II. Series.
BS2625.52.B377 2018 262

Library of Congress Control Number: 2018947147
ISBN 978-1942697626 (paperback)
ISBN 978-1942697633 (hardback)

The fonts used to create this work are available from
www.linguistsoftware.com/lgku.htm
Cover design by T. Michael W. Halcomb
Text layout and book design by Carl S. Sweatman

To Balázs and Andrew

GlossaHouse
GlossaHouse Dissertations Series

GLOSSAHOUSE DISSERTATION SERIES

The goal of the GlossaHouse Dissertation Series to facilitate the creation and publication of innovative, affordable, and accessible scholarly resources, whether print or digital, that advance research in the areas of both ancient and modern texts and languages.

Table Of Contents

ABBREVIATIONS

The abbreviations used throughout this work follow the standard forms, as established by and found in the *SBL Handbook of Style*, 2nd edition (2014). Those employed in this work, but not appearing in the *Handbook*, are listed here according to abbreviation:

BHHB	Baylor Handbook on the Hebrew Bible
COTC	Calvin's Commentary on the Old Testament
EBC	Expositor's Bible Commentary
JLS	*Journal of Literary Studies*
JPSBC	JPS Bible Commentary
JPSTC	JPS Torah Commentary
THL	Theory and History of Literature

PREFACE

This work was initially motivated by the simple purpose of achieving a narrative critical study of Acts 10:1–15:35. During the course of interpretation, the selected text's connections with utterances from the Old Testament (OT) were examined. The intertextual dimension of the narratives in Acts, however, demanded attention on its own right and thus became the primary focus of study.

The shift of focus from narratology to intertextuality came with the challenge of presenting a comprehensive methodology for studying textual correlations in the book of Acts. The conversion of the Gentiles along with related narratives in the six chapters in Acts offer multiple instances of intertextuality. Quotes, allusions, and verbal correspondences are easily detectable in the text. Narratives and utterances in Acts, moreover, evoke themes and forms of the OT without making reference to individual passages. When examining the rich and multi-layered connectedness between narratives in Acts and the OT, a reader can feel overwhelmed and puzzled. In an earnest search for a comprehensive methodology, the notion of establishing a single unified mode of evoking Scripture had to be rejected. Although during my research I was inspired by many proposals of intertextuality from the field of biblical scholarship, in the end the methodology applied in this work was based on an understanding of textual correlation as proposed by French literary scholar Gérard Genette.

Matters related to methodology, however, do not constitute the main subject of this work. The primary purpose is to offer a precise and sensitive intertextual reading of narratives in Acts that helps to appreciate the plurality of textual connections. Luke writes of "events that have been fulfilled among us" (Luke 1:1) in reference to what is recounted in Luke-Acts. Luke understands the events he wrote down as being fulfillments of God's will. The OT represents most clearly God's ancient purpose. Narratives of the early church, therefore, are told in relation to the will of God revealed in the OT. A continuous dialogue is achieved in Acts between God's faithfulness to his people in the past and the stories of mission and conversion among the Gentiles. Discerning formal and substantial patterns of that dialogue is the task undertaken in this work.

Chapter 1
METHOD OF STUDY AND THE SELECTED TEXT

1.1. Introduction

The aim of this work is to study the intertextual correlations of a central section in the book of Acts of the New Testament (NT). Acts 10:1–15:35 takes the readers on a journey from the conversion of a Roman Centurion through ambiguous events and debates to the decree of the Jerusalem Council on receiving the Gentile converts in the church. These chapters in Acts reveal the challenges, the theological debates, and the evaluation of the events that shaped and redefined the very identity of the early church at a crucial turning point in its history.

Undoubtedly, a vital aspect of the process is the use of Scripture. The Scriptures of Israel play a crucial role in framing the dilemmas and offering solutions on the matter. Events are thus portrayed in conformity with certain narratives of the OT, Scripture verses are quoted by missionaries and leaders to support certain arguments, characters are shown in contrast and harmony with well known figures of the ancient holy narratives. The challenge lies not so much in identifying the right words, phrases, narratives, themes or books of the OT that are evoked in Acts but much rather in defining patterns of textual correlations. This is precisely the goal of this work. Mainly but not exclusively relying on French literary theorist Gérard Genette's map of transtextuality, it is the goal of this study to enumerate, to group and to evaluate textual connections in Acts 10:1–15:35.

Thus, the primary intention of this study is to arrive at a better understanding of what is commonly designated as intertextuality of the selected portion of Acts. However, this undertaking will have both methodological and theoretical implications for biblical scholarship. This will be especially true if one considers that, apparently, there were no attempts made in biblical scholarship to accommodate the types of transtextuality Genette proposed. This makes methodological considerations inevitable. The relevant segments of Genette's theory will be introduced, evaluated, adjusted, and modified as necessary; thus, new suggestions will be made within the frame of the Genettian textual correlations. All this work, however, will be undertaken with the intention to keep the primary focus on the text itself.

1.2. Intertextuality, Transtextuality, and the Nature of Dialogue

When pursuing an intertextual interpretation of a selected text within the Bible one is faced with the double task of clarifying a theory of intertextual relations and demonstrating a methodology. Both tasks are to be performed against the backdrop of a flourishing and occasionally confusing complexity of definitions and methodologies within the field of biblical scholarship. It is the goal of this chapter to reveal the theoretical basis for interpreting textual connections in general and in Acts 10:1–15:35 in particular.

The term intertextuality was introduced to French academic circles by Julia Kristeva in the 1960s in her attempt to introduce Russian literary theoretician Mikhail Bakhtin. Kristeva's views on the subject are most articulate in a chapter titled "Le mot, le dialogue, le roman" published in her book, *Sèméiotikè* in 1969.[1] In an attempt to correct structuralism, the dominant approach of the time, Kristeva envisioned a different understanding of texts. In contrast to structuralist thinking, she proposed that structures do not exist in themselves: they are to be seen and examined in their relations to other structures. As a result of her efforts, the generation of meaning was relocated in a wholly new context. Kristeva held that "any text is constructed as a mosaic of quotations; any text is an absorption and transformation of another."[2] She argued that the literary word is "an intersection of textual surfaces rather than a point (fixed meaning) … a dialogue among several

[1] Julia Kristeva, *Sèméiotikè: recherches pour une sémanalyse* (Paris: Éditions du Seuil, 1969).

[2] Julia Kristeva, *The Kristeva Reader*, ed. Toril Moi (New York: Columbia University Press, 1986), 37.

writings: that of the writer, the addressee (or the character) and the contemporary or earlier cultural context."[3] Stefan Alkier, a noted German scholar of biblical intertextuality, pointed out that Kristeva's theory of text extends to the semiotics of culture. Kristeva treated the text not as a closed structure but as a relational phenomenon: "It maintains relationships to other texts and to the one "general text," which Kristeva designates as "culture.""[4]

Kristeva's main concern appears to promote a poetics that treats dialogue and ambivalence as essential aspects of the poetic word. Those two terms are taken from the work of Russian literary theorist Mikhail Bakhtin (Михаи́л Миха́йлович Бахти́н). Indeed, the very notion and concept of intertextuality was first presented as an interpretation of Bakhtin's views.[5] Some of Bakhtin's ideas are presented here to introduce the main questions of intertextuality.

From the early 1920s Bakhtin emphasized the social and historical context of all utterances. He claimed that language does not exist in isolation but is utilised by people in certain contexts. Sentences that can have one meaning on an abstract level can have very different meanings depending on the situations in which they are uttered. Words that have no meaning at all in themselves can say much if the situation of the addresser and of the addressee in taken into consideration. It follows from this argument, that language is always in relation to what has been said before. All utterances are in relation to patterns of previous and future forms and modes of communication. It this sense, each utterance is dialogic inasmuch as it is understood in the light of what has been said before. It is concluded therefore that no abstract linguistic system is able to convey the sense of dialogic vividness

---

[3] Ibid., 36.

[4] Stefan Alkier, "Intertextuality and the Semiotics of Biblical Texts," in *Reading the Bible Intertextually*, ed. Richard B. Hays, Stefan Alkier, and Leroy A. Huizenga (Waco, TX: Baylor University Press, 2009), 4.

[5] Bakhtin has many followers among theologians. Barbara Green recently wrote a summary on how Bakhtin is followed by biblical scholars. See Barbara Green, *Mikhail Bakhtin and Biblical Scholarship: An Introduction* (Atlanta: Society of Biblical Literature, 2005).

present in each utterance. The relational character of words is not limited to relations within an abstract system but much rather stands in connection with concrete social situations. Each word is determined, according to Bakhtin, by those who speak and those to whom the utterance is addressed. There is, therefore, a relation with the other that determines the concrete utterance.[6] Dialogism that characterizes all of language serves as a central concept.

In Bakhtin's opinion it is necessary, but at the same time insufficient to examine literary works purely on linguistic grounds. Linguistics can only concentrate on semantics and therefore loses sight of the dialogic nature of utterances. Bakhtin does not only concentrate on language when proposing theories of literature but advocates for examining discourse: "Discourse, that is, language in its concrete living totality, and not language as the specific object of linguistics, something arrived at through a completely legitimate and necessary abstraction from various aspects of the concrete life of the word."[7] This task can be achieved by metalinguistics with which linguistics shares a common ground but should not be confused with it.[8]

The most influential work by Bakhtin on the subject relevant for the purpose of this study is, *Проблемы поэтики Достоевского*[9] (*The Problems of Dostoevsky's Poetics*). At the centre of the book stands an evaluation of Dostoevsky's voluminous work. On the one hand, it is not without challenge, as has been pointed out by Allen,[10] to read Bakhtin as the forerunner of Kristeva's intertextuality. As the title, *The Problems of Dostoevsky's Poetics*, suggests, the book deals with issues pertaining to the work of the Russian novelist and not to a general theory of texts and even less to a model to be followed by contemporary writers. On the other hand, Bakhtin's observations

---

[6] Graham Allen, *Intertextuality* (London: Routledge, 2000), 17–20.

[7] Mikhail Bakhtin, *Problems of Dostoevsky's Poetics*, ed. Caryl Emerson, trans. Caryl Emerson (Minneapolis: University of Minnesota Press, 1984), 181.

[8] Ibid., 181–85.

[9] Михаил Михайлович Бахтин, *Проблемы поэтики Достоевского* (Москва - Augsburg: Werden-Verlag, 2002).

[10] Allen, *Intertextuality*, 42.

regarding certain aspects of Dostoevsky's novels are linked to general observation about dialogue and doubleness potentially present in all of human utterances and to some extent in culture in general. Added to this, one cannot escape noting how committed Bakhtin's text proves to dialogue when reading lines like this: "Two voices is the minimum for life, the minimum for existence."[11] More than this, Bakhtin suggests that dialogue constitutes an integral part of human existence and that it was demonstrated in an unprecedented, unique way in Dostoevsky's artistic achievement. To take this point further, one can learn more about the nature of this dialogue:

> The polyphonic approach has nothing in common with relativism (or with dogmatism). But it should be noted that both relativism and dogmatism equally exclude all argumentation, all authentic dialogue, by making it either unnecessary (relativism) or impossible (dogmatism). Polyphony as an artistic method lies in an entirely different plane.[12]

At the very least one can detect a sense of determination to dialogue that is achieved by polyphony and finds at times more limited expression in several areas of literature.

Bakhtin begins by observing that characters in Dostoevsky's novels have a great deal of complexity and autonomy in relation to that of the author. Bakhtin admires the way Dostoevsky endowed his characters with independence and freedom.[13] They are "not voiceless slaves…but *free* people, capable of standing alongside their creator, capable of *not agreeing* with him and even of *rebelling* against him."[14] Bakhtin characterized this phenomenon by the word *polyphonic* and sees in Dostoevsky the creator of a new invention, the polyphonic novel: "A plurality of independent and unmerged voices and

---

[11] Ibid., 252.

[12] Bakhtin, *Problems*, 69.

[13] Ibid., 5.

[14] Ibid., 6.

consciousnesses, a genuine polyphony of fully valid voices is in fact the chief characteristic of Dostoevsky's novels."[15]

The world of this new type of novel may seem chaotic and unorganised at times. Only an understanding of Dostoevsky's artistic design will enable the readers to see cohesion and overall consistency in the novel.[16] However, the independence of characters will not result in falling out of the overall artistic plan. The incorporation of independent ideas presented by very different characters will not break the organic unity of Dostoevsky's work:

> His task: to overcome the greatest difficulty that an artist can face, to create out of heterogeneous and profoundly disparate materials of varying worth a unified and integral artistic creation. Thus the Book of Job, the Revelation of St. John, the Gospel texts, the discourses of St. Simeon the New Theologian, everything that feeds the pages of his novels and contributes tone to one or another of his chapters, is combined here in a most original way with the newspaper, the anecdote, the parody, the street scene, with the grotesque, even with the pamphlet. He boldly casts into his crucibles ever newer elements, knowing and believing that in the blaze of his creative work these raw chunks of everyday life, the sensations of boulevard novels and the divinely inspired pages of Holy Writ, will melt down and fuse in a new compound, and take on the deep imprint of his personal style and tone.[17]

However, Bakhtin is eager to point out that dialogue is not simply a device subordinated to a hidden authorial agenda, but in fact

---

[15] Ibid.

[16] Bakhtin, *Problems*.

[17] Леонид Петрович Гроссман, *Поэтика Достоевского* (Москва: Государственная академия художественных наук, 1925), 175–76 in Bakhtin, *Problems*, 15.

constitutes the very fabric of the novel. And he is even more eager to demonstrate that artistic design in not achieved by monologic strategy:

> Dostoevsky's world is profoundly pluralistic. If we were to seek an image toward which this whole world gravitates, an image in the spirit of Dostoevsky's own worldview, then it would be the church as a communion of unmerged souls, where sinners and righteous men come together; or perhaps it would be the image of Dante's world, where multi-leveledness is extended into eternity, where there are the penitent and the unrepentant, the damned and the saved. Such an image would be in the style of Dostoevsky himself, or, more precisely, in the style of his ideology, while the image of a unified spirit is deeply alien to him.[18]

The idea, or to be more precise, the interaction with the idea is of central significance in understanding the artistic word of Dostoevsky: "the idea really does become almost the hero of the work."[19] There is a special role to ideas throughout the novels since each character seems to be possessed by an idea. More than this, there is an endless interaction, a never-ending quarrel between characters and ideas. Dostoevsky's world is characterised primarily by coexistence and interaction of ideas and characters. He writes:

> Dostoevsky neither knows, nor perceives, nor represents the "idea in itself" in the Platonic sense, nor "ideal existence" as phenomenologists understand it. For Dostoevsky there are no ideas, no thoughts, no positions which belong to no one, which exist "in themselves." Even "truth in itself" he presents in the spirit of Christian ideology, as incarnated in Christ; that is, he

---

[18] Bakhtin, *Problems*, 26–27.

[19] Ibid., 78.

> presents it as a personality entering into relationships with other personalities.[20]

The interaction between ideas and characters contributes toward changing both. Characters identify with ideas, whereas ideas receive a personal flavour. Bakhtin writes: "And the result is an artistic fusion, so characteristic for Dostoevsky, of personal life with worldview, of the most intimate experiences with the idea. Personal life becomes uniquely unselfish and principled, and lofty ideological thinking becomes passionate and intimately linked with personality."[21]

An even further aspect of the interaction receives articulation. The on-going dialogue in Dostoevsky's work is not limited by time:

> "Reality in its entirety," Dostoevsky himself wrote, "is not to be exhausted by what is immediately at hand, for an overwhelming part of this reality is contained in the form of a *still latent, unuttered future Word*." In the dialogue of his time Dostoevsky also heard resonances of the voice-ideas of the past—both the most recent past ... and the more remote.... Thus on the plane of the present there came together and quarrelled past, present, and future.[22]

In a world of dialogue, it is nearly impossible to identify certain words with certain individuals in separation. Every word is mediated by others thus modifying its meaning and altering its path: "Our practical everyday speech is full of other people's words: with some of them we completely merge our own voice, forgetting whose they are; others, which we take as authoritative, we use to reinforce our own words; still others, finally, we populate with our own aspirations, alien or

[20] Ibid., 31–32.
[21] Ibid., 79.
[22] Ibid., 90.

hostile to them."[23] Words are never owned by anyone and yet they are used and mediated by a great number of characters.

Kristeva used Bakhtin's thoughts on dialogue, polyphony, ambiguity, mediated word and on the innumerable voices in the text to propose a general idea of what she called intertextuality. Following Kristeva's engagement with Bakhtin, the concept of intertextuality was examined and adapted by structuralist theoreticians. Allen suggests that from the 1960s onwards one could detect the presence of a more circumscribed form of intertextuality distinct from the one initially based on a post-structuralist frame of thought.[24] My own reading of Acts 10–15 has been greatly inspired and influenced by French literary theorist Gérard Genette's thoughts on intertextuality or transtextuality as he prefers to term it. His general considerations and the five types of transtextuality in particular provide the framework for my own interpretation of the selected texts in Acts. It is necessary therefore to outline his propositions regarding textual relations.

In his trilogy *Introduction à l'architexte* (1979),[25] *Palimpsestes* (1982)[26] and *Seuils* (1987)[27] Genette produces a coherent theory and a complete map of what he terms as transtextuality.[28] In *The Architext*,[29] Genette starts by exploring the classical triad of genres—lyric, epic and drama—generally attributed to Plato and Aristotle by a great number of scholars.[30] The author soon proposes that a confusion in treating the triad stems from the inability to distinguish mode from genre. Lyric, epic and drama appear to refer to at least two partly

---

[23] Ibid., 195.

[24] Allen, *Intertextuality*, 95.

[25] Gerard Genette, *Introduction à l'architexte* (Paris: Seuil, 1979).

[26] Gérard Genette, *Palimpsestes. La littérature au second degré* (Paris: Seuil, 1982).

[27] Gérard Genette, *Seuils* (Paris: Seuil, 1987).

[28] Allen, *Intertextuality*, 98.

[29] Gérard Genette, *The Architext: An Introduction*, trans. Jane E. Lewin (Berkeley: University of California Press, 1992).

[30] A similar treatment is achieved by Northrop Frye—see *Anatomy of Criticism: Four Essays*, 15th ed. (Princeton: Princeton University Press, 2000).

overlapping categories. On the one hand, the above-named terms can simply mean modes of enunciation: in lyric only the author speaks, in epic both the author and the characters speak, in drama only the characters speak. On the other hand, one can also describe genre defined by content or thematic elements using the same triad. The modes of enunciation can be referred to as natural forms the same way as one can speak of natural languages.

The main difference according to Genette stands in the fact that genres are literary categories whereas modes are categories that belong to linguistics.[31] Therefore, one should really speak of modes (pure narration/mixed narration/pure dramatic imitation) and genres (lyric/epic/dramatic) as two separate types that have a complex relationship with one another not based solely on inclusion. Genette has effectively demonstrated that the confusing and insufficient categories cannot be the building blocks for poetics. At this point he turns to what is called transtextuality in his work: "The text interests me (only) in its textual transcendence—namely, everything that brings it into relation (manifest or hidden) with other texts."[32] According to Allen transtextuality "includes issues of imitation, transformation, the classification of types of discourse, along with the thematic, modal, generic and formal categories and categorizations of traditional poetics."[33]

In *Palimpsests* Genette takes up again and further clarifies the subject of transtextuality. He declares that the text should not be read as a singularity but in all its transtextual relations and goes on to propose a "kind of open-structuralism."[34] In the Genettian system, transtextuality can be considered as the equivalent of Kristeva's intertextuality and what most scholars today call intertextuality.

---

[31] Genette, *Architext*, 63–64.

[32] Ibid., 81.

[33] Allen, *Intertextuality*, 100.

[34] Gérard Genette, *Palimpsests: Literature in the Second Degree*, trans. Channa Newman and Claude Doubinsky, 8th ed. (Lincoln: University of Nebraska Press, 1997), 399.

Genette makes a further significant observation with regard to the orientation of his notion of transtextuality. While another great theorist of the time Riffaterre observes intertextuality at the level of sentences and fragments, that is to say on a semantic level, Genette is mainly interested in the "work considered as a structural whole."[35]

Genette divides transtextuality into five types. He lists them "in increasing abstraction, implication, and comprehensiveness."[36] *Intertextuality* as the first type is defined "as the actual presence of one text within another."[37] Quotations, plagiarism, and allusions are included in this type. With regard to the latter, Genette argues that allusion will contribute toward an understanding of the full meaning of the enunciation whereas the opposite will render the text unintelligible.

The second type, *paratextuality* is of such great importance to Genette that he devoted an entire book.[38] Paratext is related to the pragmatic dimensions of the text. It includes notices, forewords, illustrations, book covers, commentary, etc. These markers show the potential of influencing readers and of determining interpretation.[39] Paratextual dimensions of Acts 10:1–15:35 will not be examined in the dissertation for two reasons. First, paratext is said to be of liminal character since it surrounds the text itself. It is a threshold, "a zone between text and off-text."[40] Paratextuality is concerned with reception and reading. In this regard paratextuality can be separated from the other types of transtextuality. The second reason for not discussing paratextuality is more practical. Genette claims that "The paratext...is empirically made up of a heterogeneous group of practices and discourses of all kinds and dating from all periods."[41] Once this remark is applied to the vast number of paratexts added to the Bible, it will

---

[35] Ibid., 2–3.

[36] Ibid., 1.

[37] Ibid., 2.

[38] Gérard Genette, *Paratexts: Thresholds of Interpretation*, trans. Jane E. Lewin (Cambridge: Cambridge University Press, 1997).

[39] Genette, *Palimpsests*, 4.

[40] Genette, *Paratexts*, 2.

[41] Ibid.

become clear that biblical paratextuality deserves academic attention on its own.

The third type, *metatextuality*, remains somewhat underdeveloped in Genette's work. The term is identical with commentary. A text can speak of another text without necessarily citing or even naming it. Metatextuality mainly concerns silent evoking.[42] In addition, the term *metatext* in today's academic world is generally accepted to express textual relations when one text describes or explains another.

Palimpsests, Genette's second major work on transtextuality, is entirely devoted to *hypertextuality*, the fourth type. By hypertextuality he means "any relationship uniting a text B (which I shall call *hypertext*) to an earlier text A (I shall, of course, call it the *hypotext*), upon which it is grafted in a manner that is not that of commentary."[43] A text is produced by derivation of any kind from an earlier text. Still, another type might be that text B will not mention text A, but could not exist without it. In all cases an act of transformation or a transformative process has to take place. Genette puts more emphasis on silent evoking, but does not exclude citing as being part of hypertextuality.[44] It has been demonstrated that *Aeneid* and *Ulysses* are both hypertexts of the same hypotext, the *Odyssey*. The transformation leading from the work of Homer in those works is not the same though.

One could speak of a *simple* or *direct* transformation in *Ulysses* where action is transposed into a different location and different time. Virgil, on the other hand, tells a different story by imitating Homer on a generic level, thus one can speak of *imitation*. Imitation is more complex than direct transformation. Imitation requires a process of transformation through which one is able to establish a generic model from a singular performance and generate one or more mimetic performances. The two types of transformation retain two distinct characteristics of the pre-existent text. One transposes action and

---

[42] Genette, *Palimpsests*, 4.
[43] Ibid., 5.
[44] Ibid.

relationships that are treated in a different style; the other keeps the style but tells a completely different story. But this is not simply the question of telling the same thing in a different style and telling a different thing in the same style. Imitation entails identifying a certain manner of a given utterance and then producing new utterances in the same manner.[45] The boundaries are first presented to be clear cut but later Genette admits that mixed practices are a very real possibility: "The same hypertext may simultaneously transform a hypotext and imitate another."[46]

Added to the two kinds of relations of hypertextuality (i.e., transformation and imitation) Genette introduces the idea of mood, which can be playful, satirical, or serious. Consequently, there will be six major categories in this relationship: playful transformation is parody, satirical transformation is travesty; serious transformation is called transposition; playful imitation is pastiche, satirical imitation is caricature, serious imitation is forgery. It is added immediately that these boundaries are arbitrary and are more often blurred than not.[47] Genette's idea of mood is a necessary step toward determining hypertextual relations in precision.

Whereas transformation and imitation mainly concern hypertextual technique, mood enquires about the effect created in the hypertext by the presence of the hypotext. To further specify mood, Genette adds more moods to his charts imagined in a circle. The three moods are pictured as three colours with shades in between them. Between playful and satirical ironic is placed; between satiric and serious polemical is inserted; between serious and playful humorous is inserted. The mood circle runs from playful through humorous to serious; from serious through polemical to satiric; from satiric through ironic to playful again.[48] Even here the boundaries are more fluid than clear-cut. Although Genette in his book decides to interpret texts that

---

[45] Ibid., 6.
[46] Ibid., 30.
[47] Ibid., 28.
[48] Ibid., 29.

appear to be strongly hypertextual, he nevertheless argues that hypertextuality can be an aspect of any literary work.[49] Out of the several moods only serious imitation and serious transformation will be appealed to since they have relevance for Acts.

The final type is termed *architextuality*. The silent connections discussed here are questions of genre. It is by paratextual reference, titles, and subtitles that the reader is able to receive direct architectural information. Even then the readers may suspect or refuse the paratext and make their own inference. In most instances, however, works do not identify themselves as poems, or novels. Nevertheless, it is safe to claim that generic understanding will greatly bear upon every reading of every work mainly by creating expectation that potentially leads to a generic pact.[50]

In his earlier work, Genette explored more fully and more fluidly the notion of architextuality in terms of textual transcendence: "The architext is, then everywhere—above, beneath, around the text, which spins its web only by hooking it here and there onto the network of architexture."[51] It is not only genre in general that he had in view when writing of the architext. It was insisted upon that the architextual transcendence of the text should be investigated by a number of disciplines. The theory of genres is listed among the perspectives that should be employed. But others, like the theory of modes, theory of figures, theory of styles, theory of forms, theory of themes, should constitute a part in examining the architextual transcendence.[52] It is to be pointed out that Genette later employed a more precise and somewhat altered terminology. Architextuality seems to have been reduced to the question of genre in Genette's thought. Transtextuality took the place of what architextuality stood for earlier.[53] Another

---

[49] Ibid., 9.

[50] Ibid., 4–5.

[51] Genette, *Architext*, 92.

[52] Ibid., 83–84.

[53] Genette says: "Today I prefer to say, more sweepingly, that the subject of poetics is *transtextuality*, or the textual transcendence of the text, which I have already defined roughly as 'all that sets the text in a relationship, whether obvious or concealed.'

change seems to have taken place by subsuming style under hypertextuality as imitation.

In my view architextuality should include all those fields that Genette earlier assigned to it. Thematic, modal and formal connections continue to be viewed as architextual connections. With regard to style, it can be a real border case. If the style of a singular work were imitated by another work, it would rightly be seen as a case of hypertextuality. If, however, a larger corpus is imitated this could be a case of architextuality. This is the approach assumed in this work.

It is imperative to heed the warning by the theorist that the five types of transtextuality are not being viewed as entirely separate categories. On the contrary, their relationship is that of mutuality and reciprocity.[54] A reader can detect architextual relations that can be established through paratexts. For instance, the title of a given work can convey its genre by calling it poem or novel. Other times architextuality is perceived through imitation, which is to say by hypertextuality. Even further, allusions can denote a deeper connection of hypertextuality.

A further clarification is needed with regard to the nature of the five types. Genette speaks of the five types of transtextuality in two ways. First, they are aspects of textuality. There is no literary work that does not evoke other works in some way. In this sense all works are hypertextual (or intertextual and architextual). He decided however to examine works that are mainly and openly hypertextual refusing to follow what he calls "hypertextual hermeneutics."[55] Structures naturally can be observed on a large scale; therefore, such an approach is justified given that one pursues methodological goals. In the same spirit, there would be enough grounds to claim that the book of Acts as a whole could be described as a hypertextual imitation of the Greek OT—the Septuagint (LXX). I hope to prove this point later. However,

---

Transtextuality then goes beyond, and at the same time subsumes, architextuality, along with some other types of transtextual relationships" (*Palimpsests*, 1).

[54] Ibid., 7–8.

[55] Ibid., 9.

in this work the individual passages of Acts 10:1–15:35 will be examined in relation to architextuality, hypertextuality, metatextuality and intertextuality. Almost all passages have architextual relations but metatextuality and hypertextuality appear to be mutually exclusive. Again, intertextuality is most often combined in our section with one concrete hypertextual operation, imitation. Intertextuality is always in view when it comes to examining metatextuality.

It is to be noted that not all of these four types of transtextuality are equally well developed by Genette. Hypertextuality comes with a heavy taxonomy and great precision. Adjustments and occasionally modification will have to be performed in this case. Many hypertextual operations irrelevant for our text will not be discussed. Metatextuality, on the other hand, is not well developed. The challenge will be to outline distinct metatextual operation relevant for the text examined. In both cases I will attempt to proceed by considering what choices serve the study of the text at hand in congruity with Genette's general approach. At times, however, I will point out that other approaches may complement what a structuralist study offers.

Finally, a terminological explanation is needed. Genette calls transtextuality what modern biblical scholarship terms intertextuality. Genette, however, uses intertextuality, in a very strict sense. Since I try to remain in dialogue with biblical scholarship, the term intertextuality will be used in a general sense, to denote textual relations of the broadest type. At times, however, Genette's precise taxonomy will be applied. The four types of transtextuality, along with the several subcategories, will be used to achieve greater precision.

Although textual relations of biblical texts are the main focus of this study, it does not come with a suggestion that intertextual reading is the one right approach to the NT or the Bible in general. The claim that intertextuality is constitutive in the generation of meaning does not lead to a methodological monopoly. It is argued that intertextuality is an inescapable part of biblical exegesis, but it is not the only perspective texts are to be studied from.

In fact, intertextual investigation plays an integral role in the disciplined process of exegesis. In my opinion, Stefan Alkier has been most successful in grounding a comprehensive methodology of biblical exegesis in a textual theory informed by literary studies, especially semiotics. Alkier stated that the primary focus of NT studies is "linguistic signs that, organized, become texts and are received in this expectation."[56] Petőfi's definition of text is cited by Alkier to ground his claim:

> For us, *textuality* is not inherent characteristic of verbal objects. A producer or a recipient regards a verbal object as text when he or she believes that this verbal object is a cohesive and complete whole that corresponds to an actual or assumed communicative intention in an actual or assumed communication situation. A text is—according to semiotic terminology—a complex verbal sign (or a verbal sign complex) that correspond to a given expectation of textuality.[57]

This definition allows texts to be studied as "system-immanent constructions" and also according to their "functional embedding."[58] Alkier continues by claiming that text-immanent and text-external perspectives are not mutually exclusive but if practised in a disciplined way can be complementary. The text-immanent perspective comes first but that does not imply superiority. Alkier continues to propagate three realms of investigation in studying biblical texts in a particular order: intratextual, intertextual and extratextual.

Intratextual study concentrates on "syntactic, semantic and pragmatic textual relationships in connection with the models of analysis of literary structuralism and with the inclusion of ancient rhetoric."[59] This area could be termed as the universe of discourse. The

---

[56] Alkier, "Intertextuality," 7.

[57] Ibid.

[58] Ibid., 8.

[59] Ibid., 9.

text is treated as an autonomous structure in isolation from the text-external relationships. Next, the intertextual investigation considers meaning that emerges from relating one text to others.

Alkier sheds light on the different perspectives of intertextuality. The scholar speaks of *production-oriented perspective*, *reception-oriented perspective* and *experimental perspective*. The first two fall into the category of limited notion of intertextuality whereas the last one can be termed as unlimited intertextuality.[60] Finally, extratextual investigation focuses on relations with extratextual signs. Questions of introductory nature, as well as archaeological and historical observation, are taken into consideration.[61]

Text-external (both extratextual and intertextual) relationships are contained in the encyclopedia, as introduced by Umberto Eco. Alkier writes: "The encyclopedia is the cultural framework in which the text is situated and from which the gaps of the text are filled."[62] It is justifiable to separate the intertextual and extratextual investigations as subsequent steps in the process of study because of the focus on different groups of extratextual relationships. However, on a theoretical level both these areas are contained in the encyclopedia.

Attention to the proposed methodology by Alkier has been paid because it has the value of combining different perspectives on interpreting NT texts in an orderly fashion. It also has the advantage of showing the place and role of intertextual relations in the larger process of interpretation. This work aims to complete the second, intertextual, investigation of the text with the awareness that this study is part of the larger process of interpretation. Exegetical result of intratextual character will be introduced out of necessity to locate intertextual correlations. Extratextual remarks will also be listed occasionally to better establish certain intertextual readings.

---

[60] Ibid.

[61] Ibid.

[62] Ibid., 8.

1.3. Acts 10:1–15:35 as a Unit

When applying intertextual methodology in the field of biblical scholarship, especially if the method is relatively novel to the field, two courses of study appear to be relevant. A major trend seems to be focusing on how a certain narrative or book of the OT can be seen interacting with a significant portion of the NT. Leroy Huizenga's recent book, for instance, examines the use of the narrative of the binding of Isaac from Gen 22 in the entire Gospel of Matthew.[63] A similar and more recent undertaking is performed by the Library of the New Testament Series. Several authors enumerate and evaluate how individual books or an entire corpus of the OT surface throughout the NT.[64] A different approach seems to be that of considering all or nearly all intertextual connections in a given portion of the NT—be it a book, a chapter, or a corpus.

The clearest embodiment of this type of investigation is an entire commentary by several authors devoted exclusively to the use of the OT in each NT book.[65] The investigation of this dissertation follows the latter path inasmuch as intertextual correlations of a selected section of the NT, namely Acts 10:1–15:35, are mapped and studied. Although relevant treatment of the same OT passages outside the boundaries of the examined section will be occasionally introduced, it will always be performed in search of either parallel or alternate ways of evoking the same texts. The strong focus of this undertaking is motivated by an interest in the central section of Acts at hand. Events triggered by the conversion of Cornelius leading to the acceptance of Gentiles at the Jerusalem Synod are central to the narrative of Acts.

---

[63] Leroy Andrew Huizenga, *The New Isaac: Tradition and Intertextuality in the Gospel of Matthew*, NovTSup 131 (Leiden: Brill, 2012).

[64] Steve Moyise and Maarten J.J. Menken, eds., *Deuteronomy in the New Testament: The New Testament and the Scriptures of Israel*, LNTS 358 (London: T&T Clark, 2007); Maarten J.J. Menken and Steve Moyise, eds., *The Minor Prophets in the New Testament*, LNTS 377 (London: T&T Clark, 2009).

[65] G.K. Beale and D.A. Carson, eds., *Commentary on the New Testament Use of the Old Testament* (Grand Rapids: Baker Academic, 2007).

Further, the choice for examining several intertextual connections in Acts is motivated by the rich interaction of several intertexts, subtexts, hypotexts in the selected section. Texts of the OT in Acts are not evoked in singularity. Texts are evoked in relation to one another. These texts are presented as being in harmonious, complementary, and occasionally in conflicting relation with one another. The multi-voicedness of the Scripture is played out in full. Bakhtin's polyphony or even dialogue is indeed an accurate description of how several texts interact in Acts. Nevertheless, the interaction between several texts is hosted and determined to a great degree by the text of Acts. That relation is influenced by the text of Acts and therefore deserves attention.

Acts 10:1–15:35 is a central section in the whole book focusing mainly on a major development in the early Christian movement—namely the reception of Gentile Christians in the church. The first major section is Acts 10:1–11:18 centring on the conversion and baptism of a certain Roman centurion named Cornelius along with his household. Peter plays a crucial role in the events, first by being reluctant to obey God's initiative toward the Gentiles, then by convincing others to embrace the new group within the church. The episode itself breaks into two parts. First, in Acts 10:1–48 events leading to the conversion and baptism of Cornelius are told, then countering opposition in Jerusalem is recounted in Acts 11:1–18. The rest of chapter 11 tells two small episodes in the church of Antioch (cf. 11:19–30). Marguerat is right in calling these chapters the birth and life of the church in Antioch.[66]

Next, the persecution and deliverance of Christians is recounted in Acts 12 with special attention devoted to Peter. The unit only fits the larger narrative context loosely because there is a shift from Antioch back to Judea and Gentile mission appears to be of no concern.

[66] Daniel Marguerat, *Les actes des apôtres (1–12)*, vol. Va, Commentaire Du Nouveau Testament (Genéve: Labor et Fides, 2015), 407.

Witherington even suggested that this is an independent unit.[67] Persecution, however, is often portrayed as one reaction to the spreading of the word of God and to the outpouring of the Spirit. The episodes about the imprisonment and deliverance of Peter in Acts 12:1–19 and the death of Herod in Acts 12:20–25 are in accordance with the cyclical nature of Acts even if chronological and thematic concerns may be justified.

From Acts 13 onward the Gentile mission theme is resumed and dominates the scene to the end of the Jerusalem Council. Acts 13:1–14:28 is a large narrative about the first missionary journey of Paul. Two significant developments characterize this mission trip. First, an increasing response from the Gentiles to the mission is noted. Second, Paul becomes a leading figure in converting the nations. Paul's speech in Pisidian Antioch in Acts 13:16–41 provides the theological frame for the new development in the missionary activity of the church. Finally, Acts 15:1–35 tells of the Jerusalem Council along with its immediate context. The meeting in Jerusalem debates and settles the issue of Gentiles in the church by offering theological justification for welcoming them and by laying out some laws to be observed by them.

Acts 10:1–15:35 therefore is held together by the common theme of Gentile mission. The conversion of Cornelius and the outpouring of the Spirit on the Gentiles pose an obvious challenge to the community. Continuing conversions from Gentiles outside Judea primarily through Paul's missionary activity lead to a discussion and resolution of the same issue. Thematic unity, however, is only one of the determining factors in those chapters. Presenting the events in a cyclic pattern is also at work. Proclaiming the word is followed by positive responses and by the outpouring of the Spirit; hostility to apostolic preaching immediately arises which is countered by strengthening from God.

---

[67] Ben Witherington, *The Acts of the Apostles: A Socio-Rhetorical Commentary* (Grand Rapids: Eerdmans, 1997), 376.

1.4. The Book of Acts and its Architextual Correlations

Prior to investigating individual intertextual correlations of selected passages in Acts, the book's generic relationships will need to be examined. Given the significant orientation detectable in Acts toward the Holy Scriptures of Israel, the book's generic and stylistic ties with the writings of the LXX in particular, will be given priority. Nevertheless, in accordance with a trend in biblical scholarship, generic connections with relevant ancient works of history will also be dealt with briefly.

According to Genette, architextuality is the most implicit, almost exclusively silent connection between two or more texts that includes "types of discourse, modes of enunciation, literary genres"[68] out of which each text emerges. Silent does not mean however that the examination of these types of connection would be irrelevant or insignificant. On the contrary, signs of genre and sub-genre create expectations in the reader and potentially result in generic pact.[69] This is not to say that the individual work will adhere strictly to one genre or another. Every work is read in the light of what has been said before, but at the same time individual works can break, change and even transcend earlier patterns. New works can create surprise or show irony directed against existing forms. The only point made here is that neither uncritical adherence nor revolutionary attitude to existing forms is assumed at this point of interpretation.

The Acts of the Apostles is one of the most interesting and challenging books in the NT. Many readers approach the book with a simple assumption that it is a chronological account of what happened with the followers of Jesus after his resurrection and ascension. Therefore, one could turn to this writing and find out about events that

---

[68] Genette, *Paratexts*, 1.

[69] The expression *generic pact* originates from German literary theorist, Hans Robert Jauss who emphasized the role of the readers' reception in interpreting literary works. His school of thought, *receptions aesthetic*, is explained in two of his works: Hans Robert Jauss, *Aesthetic Experience and Literary Hermeneutics*, THL 3 (Minneapolis: University of Minnesota Press, 1982); idem, *Toward an Aesthetic of Reception*, THL 2 (Minneapolis: University of Minnesota Press, 1982).

took place between 30 and 60 CE. It might be puzzling from a chronological point of view that the book does not tell us of the fate of a central protagonist, apostle Paul. Yet this is the only writing in the NT that attempts to give a record of what happened with the early Christian movement beyond the life of Jesus.

Beyond the chronological approach one can notice a geographical thrust in the book. One could even argue that Acts is more interested in the map of how the Christian message was carried from Jerusalem to the ends of the world, that is the entire Roman Empire. Thus, the lack of information on how Paul's fate in Rome turned out may be due to the work's increased interest in spreading the gospel in new locations as opposed to interest in individuals however prominent they might have been.[70] It could be suggested that the places "Jerusalem, all Judea, Samaria and ends of the earth" listed in Acts 1:8 are not only stages of spreading the gospel but also provide the basic orientation of the book toward holy geography.[71]

With regard to authorship, it is important to note that Acts is anonymous and nowhere does it mention the name of the author. There are, however, several hints within the text about the characteristics and identity of the writer.[72] Added to the internal evidence, external evidence[73] also points to Luke, a companion to Paul during his mission, a pagan-born, educated man as the author of Acts.[74] Regarding the date of the final composition of the book, most scholars

---

[70] Witherington, *Acts*, 1.

[71] Joel B. Green, "Acts of the Apostles," *DLNT* 14–15.

[72] Most importantly, the writer presents himself as the companion of Paul in Acts 16:10–17, 20:5–15, 21:1–18 and in 27:1–28:16. It appears as the author knew Paul and was "at least a second-generation Christian" (see Darrell L. Bock, "Luke, Gospel of," *DJG* 495–96).

[73] Most ancient sources attest Lukan authorship. The Muratorian Canon attributes the third Gospel to a doctor and companion to Paul—see ibid., 496.

[74] There is a consensus among the biblical scholars regarding Lukan authorship. See, e.g., Joseph A. Fitzmyer, *The Acts of the Apostles*, AB 31 (New Haven: Yale University Press, 1998), 47–65, and also Witherington, *Acts*, 51–60.

name the late 70s to early 80s CE as the most likely period for writing Acts.[75]

There is very little consensus, however, beyond basic question of authorship and date of the work. To name or define the genre of Acts is among the more divisive issues in the field. Attempts have been made to locate Acts in the generic field of its age. Proposals for possible genres could be grouped along the lines of more Hellenistic and more Jewish aspects of Acts.

One the one hand, well-known Greek and Roman forms of literature were suggested as the generic background for Luke-Acts. Among them one can find a proposal reinforced recently by Adams to read Acts as an adaptation of ancient biography.[76] It can be argued safely that depicting characters like James, Peter and Paul is a central feature in the work. Nevertheless, it has also been pointed out that central characteristics of ancient biographies, such as the discussion of "birth, death, appearance, [and] remarkable character traits"[77] are of no concern for Luke. Acts seems to be interested in its characters more for what they stand for than what their attributes are. The lack of that interest takes away the claim of biography.

A much stronger case could be made in my opinion for viewing Acts as an ancient historiographical work of some kind concentrating on early Christianity. Witherington argues for this case when he lays out specifics of Lucan history writing: "Luke and Acts together must be seen as some sort of two-volume historiographical work. Luke in his second volume is writing a continuous narrative about the growth and development of a remarkable historical phenomenon, early Christianity, which he believed was the result of divinely initiated social change."[78] The motivation of the kind of history writing Luke performs is said to be theological:

---

[75] Witherington, *Acts*, 62.

[76] Sean A. Adams, *The Genre of Acts and Collected Biography*, SNTSMS 156 (Cambridge: Cambridge University Press, 2013).

[77] Witherington, *Acts*, 20.

[78] Ibid., 21.

> The manner in which Luke writes this narrative is from a theological point of view, for Luke believes that it is God, and God's salvation plan, that is the engine that drives and connects the various facets of his account. If there is any dominant actor in the book of Acts, it is God in the person of the Holy Spirit who guides and directs the words and deeds especially of the main protagonists in the narrative.[79]

Witherington makes further points about the specifics of Lukan history-writing that are worth considering. Acts is mainly theocentric, he argues. God determines the course of events in history according to his will revealed in the past. Jesus is an essential part of the God's larger salvation plan but within a larger theocentric frame. The prefaces to the Gospel of Luke (1:1–4) and to Acts (1:1–3) shed more light on how those works are to be read. The narrator claims to give "an account of the events that have been fulfilled among us" (Luke 1:1). One can detect two directions in this statement. First, since the two works cover the life of two subsequent generations, the aim of the text seems to emphasize continuity between the eyewitnesses and later followers of Jesus. They are both made part of the drama initiated by God through Jesus. With this extension, on the other hand, also comes a restriction. Luke is not aiming to write a universal history that starts from the beginning. In Luke-Acts the writer gives a portrayal of recent events covering two generations. The events that have been fulfilled nonetheless are grounded in God's past saving plan and have universal significance.[80]

By including himself among the ones who witnessed the things that were fulfilled (Luke 1:1), the "we" passages beginning in chapter 16 are foreshadowed by Luke. By being participant at least in some of the events recounted, Luke fulfils the requirements of history writing of his time, namely that he was able to make his own observations of

---

[79] Ibid.

[80] Ibid., 21–22.

the events depicted among the ones he received from other witnesses.[81] Synchronisms throughout the book ground the stories of the early church in the wider historical context. They can be understood as signals about the credibility and significance of the events for the wider world.[82]

Other scholars claim that Acts stands much closer to Hellenized Jewish historiography of the time similar to the works of Artapanos, Demetrios and Josephus.[83] Jacob Jervell even goes further when claiming that Acts stands closest to the type of history writing that can be found in Israel's Scriptures or the LXX, to be more precise. Jervell makes a strong statement by proposing the heavy term *salvation history* for Acts: "Luke does not know the term 'salvation history.' He does not employ the word ἱστορία. But he knows about one particular history, and this history has salvation as its theme. This is the history of Israel. The church, its message and life, is in itself the final part of this history. This is because Luke writes the history of the people of God."[84] This salvation history is distinguished from the history of Gentiles. Theirs is what Jervell calls an "empty" history as attested in Acts 14:16: "In past generations he [God] allowed all the nations to follow their own ways." This is a history of idolatry and ignorance[85] and the only connection that it had with God is that he gave the Gentiles "rains from heaven and fruitful seasons" (Acts 14:17). The Gentiles are now included in the latest phase of salvation history which nevertheless keeps being shaped after "the promises and

---

[81] Ibid., 22.

[82] Ibid., 23. Historic references are especially strong in Gamaliel's speech (Acts 5), in the narrative about the famine (Acts 11), the reign of Herod the Agrippa (Acts 12), the banishment of Jews from Rome (Acts 18) and the reigns of Felix and Festus (Acts 21–26).

[83] Ibid., 35.

[84] Jacob Jervell, "The Future of the Past: Luke's Vision of Salvation History and Its Bearing on His Writing of History," in *History, Literature, and Society in the Book of Acts*, ed. Ben Witherington (Cambridge: Cambridge University Press, 1996), 104.

[85] Ibid., 105.

patterns in God's word and acts"[86] in the history of Israel. Eschatology confirms what God had been doing in the past. The latest phase of salvation history is inaugurated by the coming of the Messiah.[87] Witherington arrives at a similar conclusion, although with more emphasis on depicting the events on their own right and linking them somewhat more loosely to the history of Israel: "Luke will write the story about the crucial events which began the messianic age in which the Scriptures would be fulfilled."[88] On the question of genre in Acts, Jervell's remark comes closest to giving the most precise description in relation to Acts when he writes that Luke "chose historiography even if he was aware that he transcended its limits by far."[89]

This brings us to a crucial point in making judgment about Acts' genre and style, namely its relationship with the OT. At present, however, the discussion must be limited to stylistic and generic concerns. Without doubt, the influence of the OT is considerable "on Luke's language, literary techniques, narrative style and employment of various themes,"[90] as Rosner put it. Although Acts 10:1–15:35 will be kept in view the whole time, the issue of linguistic, literary and thematic parallels cannot be addressed in isolation from the rest of the book. On the contrary, links between the LXX and the entire book of Acts need to be considered to have a more complete picture.

Scholars often point out that the Acts is heavily packed with linguistic Semitisms. It is even further specified that a more exact term would be Septuagintalism, that is to say, the close resemblance with the style of the LXX. Specific forms of Semitism apparent in the LXX seem to form a close parallel with the language of Acts.[91] The

---

[86] Ibid., 106.

[87] Ibid.

[88] Witherington, *Acts*, 14.

[89] Jervell, "Future," 126.

[90] Brian S. Rosner, "Acts and Biblical History," in *The Book of Acts in Its Ancient Literary Setting*, vol. 1 of *The Book of Acts in its First Century Setting*, ed. Bruce W. Winter and Andrew D. Clark (Grand Rapids: Eerdmans, 1993), 66.

[91] When taking into account citations and allusions in Acts, the evidence clearly points to connections with the LXX version. Witherington, *Acts*, 123–25.

proposed Septuagintalism is based on observations of various characteristics. The most important one would be to prove whether Luke takes his OT quotations from the LXX as opposed to taking them from the Masoretic Text (MT) of the OT. There are 37 places in Acts where the OT is quoted.[92] Although Wilcox argued for the influence of the MT behind Semitisms in Acts, his arguments were countered on several occasions[93] and there exists a wide consensus at present that the Bible for Acts was the LXX when it came to quoting.

Quotations, moreover, are not the only link between Acts and the OT. Jervell suggests that Luke's vocabulary is almost identical with that of the LXX.[94] The link with the LXX is further strengthened by the use of characteristic word compounds and phrases. Fitzmyer identifies a number of Septuagintalisms in Luke[95] and in Acts.[96] The few examples below are characteristic of the Septuagintalisms throughout Luke-Acts:

- *apokritheis eipen*, "answering, he said": Luke 1:19; 5:5; 7:22; Acts 4:19; 5:29; 8:24, 34; 9:37
- *anastas*, "rising up": Acts 10:13, 20, 23; 11:7, 28; 13:16; 14:20; 15:7
- *doxazein ton theon*, "glorify God": Acts 11:18; 21:20
- *ek koilias mētros*, "from mother's womb": Acts 3:2; 14:8
- *kai idou*, "and behold": Acts 10:30; 11:11; 12:7; 13:11
- *legōn*, "saying": Acts 10:26; 11:3, 4, 18; 12:7; 13:15; 14:18; 15:5, 13
- *pro prosōpou*, "before the face (of)": Acts 13:24

---

[92] Fitzmyer, *Acts*, 90.

[93] Earl Richard, "The Old Testament in Acts: Wilcox's Semitisms in Retrospect," *CBQ* 42 (1980): 330–41.

[94] Jervell, "Future," 119.

[95] Joseph A. Fitzmyer, *The Gospel According to Luke I–IX: Introduction, Translation, and Notes*, AB 28A (Garden City, NY: Doubleday, 1982), 114–15.

[96] Fitzmyer, *Acts*, 114–15.

- *pros* + acc. of verb of saying: Acts 10:3; 11:14; 12:8; 13:15; 15:7
- *enōpion*, "before, in the sight of": Acts 10:30, 31, 33. This word in not used by any of the writers of the synoptic Gospels.

This point is taken further by Alexander who sees Semitisms in Luke-Acts as very different from the ones in other synoptic Gospels. The Gospel of Mark, for example, is also flavored with Semitisms. Alexander however argues for a particular kind of Semitism in Acts:

> Mark contains more Aramaisms, is more open to loan-words, more "vulgar," probably closer to spoken language. Luke's is more literary Semitism, a conscious adoption of biblical style influenced not so much by patterns of spoken Aramaic as by the "translation Greek" of the LXX.... Luke, in contrast to other synoptics, gives his language a more elevated and dignified style associated with the peculiar style of Greek prevalent in the Greek Bible.[97]

The style of Acts observed at the level of vocabulary and semantics resembles very closely that of the LXX. The effect thus is a language of the holy stories. Alfred Wifstrand supports the idea that the effect of the use of Septuagintalisms is evoking a holy language: "Luke, in contrast to other synoptics, sought to give his narrative a more elevated and dignified style by consciously and deliberately associating it with the peculiar style of Greek prevalent in the LXX which, so often reflecting the phraseology of a different language, had acquired a sacred status in the eyes of Hellenized Jews and proselytes as well as of the first Christians."[98]

---

[97] Loveday Alexander, *Acts in Its Ancient Literary Context*, LNTS 289 (London: T&T Clark, 2007), 243.

[98] Albert Wifstrand, *Epochs and Styles: Selected Writings on the New Testament, Greek Language and Greek Culture in the Post-Classical Era*, ed. Lars

Acts most certainly has a Septuagintal tune, or humming under the words. The phenomenon could be defined along more general linguistic lines. One could in fact point out that imitation is at work not from one language to the other (Hebrew of the OT to Greek of Luke's time) but from one state of language (Greek of LXX) to the other (Luke's Greek). An expanded view of imitation that involves syntax in the broad sense, morphology and vocabulary is at work at this level.[99] A certain state of language is imitated in Acts because it is the language of a corpus—that is the Holy Scriptures of Israel.[100]

Witherington takes the question of Semitisms further by bringing into attention that there seems to be an economy of Semitic expressions at work within the entire book of Acts. There are more Semitic expressions when events in Jerusalem are recounted whereas there are fewer as the characters move to Greece and Rome. Another but not entirely separate principle behind the density of Semitic expressions appears to be the occurrence of certain themes.[101] It has been noted by scholars that the narratives centring around the time of Jesus's birth are packed with Semitisms. In a similar manner, the first fifteen chapters in Acts concentrating on the life of the church in a Jewish setting contain more Semitisms than the rest of the book focusing on Greece and Rome.[102]

However, that does not mean that Acts lost Semitisms completely as the characters move away from Jerusalem or find themselves in a different situation. Jervell notes that speeches in Acts, regardless of the

---

Rydbeck and Stanley E. Porter, trans. Denis Searby, WUNT 179 (Tübingen: Mohr Siebeck, 2005)—cited in Alexander, *Acts*, 242.

[99] Genette, *Palimpsests*, 75.

[100] My colleague, Gergely Hanula recently defended his dissertation of theoretical character on the nature of holy language with special relevance for the New Testament—see Gergely Hanula, "A „szent nyelvek" fordítása mint nyelvészeti kérdés, különös tekintettel az Újszövetségre" (Ph.D. diss., Eötvös Loránd University, 2015). Many of his general observations seem promising for future discussions on the language of the NT and Acts.

[101] Witherington, *Acts*, 43–44.

[102] Rosner, "Acts," 70.

addressees, demonstrate the same patterns of Semitism influenced by the LXX: "The missionaries do speak in exactly the same way to Jews and Gentiles, *in casu* God-fearers."[103] Jervell proposes the reason behind the unified style of speeches:

> The Semitic elements, the Septuagintalisms, are to Luke the language of the Scriptures. And the apostles and missionaries always preach the same message the same way, and the church preaches exactly the same way the Apostles did. The idea is not to imitate a historical epoch of the church, the language of the apostles (this as a parallel to the Greek *mimesis*), but to show that the speeches represent the Word of God as it always has been proclaimed and still will be. There is no Greek rhetoric in the missionary speeches.[104]

Even in the narratives about the most Gentile regions Acts remains faithful to its style shaped by the holy narratives of the Septuagint.

In concluding the general considerations regarding the genre of Acts, it can be stated that a modified version of historiography is at work. Scholars remain divided whether the kind of history Luke wrote stands closer to the Hellenistic or Jewish patterns. It is also difficult not to notice the claims of history writing according the standards of the age expressed especially in the prefaces but present throughout the entire work. The link with the holy narratives in the LXX, however, based on linguistic, literary and thematic levels remains a key factor in interpreting Acts. While Acts is firmly rooted in the holy narratives of Israel, a clear effort to present the events related to the Christian church in Hellenistic cultural terms is a determining one.

1.5. Texts, Translations, Chapters, and Verses of the Bible

Before going on to discuss intertextual connections in the Bible, some preliminary remarks concerning the texts of the Bible used in this

---

[103] Jervell, "Future," 120.

[104] Ibid., 121.

study are necessary. First, in accordance with most biblical scholars, for English language translations of the OT and NT, the *New Revised Standard Version* (NRSV) will be used.[105] Occasionally my own translation will be offered to better show resemblance and contrast between texts of the two testaments. Quotes from the Hebrew OT will be taken from the *Biblia Hebraica Stuttgartensia*.[106] For Greek NT, the 27th edition of the *Novum Testamentum Graece* will be used.[107] For the LXX, Alfred Ralphs's revised edition will serve the purpose.[108] For the English translation of the LXX, due to the lack of better options, *A New English Translation of the Septuagint* (NETS) will be employed.[109] Most often, however, my own translation will be offered to better reflect correspondence with NT passages. Even when the NETS is quoted, the English versions of names of persons and places in the Bible are taken from the NRSV.

I am deeply aware that none of these choices are without problems. From time to time textual variants will be discussed to consider options that a monolithic notion of biblical texts would hide. The limits of this work allow no more than that the choice of manuscripts, of editions and versions of the Bible potentially determine intertextual readings. Linking the results of textual criticism with intertextual investigation on a systemic level lies outside the scope of this work.[110]

---

[105] *The Holy Bible: Containing the Old and New Testament: New Revised Standard Version* (New York: Oxford University Press, 1989).

[106] Karl Elliger and Willhelm Rudulph, eds., *Biblia Hebraica Stuttgartensia* (Stuttgart: Deutsche Bibelgesellschaft, 1990).

[107] Barbara Aland et al., eds., *Novum Testamentum Graece*, 27th rev. ed. (Stuttgart: Deutsche Bibelgesellschaft, 1993).

[108] Alfred Rahlfs, ed., *Septuaginta* (Stuttgart: Deutsche Bibelgesellschaft, 1979).

[109] Albert Pietersma and Benjamin G. Wright, eds., *A New English Translation of the Septuagint* (New York: Oxford University Press, 2007).

[110] For an introduction to the Hebrew text see Alexander Achilles Fischer and Ernst Würthwein, *Der Text des Alten Testaments: Neubearbeitung der Einführung in die Biblia Hebraica von Ernst Würthwein* (Stuttgart: Deutsche Bibelgesellschaft, 2009). For the same on the NT see Bruce M. Metzger and Bart D. Ehrman, *The Text of the New Testament: Its Transmission, Corruption, and Restoration*, 4th ed. (New

Finally, the issue of verse and chapter numberings, along with different names of the books of the Bible, will be addressed. Given the fact that connections between the LXX and the Greek NT are in the focus, it would seem natural that this study would follow names and numbers of the LXX. There are two main reasons why I decided to use both the MT and the LXX numbering in cases when they depart from one another. First, adherence to the LXX will be continually put to the test by contrasting it with the MT. This makes it necessary to present the numbers of both versions. Second, the majority of biblical scholars use the numbering of the MT, and only occasionally indicating the LXX numbering. Thus, when the two versions of the OT use different numbering, the MT chapter and verse numbers will be put in the first position and the LXX in the second. In a few cases the NRSV numbering departs from both the MT and the LXX. The departure will be noted in brackets.

The names for the books of the OT are a different matter. I simply judge the names of the MT, as translated in the NRSV for such books, as the ones best known; therefore, they will be given priority. This choice is motivated by the desire to reduce confusion without hiding complexity.

York: Oxford University Press, 2005). Hanula demonstrates well the problems with the main approach—see "Szent nyelvek," 134–48.

Chapter 2

PETER AND THE CONVERSION OF THE GENTILES:
ACTS 10:1–11:18

2.1. Introduction

The narrative unit at hand tells the story of the conversion of Cornelius and his household witnessed and led by the initially reluctant apostle Peter. Readers are introduced to Cornelius, a high-ranking Roman military official, who lived in the city of Caesarea. The centurion was instructed by an angel of God to send messengers for Peter, who resided in the city of Joppa. At the word of the Spirit the apostle agreed to go. When the apostle entered the house of the Roman solider, he spoke about a new understanding of God's graciousness toward the Gentiles: "I truly understand that God shows no partiality, but in every nation anyone who fears him and does what is right is acceptable to him" (Acts 10:34–35). As Peter preached the gospel in the house of Cornelius, the Spirit descended upon the audience of Gentiles, thus proving God's favor towards them. Acts 11 tells of the tensions created by the conversion of the Gentiles in the early church and the response given to the challenge. Peter presented the events along with his arguments to receive the Gentiles in the church. The meeting in Jerusalem was concluded in favour of the Gentiles.

2.2. Architextual Correlations

Here architextual correlations of Acts 10:1–11:18 are examined along the lines of generic, sub-generic, thematic, and stylistic lines.

2.2.1. Believing Pagan Officials

Unexpected signs of faith shown by high-ranking foreign officials attested by prophets or prophetic figures are not unknown phenomena either in the NT or the OT. More than this, based on the frequency of stories of pagan individuals showing extraordinary faith, it is to be established as a literary *topos* within the Bible. The motivation behind applying such a *topos* in Acts lies in the book's invested interest in telling the story of Gentiles being incorporated in the church. In addition, it is to be pointed out that Acts follows up carefully on the responses Roman and Jewish officials give to the Christian proclamation. Indeed, the entire book is dedicated to a powerful Christian patron named Theophilus. It is not surprising therefore that encounters between power figures and prophets from the OT are evoked throughout Acts.

The most prominent instance within the OT for a pagan official to receive the grace of the God of Israel through the interaction with a prophet is the story of Naaman the Syrian as recounted in 2 Kgs 5:1–19. A powerful military leader, deliverer of his nation, fell ill with leprosy. At the word of a Jewish girl slave the commander decided to journey to Israel and to seek healing from the prophet in Samaria. Eventually Naaman proceeds to meet with Elisha at his place. But the prophet only sends a message to the powerful man to wash himself in the Jordan River without going out to meet him. The instruction is understood as a sign of disrespect and is obeyed reluctantly. When the bath is performed, the man is miraculously cleansed from leprosy.

After the healing Naaman makes a powerful confession of faith about God: "Now I know that there is no God in all the earth except in Israel" (2 Kgs 5:15). In addition, he pledges to worship no other gods, but the God of Israel (2 Kgs 5:17). The healed commander will worship the God of Israel but asks for permission to enter the temple of Rimmon once a year: "When my master goes into the house of Rimmon to worship there, leaning on my arm, and I bow down in the house of Rimmon, when I do bow down in the house of Rimmon, may the LORD pardon your servant on this one count" (2 Kgs 5:28). The rest of the chapter revolves around the gift the Syrian army commander intends to give to the prophet.

Another typical instance for an unexpected proof of faith from a powerful pagan man is when the king of Nineveh, condemned by

Jonah the prophet, decides to hold a fast, put on sack cloths, and sit in ashes (Jonah 3:6–7) in seeking God's favor. Since connections with the story of Jonah will be discussed later in some length, it is sufficient to point out that the unexpected positive reaction from a pagan king in response to the prophet is at work in the book of Jonah.

A more distant and modified version of the same *topos* can be found in the story of Ebed-melech as written in the book of Jeremiah (Jer 38/45). The Ethiopian eunuch working for the king of Judea in the days of the Babylonian siege carries out a complicated rescue mission to save the prophet from the pit he had been thrown into. This time it is the prophet who is in need, not the foreign official. Therefore, in one respect the two characters are in a reversed situation. However, the narrative portrays Ebed-melech as an example of faith and is later rewarded for obeying God. The prophet mediates the reward. Jeremiah is commanded to deliver the message from God: "For I will surely save you, and you shall not fall by the sword; but you shall have your life as a prize of war, because you have trusted in me, says the LORD" (Jer 39:18/46:18). Ebed-melech therefore is saved from the doom because he proved his trust in the Lord.

Two more examples will follow from the NT to shed more light on the use of the *topos*. The first one, the healing of a centurion's slave[1] is from a book by the same author, the Gospel of Luke in 7:1–10.[2] When

---

[1] Witherington proposes that Theophilus might have remembered "the somewhat similar story involving a centurion" (*Acts*, 347). This implies an intertextual connection between 2 Kgs 5 and Acts 10.

[2] Some NT scholars noted a closer connection between the story of Naaman and that of the healing of the centurion's slave. There is an allusion to the story of Naaman in Luke 4:27: "There were also many lepers in Israel in the time of the prophet Elisha, and none of them was cleansed except Naaman the Syrian" (Joel B. Green, *The Gospel of Luke*, NICNT [Grand Rapids: Eerdmans, 1997], 286). Green speaks of "vibrant echoes" while comparing key elements in both narratives.Both stories start with a well respected Gentile officer followed by an intercession of Jewish elders, on the one hand, and of the Jewish slave girl, on the other. In both stories the meeting between the pagan official and the man of God does not take place. Both stories result in healing from a distance. However, Green's proposal of intertextual connection is left undeveloped in his commentary. A more compre-

Jesus enters Capernaum, a certain centurion sends for the master to heal one of his slaves. The Jewish leaders of the place praise the solider as someone who "loves our people, and it is he who built our synagogue" (Luke 7:5). On his way to heal the servant, Jesus receives another message from the friends of the centurion: "Lord, do not trouble yourself, for I am not worthy to have you come under my roof; therefore I did not presume to come to you. But only speak the word, and let my servant be healed" (Luke 7:7). Jesus, faced with the trust of the pagan official, makes an important statement about his faith contrasting it with that of the people of Israel: "I tell you, not even in Israel have I found such faith" (Luke 7:9). When the messengers returned home, they found the slave in good health. In this story, which closely follows the pattern outlined above, Jesus pronounces the faith of the centurion as bigger than the faith he found in Israel.

The final example comes from Acts itself. In the story of Philip and the Ethiopian eunuch (Acts 8:24–40) the pagan character is taken one step further than all his predecessors. On a journey home from the Jerusalem Temple, Philip the evangelist accompanies a high-ranking man. During the course of their conversation, the eunuch expresses that he does not understand a certain passage in the book of Isaiah, namely Isa 53:7–8 and requests interpretation from the man of God. There is a need for proper interpretation of a certain passage in the Bible. Philip responds by "starting with this scripture", then proclaims "to him the good news about Jesus" (Acts 8:35). Finally, the Ethiopian man expresses his wish to be baptised: "Look, here is water! What is to prevent me from being baptized?" (Acts 8:36). Philip administered baptism to the eunuch, who then continued his travel rejoicing.

---

hensive study was undertaken by John Shelton along the lines of literary dependence—see "The Healing of Naaman (2 Kgs 5.1–19) as a Central Component for the Healing of the Centurion's Slave (Luke 7.1–10)," in *The Elijah Elisha Narrative in the Composition of Luke*, ed. John S. Kloppenborg and Joseph Verheyden (London: T&T Clark, 2014), 65–87. It is sufficient to note that beyond architextual connection there probably exists another type of textual connection.

There are more passages in both Testaments where the same *topos* appears to be at work. A few relevant observations for interpreting Acts 10:1–15:35 can be made at this stage. The most complete and powerful embodiment of the *topos* for Luke seems to be the story of Naaman the Syrian. The elements of the *topos* can be outlined as the following: (1) a powerful pagan man is in need; (2) the man seeks assistance from the man of God showing faith during the process and finally (3) God's grace is mediated through the man of God. These seem to be the three basic steps in the process.

There are serious modifications in each embodiment but only the ones present in our passage are of concern here. Luke's application of the *topos* in Luke-Acts can be defined along shifts of emphasis. First, the faith of powerful men of the pagan world is provisional and somewhat still lacking compared to the faith of both Roman centurions in Luke 7 and Acts 10. The believing Gentiles of the OT prove their faith through one action of faith. Further, their faith is neither presented as superior to the faith of Israelites nor does it change their status as aliens to the covenant with God. Luke, however, takes the *topos* more seriously on several levels. Jesus is said to pronounce the faith of the Roman soldier to be superior to that he found in Israel.

Second, already implicit in the story of the Ethiopian eunuch is the reception of the Gentiles into the community of the people of God. It will become more explicit in the conversion of Cornelius's household. Following the account of Cornelius and the outpouring of the Spirit on the Gentiles, Peter understands that God welcomes all the Gentiles, not just the ones with whom he came into contact. From a singular event Peter makes a general assumption. The Gentiles in Luke's use of the *topos* show more faith than their predecessors did. The approval of their faith by the outpouring of the Spirit leads to more radical conclusions regarding the status of the Gentiles in relation to the people of God.

2.2.2. Complementary Visions

The other significant phenomenon of generic character is the presence of visionary experiences. There are two visions in Acts 10:1–11:18. The first one in Acts 10:1–8 tells of an angel appearing to Cornelius, the Roman centurion, giving him instruction about sending messengers to Peter in Joppa. The second vision is that of Peter in Acts 10:9–16 told again later in 11:5–10 about the descending vessel and the voice telling him to eat the animals in it. Visions involving angelic figures are not rare phenomena in the Bible.[3] Talbert calls the one in Acts 10:9–16 an *angelophany* and proceeds to identify a set number of components belonging to the genre. Normally, as Talbert claims, such an occurrence starts with an (1) introduction followed by the (2) appearance of an angel; the one who sees the angel (3) expresses amazement but most often fear; (4) the angle communicates God's will, whereas (5) the addressee obeys the command.[4] Such a pattern is easily discernible in the depiction of Cornelius's vision: following a brief introduction (Acts 10:1–2) the angel is said to appear and to address the soldier (10:3) who reacts in fear (10:4); the angel brings news about the acceptance of Cornelius's prayers and gives instruction to send for Peter (10:5–6); finally, the command is carried out without hesitation (10:7–8).

The two visions in the passage do not stand in isolation. As Goulder noted, there is a detectable pattern present in Luke's works to interlock pairs of visions. He named them *complementary visions*.[5] The first instance of such visions would be the ones seen by Zechariah and Mary as told in Luke 1. The old priest sees an angel of the Lord while performing his service at the Temple. He is told, that despite his old age, he will have a son who will be instrumental in returning the people of Israel to God. In the well-known story of annunciation in the

---

[3] See for example in Gen 19:1–22; Josh 5:13–15; 1 Chr 21:15–30.

[4] Charles H. Talbert, *Reading Acts: A Literary and Theological Commentary on the Acts of the Apostles*, rev. ed. (Macon, GA: Smyth & Helwys, 2005), 93.

[5] Michael D. Goulder, *Luke: A New Paradigm*, JSNTSup 20 (Sheffield: Sheffield Academic Press, 1989), 205–6.

Gospel of Luke, Mary is to learn from Gabriel that she will have a son who will reign forever on the throne of David. Mary is also told about the child Zechariah and his wife Elisabeth will have. Another example can be noted: the resurrected Jesus's appearance to Peter, on the one hand, and to Cleopas and his companion, on the other, in Luke 24, which resulted in sharing their experiences.

The complementary visions of Saul and Ananias in Acts 9:1–19 can be seen as a further example of the same technique applied in Acts. Saul's visionary experience on the road to Damascus is brought into connection with the vision of Ananias, a prominent Christian disciple of the city. In a vision he is told to go to Saul and baptise him. The two human agents are to meet and to share God's initiative.

After rightly noting the phenomenon, Dunn takes it to convey divine approval that puts the issue at hand beyond dispute.[6] His argument is based on observing the various repetitions (Paul's conversion and Peter's vision in Acts) that add more emphasis to certain contents in Acts. Dunn understands the dual visions as expressing the same truth. It is argued, therefore, that the same truth is established twice in visions thus contributing to a more powerful statement. Thus, establishing certain truths might very well be the effect of employing complementary visions. There seems to be much more at stake here, though. Green gives a more nuanced evaluation of the effect of these complementary visions by saying: "These are 'complementary' inasmuch as in each case visionary experiences are related in tandem, and the successful completion of the one act of God through a human agent is related to the response of the other."[7] The plan God wants to carry out involves two parties that might be neutral (Zechariah/Mary) or hostile to one another (Saul/Ananias). The two sides have to cooperate to fulfil God's plan.

---

[6] James D.G. Dunn, *The Acts of the Apostles* (Valley Forge, PA: Trinity Press International, 1996), 131.

[7] Joel B. Green, "The Problem of a Beginning: Israel's Scriptures in Luke 1–2," *BBR* 4 (1994): 80.

Juxtaposing two visions as part of the same divine initiative is not a Lukan invention. Goulder proposed that there might be an OT model as attested in chapter 3 of the book of Tobit, from which Luke derived his version.[8] The merit of this argument is best understood in pointing to the use of the same technique as opposed to setting up a path of influence. Talbert proposes that dual visions are a general literary phenomenon well attested in ancient literature. Talbert gives examples of "double revelations" in ancient sources before and after the 1st century.[9] Based on those sources, he assumes that legitimizing is the main purpose of such visions.

Luke's artistry however does much more than legitimizing or enforcing certain contents in the visions of Cornelius and Peter. It is somewhat surprising that one of the seers of vision is a Gentile, a Roman soldier. More than this, Cornelius's experience is recounted first, thus giving it a prior position. The relationship of the two parties involved is that of opposition and possible conflict. The Roman centurion was unclean therefore unfit for a communion with Jews. The complementary visions place two people together as receivers of divine instruction one of which is incompatible with God and his people.

In both visionary experiences there is a clear reference to the other party involved: Cornelius is commanded to send for Peter whereas the apostle is told by the Spirit not to hesitate to fulfil the request of the messengers. At first, Cornelius seems to be the one characterized by need: he needs to receive word from a prominent Christian leader. The

---

[8] Goulder, *Luke*, 206.

[9] "Livy 8.6.8–16; Dionysius of Halicarnasus, *Roman Antiquities* 1.55–59; Strabo, *Geography* 4.1.4—a group is told to use for their voyage a guide received from the goddess Artemis, while a woman devotee of Artemis is told in a dream to sail with the group as their guide; Achilles Tatius, *Clitophon and Leucippe* 4.1.4–8; Apuleius, *Golden Ass* 11.6.13; 11.22; *Joseph and Aseneth* 14–15—an angel communicates different things to both parties to get them together; Eusebius, *Church History* 6.11.1–3—a bishop elsewhere has a vision that indicates he will be bishop in Jerusalem, a similar vision is also given to the Jerusalem Christians" (Talbert, *Reading Acts*, 94–95).

narrative however portrays Peter just as much in need as Cornelius. Peter is in need of food when hearing instructions from heaven. During his visions he proves reluctant to obey and appears in need of convincing. He also needs to understand the meaning of God's grace in relation to Gentiles. Along the lines of complementary visions, Luke gives priority to an unlikely hero and at the same time shows Peter in a more fragile state.

2.2.3. Septuagintal Phrases

The question of style with regard to Acts was discussed above. In this section a few examples of Septuagintalism in Acts 10:1–11:18 will be explored.

First, an instance for a special vocabulary is at focus. When the narrator introduces Cornelius as "a devout man who feared God with all his household" in Acts 10:2, a special phrase, *God-fearer* (φοβούμενος τὸν θεὸν), is used in pair with the word *devout* (εὐσεβής). Academic literature on the use of the phrase *God-fearer* in the NT is indeed enormous.[10] The debate related to the term focuses on whether it is technical terminology for proselytes converted to the Jewish faith, or the word may denote a general attitude toward God. A still further suggestion is that the class of people described by the words εὐσεβὴς καὶ φοβούμενος are neither Jews nor proselytes but those who showed sympathy toward Jewish ways of life without entering the group of converts or would-be converts.[11]

What is of interest here is that the term *God-fearer* used in Acts in several passages (e.g., Acts 10:2, 22, 35; 13:16, 26) in its plural form features prominently in the LXX. The term, οἱ φοβούμενοι with the word *God* but most often with *Lord* as the object in the book of Psalms refers to the worshipping community of the Temple. One can read

---

[10] C.K. Barrett, *The Acts of the Apostles*, vol. 1, ICC (Edinburgh: T&T Clark, 1994), 500–501.

[11] Ibid., 1:500.

several[12] calls to worship to those who *fear the Lord*. The one in Ps 22:23/21:24 is a good example: "You who fear the LORD, praise him!" In other parts of Wisdom literature, Sirach in particular, the term points to a general attitude of the listeners the speaker appeals to.[13]

It is noteworthy that in three similarly structured passages in the Psalms (115:9–11/113:17–19; 118/117:2–4; 135/134:19–20), those who fear the Lord are listed among "Israel" and the "house of Aaron"—most likely referring to the same group. In Mal 3:16 the term clearly denotes Israelite believers. The most interesting passage comes from 2 Chr 5:6, especially if compared with the MT text of the same passage. The MT only knows of "King Solomon and all the congregation of Israel" whereas the LXX text adds another group, the fearers: ὁ βασιλεὺς Σαλωμων καὶ πᾶσα συναγωγὴ Ισραηλ καὶ οἱ φοβούμενοι. Clearly the extra phrase must convey a group of people distinct from the congregation of Israel, thus must refer to Gentiles. Witherington claims that the evidence is sufficient to safely conclude that Luke used the word to refer to Gentiles who have some sort of relationship with Jewish religion.[14] Relevant for the present evaluation is that the term has a very strong Septuagintal ring denoting general piety, possibly with an openness to include Gentiles among the God-fearers as it is attested in the LXX.

The examples so far discussed pertained to fixed words from the LXX that came to be technical terms. The phrases below contain more words and allow greater variety. Nevertheless, the LXX phrases are often used in connection with certain contents in the NT.

To begin with, when describing the piety of Cornelius, the text mentions prayer and alms-giving: "He gave alms generously to the

---

[12] Further examples can be found for οἱ φοβούμενοι in cultic contexts in LXX Ps 65:16; 113:49; 117:4; 127:1; 134:20.

[13] Most references to the right attitude toward God are found in Sir 2—esp. 2:7, 8, 9, 16, 17.

[14] Witherington, *Acts*, 342. The LXX in fact has another extra phrase: *the ones who were gathered*. In the MT the word seems to refer to the entire community whereas in the LXX they appear to be a distinct group.

people and prayed constantly to God" (Acts 10:2). Similar descriptions of piety that contain alms-giving are found in the Tobit (e.g., 1:3, 16; 2:14). A remarkable example of both prayer and alms-giving occurring together can be found in a description of the old Tobit in 14:2: "And he gave alms, and he continued to fear the Lord God and to acknowledge him." It should be noted again that the stereotypical descriptions of certain individual's piety are all about Jewish people whereas in Acts 10 the same language is applied to a Gentile person.

A further instance of Septuagintal phrases is found in the description of divine communication with Israel through Jesus in Acts 10:36: "You know the message he sent (τὸν λόγον ὃν ἀπέστειλεν) to the people of Israel." In the Psalms, the phrase *sending the word* is regularly used to refer to God's interaction with creation. God is said to send his word in several passages—e.g., Pss 107/106:20, 147:15/147:4, and 147:18/147:7. Jesus preaching activity is thus portrayed as God's continuing interaction with his people.

The second half of Jesus's preaching activity, *preaching peace* (εὐαγγελιζόμενος εἰρήνην), in Acts 10:36 is almost a technical term in the OT for bringing good news of deliverance. Isaiah rejoices at the sight of the messenger who brings news of peace: "Like the feet of one bringing glad tidings of a report of peace [εὐαγγελιζομένου ἀκοὴν εἰρήνης], like one bringing glad tidings of good things" (Isa 52:7). Similarly, the prophet Nahum envisions a messenger on the mountain carrying news of deliverance: "Behold, on the mountains are the feet of one who brings good tidings and who announces peace [ἀπαγγέλλοντος εἰρήνην]" (Nah 1:14). Jesus Christ's preaching activity is not only set in the context of God's on-going communication with the world but also with the strong message of deliverance from a great evil.[15]

---

[15] Haenchen seems to attribute the complicated syntax of Acts 10:36 to the influence of two verses: Ps 107/106:20 and Isa 52:7—see *The Acts of the Apostles: A Commentary*, trans. Bernard Noble and Gerald Shinn, rev. and upd. R. McL. Wilson (Oxford: Basil Blackwell, 1971), 351–52. In my view this is another case of

Further, sacrificial connotations of a verse deserve some attention. In Acts 10:4 the angel tells Cornelius that his "prayers and...alms have ascended as a memorial before God" (ἀνέβησαν εἰς μνημόσυνον ἔμπροσθεν τοῦ θεοῦ). The language of this verse is reminiscent of numerous descriptions of sacrifices in the LXX.[16] Esler draws attention to the fact that the words of the angel sound in the ninth hour which is the time for the evening sacrifice. He thus concludes:

> Putting these two features together, then, we see that Luke is suggesting that the prayers and the alms of this Gentile were accepted by God in lieu of the sacrifices which he was not allowed to enter the Temple to offer himself. In other words, God has acted to break down the barriers between Jew and Gentile by treating the prayers and alms of a Gentile as equivalent to the sacrifices of a Jew.[17]

These words reflect Esler's interest in the social interpretation but they also point to the use of sacrificial language in relation to a Gentile person's piety.

Finally, applying creation language is at work in the parallel statements of Acts 10:12 and 11:6. When Peter recounts his vision in Jerusalem, he vividly portrays the abundance of animals in the vessel: "I saw four-footed animals, beasts of prey, reptiles, and birds of the air" (Acts 11:6). The list of animals evokes the language of creation as used in several parts of the OT.[18] Nothing more is argued here than that, when describing the vision, the elevated language of creation is evoked to a certain effect.

---

ungrammaticality as explained by Michael Riffaterre suggesting intertextual connection—see *Text Production* (New York: Columbia University Press, 1983), 7.

[16] For example Lev 2:2, 9; 6:15; Sir 45:16.

[17] Philip F. Esler, *Community and Gospel in Luke-Acts: The Social and Political Motivations of Lucan Theology* (Cambridge: Cambridge University Press, 1989), 162.

[18] Clear examples can be found in Gen 1:24, 6:20, and in Lev 11:46–47.

The examples for Septuagintal style are different in character but they all add to the same impression: the stories are told in a way similar to religious stories recounted in the LXX. Special words, phrases, stereotypical descriptions of creation, and religious activities all set in a new narrative are used to tell the story of Gentiles who do not fit easily this context. This way the narrative builds on ambiguity that allows the reader to include the unlikely people in the on-going story of the people of God through dissonance. The use of the old language in a new context is the challenge our text faces.

2.3. Hypertextual Correlations

It is proposed in this section that two hypertextual correlations of different character are present in Acts 10:1–11:18. On the one hand, readers are justified in considering the book of Jonah to be the hypotext for the entire narrative unit at hand in Acts. The nature of correlation between the hypertext and hypotext is that of direct transposition. It is claimed below that the primary point of correlation is the plot of Jonah, which shapes the narrative of the conversion of Cornelius and of his friends along with his household. On the other hand, it will be also argued later that the hosting of the three messengers by Abraham as told in Gen 18 is imitated by serious imitation in the narrative of receiving the three messengers by Peter in Joppa. The imitation detectable in Acts 10:10–23 rests on similar settings of the two hosting events, on the one hand, and on verbal correspondence, on the other. Verbal correspondence between the two narratives, that is, intertextuality in the sense Genette proposed, is treated as part of a hypertextual connection. The precise nature of the two types of hypertextuality, imitation, and transposition will be discussed along with the passages below.

2.3.1. Jonah and Peter, the King of Nineveh and Cornelius: A Case of Direct Transposition

To begin with, it is argued in this section that the connection between the Cornelius narrative as recorded in Acts 10:1–11:18 and Jonah can most accurately be described as a hypertextual one. It is proposed that the story of Jonah with its focus on the disobedient prophet and on the repentant king with the people of Nineveh can be viewed as a hypotext for the story of Peter the apostle and the conversion of Cornelius along with the community in his house.

The narrative of Acts 10:1–11:18 naturally divides into two parts. Acts 10 tells the story of Peter and Cornelius and the conversion of the latter along with his household. Acts 11:1–18 presents the probing and justifying of the conversion of the Gentiles by the so-called Jerusalem brothers who initially disapproved the new development. As part of his effort to convince the doubters in Jerusalem, Peter tells of the conversion of Cornelius again. There are two parallel accounts of the same events, once told by the narrator and once by Peter himself. Not every detail of Acts 10 is recounted in Acts 11. Acts 10 is a narrative while Acts 11 is a speech aimed at convincing. The two accounts will provide fertile ground for attesting intertextual connections.

Acts 10 begins by telling the story of two visions. First, according to Acts 10:1–8 in Caesarea an angel visits Cornelius, a pagan soldier. The messenger calls the soldier by name, assures him of God's favour and commands him to send to Joppa for Peter. After this incident, the readers are told about Peter's vision in 10:9–16. While staying on the rooftop of the house, the apostle saw a vision of an object similar to a large sheet descending from heaven. The object was filled with animals. A voice commanded the apostle to kill and eat the creatures. In reaction to Peter's objection, the voice instructs him not to call anything profane that God has made clean. While Peter meditates on the meaning of the vision, three messengers arrive. After they deliver their message, Peter invites them to feast together. The following day they all start their journey toward Caesarea, as recounted in Acts 10:17–23. The rest of the narrative gives detailed account of Peter's encounter with Cornelius and his household. Cornelius greets Peter. While the apostle preached to the Gentiles, the Spirit descends on the audience. Peter in return decides to baptize the converts.

Acts 11 introduces a hostile response to the conversion event. Later, this led to arguments concerning the status of Gentile converts. The heart of the debate was that Peter ate with uncircumcised people. The agreement is facilitated by Peter's account of the conversion. Special emphasis is laid on the vision of Peter while the vision of Cornelius is not even mentioned. The consensus reached on this matter comes in verse 18: "Then God has given even to the Gentiles the repentance that leads to life."

Before demonstrating hypertextual relation between Acts 10:1–11:18 and Jonah, some methodological remarks are necessary. Serious transformation, or transposition, is regarded by Genette to be the most important hypertextual practice. This observation is not only supported by great literary achievements that fall into this category, but also by the extent of the works following the practice. Imitation tends to give rise to shorter works (except for continuation), while transposition, with its diversity of transformational procedures, is capable of being applied in vast works of literature.[19] Genette continues by introducing several hypertextual operations that do not stand in hierarchical connection with one another. On the contrary, it is claimed that "all specific transpositions (all transpositional *works*) depend upon several of these operations at once and cannot be reduced to any one of them except in terms of dominant characteristics."[20]

Nevertheless, Genette was able to divide hypertextual operations into two categories: *purely formal* and *purely thematic*. In case of the former, it is argued, meaning is only affected by accident or as an unintended consequence. In case of the latter, meaning is affected overtly and deliberately. Genette admits that the distinction between purely formal and purely thematic transposition is a hard one to maintain when it comes to reading concrete works.[21] Distinction proves even harder to maintain in case of quantitative transpositions. Genette orders quantitative transpositions into two groups: *reduction*

---

[19] Genette, *Palimpsests*, 212–13.

[20] Ibid., 213.

[21] Ibid., 214.

and *augmentation*. The former concerns abridging the text, whereas the latter concerns extending the text. It stands as self-evident that neither of these operations can be performed without affecting and thus altering the structure and substance of the hypotext.[22]

Reductive and augmentative alterations can be achieved in a number of ways but they will always result in different texts. Since purely quantitative transposition is not relevant for the examined narrative in Acts, the rich taxonomy[23] Genette proposed to cover the field will not be introduced here. It is essential, however, to point out that thematic transposition will always result either in diminishing and even dismissing or expanding and extending certain aspects of the hypotext. In other words, thematic transformations will always involve and will be based on quantitative ones, and all purely formal transformations show potential thematic power.[24]

The other type of transformation is defined as *purely thematic*. Genette writes: "The dominant effect that concerns me now is, as stated, a thematic transformation bearing on the very significance of the hypotext; to a transformation of that type I shall assign the term *semantic*, which speaks for itself."[25] This particular transformation is said to rely on two further transformational devices: *diegetic* transposition or *pragmatic* transposition. The adjective *diegetic* is accepted by Genette to mean the spatio-temporal world in which the story takes place. Diegetic transposition quite simply is achieved by changing the time and the location of a certain action or by changing both. Pragmatic transposition, on the other hand, concerns changing the action itself.[26] The distinction between the two transpositional

---

[22] Ibid., 223–24.

[23] The purely formal transpositions are: translation, versification, prosification, transmetrification, and transtylization. Still purely formal but quantitative transformations are: excision, concision, condensation, digest, on the one hand, and extension, expansion, and amplification, on the other. Transmodalization is also categorized as purely formal. Ibid., 212–93.

[24] Ibid., 228.

[25] Ibid., 294.

[26] Ibid., 294–95.

devices is of theoretical character. Changing the settings of a narrative naturally will result in an altered action in practice.

A further significant aspect of diegetic transpositions is to what extent the identity of the characters is changed or kept. Genette calls keeping the characters' names, gender, age, nationality, social status, etc., diegetic faithfulness. Pure diegetic faithfulness, however, can hardly be found in literary works. Most often one or more attributes of the characters are altered in the new settings, resulting in a peculiar mix of strangeness and recognizability.[27]

It should be stressed, that pragmatic transformation can simply be the by-product of a diegetic one. As was mentioned earlier, transposing action from one period and location to another will inevitably result is a different action. Genette claims the distinction between what could be called purely diegetic transposition and a purely pragmatic one can be maintained. It is argued that pragmatic transposition is specifically performed to transform the message of the hypotext. Correcting the message of the hypotext in the hypertext would be a clear example of pragmatic transposition.[28]

For reasons of clarity, I judge it necessary at this point to link theoretical considerations directly with the subject at hand. It will be argued below that Acts 10:1–11:18 is best understood as a diegetic (thus thematic) transposition of significant portions of the plot of the Jonah narrative. This claim comes with a strong disclaimer: this is not to claim that the Cornelius episode is simply the product of a rewriting of Jonah by changing the names and keeping some attributes of the characters and transposing the plot into first century Judea. Instead, it is proposed that the story of Peter and Cornelius is presented by the narrator in accordance with the plot of Jonah. In order to demonstrate the hypertextual correlation, Jonah is to be considered as hypotext for Acts 10:1–11:18.

---

[27] Ibid., 296.

[28] Ibid., 311–12.

2.3.1.1. The Book of Jonah

Commentators date the book of Jonah during either the exile or the restoration period that is between 586 and 438 BCE.[29] Questions of captivity, interaction with Gentiles and deliverance, prominent within the book, harmonise well with the challenges of the age.

The book of Jonah is part of the prophetic literature within both the Hebrew and the LXX canon. Although Jonah, with its narrative character, differs significantly from the other prophetic books, its position within "The Twelve" or the "Minor Prophets" is well attested.[30] Reflecting on both the strong narrative character of the ancient writing and on the lack of longer prophetic addresses, Ben Zvi proposed that Jonah be viewed as a meta-prophetic book inasmuch as it reflects on the role of prophets and the nature of prophecy.[31] The message of the book is conveyed with high literary skills. The literary quality of the book is noted and praised by biblical and literary scholars alike.[32]

The story begins with a commission in 1:1–3 given by the Lord to communicate God's message in the Assyrian capitol Nineveh. God makes it his prophet's mission to travel to the great city on account of its sin: "Go at once to Nineveh, that great city, and cry out against it; for their wickedness has come up before me" (Jonah 1:2). There is significant difference between the MT and LXX in the wording of the prophetic commission. In the MT Jonah is entrusted with a harsh message against Nineveh, to "cry out against it" (וּקְרָ֣א עָלֶ֑יהָ).[33] The commission is given again to Jonah in 3:1 after he is delivered from

---

[29] Jack Sasson, *Jonah: A New Translation with Introduction, Commentary, and Interpretations*, AB 24B (New York: Doubleday, 1990), 26–28.

[30] Ibid., 14–15.

[31] Ehud Ben Zvi, *Signs of Jonah: Reading and Rereading in Ancient Yehud*, JSOTSup 367 (London: Sheffield Academic Press, 2003), 80–98.

[32] Jauss gives an excellent study from a literary perspective—see Hans Robert Jauss, "The Book Jonah—A Paradigm of the 'Hermeneutics of Strangeness'," *JLS* 1 (1985): 1–19.

[33] W. Dennis Tucker, *Jonah: A Handbook on the Hebrew Text*, BHHB (Waco, TX: Baylor University Press, 2006), 14.

the fish, but there is a slight change. Jonah is commanded "to proclaim to it" (וּקְרָא אֵלֶיהָ). The Hebrew verb is the same, but the relative pronoun is changed from על to אל. Certainly, they can be read as equivalents as the context would suggest. It has been shown that אל and על can be interchanged.[34]

The phenomenon can also be explained as that the use of אל in Jonah 3:1 would foreshadow the reaction of the Ninevites in 3:8, where it is said that they must "cry *to* God" (וְיִקְרְאוּ אֶל־אֱלֹהִים). It does not change the fact, however, that the commission in 1:2 "carries at the very least the potential to connote a sense of a coming disaster for the object of the proclamation,"[35] whereas 3:1 knows of proclamation without further specifications. Ben Zvi argues for the possibility of dual reading typical throughout Jonah, and labels the two verses as open text, meaning that it allows for a simpler and a subtler reading. The simpler reading would be to treat the two commissions as equal in content. Another, more subtle reading would be that already in the second commission Jonah should have understood that the prophetic message might not be that of destruction.[36]

The LXX wording does not embrace ambiguity in the commissions in Jonah 1:2 and in 3:1. Both verses use exactly the same expression "make a proclamation in it" (κήρυξον ἐν αὐτῇ). Jonah is entrusted with the mission of witness without any hint of the nature of the witness. Only the reference to the sins of the city gives clues about what kind of witness Jonah is to bear. In the MT Jonah's prophetic commission entails a harsh message whereas the LXX puts more emphasis on witness.

---

[34] There are several passages where the latter can take the meaning of the former: 2 Kgs 23:29; Neh 6:17; 1 Sam 25:17—cf. Ben Zvi, *Signs of Jonah*, 34. Ben Zvi demonstrates that ambiguity is at work in several passages. One more example should suffice to prove his point: "As it is well known, Jonah's proclamation וְנִינְוֵה נֶהְפָּכֶת in Jon. 3:4 creates another level of textual ambiguity..., because the text may be understood as 'Nineveh is to be overturned' (i.e. destroyed) or 'Nineveh is to turn over' (i.e. to reform itself, as it actually does in the narrative)" (ibid., 22).

[35] Ben Zvi, *Signs of Jonah*, 35.

[36] Ibid., 34–39.

Another significant difference between the two versions can be found still in the same verse, in the wording of the wickedness of the Ninevites that reached God. The MT renders the cause of the commission by the phrase “their wickedness has come up before me.” The LXX, however, knows of “the *cry* of its wickedness” (ἡ κραυγὴ τῆς κακίας αὐτῆς) that went up before the Lord, thus adding extra emphasis.[37]

As opposed to the standard prophetic behaviour to say *here I am* in response to God’s command, Jonah rose up to flee from the presence of the Lord to Tarshish, a faraway place. He went to the port city of Joppa on the northeastern shore of Israel and got on a ship. Readers will soon learn that the Lord cast a great wind[38] on the sea, and that there was a mighty storm, as a result. The two versions of the text show alternative readings in Jonah 1:4. According to the MT, “the LORD hurled a great wind upon the sea” (וַיהוָה הֵטִיל רוּחַ־גְּדוֹלָה אֶל־הַיָּם). There is no adjective preceding the word wind/spirit (κύριος ἐξήγειρεν πνεῦμα εἰς τὴν θάλασσαν) in the Greek text making it stand out. God uses his mighty force, the wind/spirit to signal Jonah and his travelling companions about his displeasure and to direct Jonah to his prophetic commission.

In the following section of Jonah 1:5–17, the sailors are introduced as being more religious than the prophet of God. Jonah was sleeping[39] while they were crying to their own gods. At their inquiry Jonah admits that he is the cause of the waves and agrees to be thrown into the sea to save the sailors. Again, there is a significant divergence in

---

[37] A similar expression can be found in Gen 18:13 and 19:13 when the fate of Sodom and Gomorrah is discussed.

[38] The Hebrew expression to *cast wind* seems to be justified by its connectedness with other uses of the same verb. The *casting* of the cargo into the sea was useless (1:5); Jonah understood that being *cast* into the see is the only action that can save the ship (1:12, 15)—see Uriel Simon, *Jonah: The Traditional Hebrew Text with the New JPS Translation*, trans. Lenn Schramm, JPSBC (Philadelphia: Jewish Publication Society, 1999), 8.

[39] The LXX text dramatizes the situation by adding that Jonah was snoring in his sleep (Jonah 1:5).

the two versions with regard to the self-identification of Jonah. According to the Hebrew text of 1:9 he confesses himself to be a Hebrew. In the LXX, however, a longer and different confession is offered: "I am a slave of the Lord." Simon proposes this to be a logical misunderstanding of the Hebrew text.[40] Sasson however, doubting that an original Jonah text ever existed, proposes that the influence of 2 Kgs 14:25 describing a Jonah who was seen to be the same person is behind the alteration.[41]

It is also noteworthy that the effort of the sailors to save the ship is described twice: once in 1:5 before Jonah's confession and once following it in 1:13. Their efforts are depicted in relatively great details. Finally, Jonah is thrown into the waves where the fish sent by God swallows the prophet. The belly of the fish contains Jonah for three days and three nights.

Following a prayer of chapter 2, Jonah reaches dry land to be commissioned again in 3:1–4a. The second command in the MT and LXX of Jonah 3:2 show differences with regard to the tense of the verb *to speak*. The Hebrew text stresses that the command is given at the time God speaks to Jonah again: "proclaim to it the message that I tell you." The Greek translation places emphasis on the previous command: "proclaim in it according to the previous proclamation that I spoke to you." The Greek version unites the two commissions whereas the Hebrew version is more ambiguous. The LXX already made the alternate wordings of the two commissions as found in the MT identical. Linking the latter commission to the former follows the tendency to recognize no difference between them.

According to the next section in 3:4b–10, following God's new or repeated command, Jonah went to Nineveh, the great city and cried/proclaimed (ἐκήρυξεν) as God had commanded. While the MT is more generous in giving forty days to repent, the Greek translation only leaves three according to Jonah 3:4. This change quickens the reaction of the Ninevites and leaves a shorter time for Jonah to wait

[40] Simon, *Jonah*, 10.
[41] Sasson, *Jonah*, 116.

outside the city.[42] The people of Nineveh believed God and proclaimed a fast to turn away the doom. The king of Nineveh, upon receiving word about the impending judgment, decides to join the fast with his nobles. In the last verse of the chapter it is written that God decides to spare the city from destruction.

The final scene in chapter 4 focuses on God's interaction with Jonah over the prophet's anger. Jonah is displeased with God's decision to have mercy on the city. The prophet positioned himself outside the city, wishing to see what would happen to it. He built a booth for protection against the heat of the sun. God caused a plant to grow there to provide shade over Jonah's head. God, however, sent a worm to smite the plant. When the wind ("east wind" in the MT, "scorching wind of heat" in the LXX) brought heat over Jonah, the prophet became sick wanting to die. The point of these happenings is to show Jonah how much God cares about people, who are worth more than the plant. The narrative ends with God's question whether He should not spare the city that is much greater than a plant.

Observing the repetitions of phrases in the two halves (1–2 and 3–4) of the book, Simon suggests a symmetrical structure for the book. There are two commands to go to Nineveh: one in 1:1–3 and one in 3:1–3. Further, Gentiles show exceptional faith in both parts: in the storm the sailors pray in 1:5 while Jonah stays in rebellion. To the message of doom the Ninevites repent in 3:6–9 while Jonah insists on destruction. Finally, Jonah wants to die in both parts, once in 1:12 and once in 4:3. The prophet is in submission in the belly of the fish while the readers do not know what result the conversation with the prophet might yield.[43] It is sufficient to note that the two halves of the book reflect one another around the issues of rebellion, faith of Gentiles and God's intervention to convince his servant.

---

[42] Ibid., 233.

[43] Simon, *Jonah*, xxiv–xxv.

2.3.1.2. Jonah and other texts of the Old Testament

The book of Jonah is deeply immersed in the OT canon as seen in interaction with a number of texts. An inner-biblical investigation of the book is not without merit since it sheds light on dominant themes, characters, and sequences that link it with the rest of the OT.

First, the prophet Jonah was often seen in connection with a character of identical name in an account about Jeroboam II and his reign in 2 Kgs 14:23–39. Both men have the same name, the same father's name, they are both prophets and it is implied that they lived in roughly the same time before the destruction of Nineveh. But this remains strictly extratextual knowledge since nothing in the narratives bind them together apart from the identical name and the shared literary corpus they are in. Nevertheless, viewing them as identical figures and using the details about each to build a unified image is well attested in ancient sources and is not contradicted in the Bible.[44] King Jeroboam II is said to have restored the northern border of Israel along the same lines as king Solomon did (1 Kgs 8:65). Jonah is portrayed as a court prophet associated with a successful but sinful king in the northern kingdom who realized national ambitions.

Further, a web of connection is created by the poem in Jonah 2, generally referred to as the psalm of Jonah. The prophet is said to have prayed while in the belly of fish. A number of psalms are alluded to[45] and the style of psalms is at work in the prayer. Moreover, the figure of Jonah is said to be reflected on in Ps 107/106.[46] Jonah is portrayed as a figure in conversation with God and that finds resonance with a number of psalms.

Another vital group of intertextual connections is with that of prophetic figures in the OT, especially the ones associated with judgment of devastating proportions. The rather obvious correlation

---

[44] Ben Zvi, *Signs of Jonah*, 44.

[45] Ben Zvi lists the following MT Psalms: 3, 5, 18, 30, 31, 42, 50, 66, 69, 71, 88, 118, 120, 130, 142, and 143—see ibid., 49.

[46] Timothy J. Stone, "Following the Church Fathers: An Intertextual Path from Psalm 107 to Isaiah, Jonah and Matthew 8:23–27," *JTI* 7 (2013): 37–55.

with Nahum is provided on grounds of the same theme: both Jonah and Nahum cover the fate of Nineveh. Association between the two prophets is further strengthened by use of the same traditional formula confession from Exod 34:6–7 concerning God's mercy. Both Jonah and Nahum appeal to God's mercy and graciousness even if with varying degree of enthusiasm. A closer look at the three passages should suffice to present the case of similar language:

Exod 34:6–7	**Nah 1:3**	**Jonah 4:4**
The *LORD, the LORD, a God merciful and gracious, slow to anger, and abounding in steadfast lov*e and faithfulness, keeping steadfast love for the thousandth generation, forgiving iniquity and transgression and sin, *yet by no means clearing the guilty*, but visiting the iniquity of the parents upon the children and the children's children, to the third and the fourth generation.	The *LORD is slow to anger* but great in power, and the LORD *will by no means clear the guilty.*	I knew that you are a *gracious God and merciful, slow to anger, and abounding in steadfast love*, and ready to relent from punishing.

Other prophetic figures are also echoed in Jonah—mostly in a manner of contrast. This is related to Jonah being a caricature of prophets in behaving exactly the opposite way a prophet is expected to act. In his commentary, Simon demonstrated well the correspondence between Jonah and Elijah[47] as recounted in 1 Kgs 17 and also with Jeremiah.[48]

Furthermore, some strong parallels with the narrative of the flood have been observed by number of ancient and modern readers of the OT.[49] The massive destruction promised, the threat of water and deliverance on dry land and further motifs of wind, forty days, the turning away of God from evil, the focus on animals, the dove, and the ship/ark—all yield to an intertextual reading of the two narratives. The presence of water and sinking into the deep led to association with baptism.[50]

Finally, a further correspondence with the figure of Abraham in Gen 18–19 deserves some attention. When considering the ultimate destruction of Nineveh as known by the ancient readers, Ben Zvi related the city to the fate of the cities of Sodom and Gomorrah:

> It is most likely that the story of the judgement of Sodom and Gomorrah and of the related conversation of YHWH and Abraham (Gen. 18–19) informed the composition and rereadings of the book of Jonah within the circle of literati for whom the book was written. One may point to the probable relation between Gen. 18.20 and Jon. 1.2…and to the reversal of expectations, as Abraham cannot save the sinning city from destruction despite his efforts and stature, whereas Jonah, a more than reluctant prophet who does not argue for the sinning city, is instrumental in its salvation. The LXX seems to reflect a tradition of interpretation that associates the text of Jonah with that of Gen. 18.20.[51]

---

[47] Simon, *Jonah*, xxxvi, 4–5, 8–9, 38.

[48] Ibid., xxxvii–xxxix.

[49] For an extensive discussion on correspondence with Noah see Hyun Chul Paul Kim, "Jonah Read Intertextually," *JBL* 126 (2007): 3–8.

[50] Ben Zvi, *Signs of Jonah*, 139.

[51] Ibid., 16–17.

It was revealed to both Jonah and Abraham that pagan cities will be destroyed on account of evil. In his commentary on the book of Jonah, Jerome—commenting on both the LXX and the Hebrew text—pointed out that in the former the wording of the sin of the Ninevites resembles that of the sin of Sodom and Gomorrah. It is written that "the cry of its wickedness has come up to me" (ἀνέβη ἡ κραυγὴ τῆς κακίας αὐτῆς πρός με) in Jonah 1:2 resembling the statement "the cry of Sodom and Gomorrah has multiplied" in Gen 18:20.[52] Furthermore, Sasson noted that the LXX makes the connection observed in the Hebrew text of Gen 18:20 with Jonah 1:2 even more explicit:

Gen 18:20	Jonah 1:2
The outcry concerning Sodom and Gomorrah has been increased, and their sins are very great!	Arise, and go to Nineveh, the great city, and make a proclamation in it, because the cry of its wickedness has come up to me.

The similar wording of the two verses led Sasson to suggest influence.[53]

Beyond revelation about the plan of God regarding the two sinful cities in view,[54] the relationship between Abraham and Jonah follows an antithetical course. Abraham pleads with God for the people of Sodom and Gomorrah whereas Jonah first accepts the call but then later wishes the destruction of Nineveh.

While commenting on Jonah 4:5, Simon noted a further correlation that denotes contrast between the two protagonists. They interact with God to change the fate of the cities. While interceding, Abraham stood

[52] Timothy M. Hegedus, "Jerome's Commentary on Jonah: Translation with Introduction and Critical Notes" (MA thesis, Wilfrid Laurier University, 1991), 5.

[53] Sasson, *Jonah*, 75, 87.

[54] Ephros juxtaposes the description of Nineveh and Sodom claiming several points of contact—see Abraham Ephros, "Nineveh and Sodom Juxtaposed: Contrasts and Parallels," *JBQ* 30 (2002): 242–46.

before the Lord (Gen 18:22) and even "came near" (Gen 18:23). Jonah in contrast silently escaped from the Lord. Later he also pleaded with God but wanted the opposite of what Abraham asked. Jonah wanted destruction. Abraham went out in the morning and "looked down toward Sodom and Gomorrah and toward all the land of the Plain" (Gen 19:28) to see if his appeal has been accepted. Jonah in contrast positioned himself outside of the city to see (Jonah 4:5) if it would be destroyed. Simon sums up the correlation of contrast: "Both Jonah and Abraham are courageous enough to appeal against the decisions of the Judge of all the earth—one championing greater leniency, the other holding out for greater stringency."[55] The figure of Jonah appears to be constructed in such a way as to reflect on great prophetic figures like Noah, Abraham, Elijah, and Jeremiah to show contrast with a traditional understanding of the prophet. Jonah is a caricature of a prophet.

2.3.1.3. Jonah as Hypotext for Acts 10:1–11:18

During the period of pre-critical biblical exegesis, the story of Jonah was most often read in relation to Jesus's death and resurrection. The clearest point of contact was provided by the motif of *three days and three nights* the prophet spent in the belly of fish. This was widely understood as prefiguring Jesus's passion and resurrection. It follows for this type of interpretation that the section depicting Jonah's troubles and deliverance in Jonah 1:1–2:10/1:1–2:11 stood at the centre of attention.

There were however readings that went beyond the Jonah-Christ typology and paid attention to other details in other parts of the book. The repentance and faith of the Ninevites was a fertile ground for explaining the inclusion of the Gentiles in God's community as recounted in Acts. Augustine gives a clear example of moving the interpretation further in his Epistle 102. When comparing Jonah's

[55] Simon, *Jonah*, 40.

experience with Jesus's death, he progresses to make a statement about the status of the Gentiles:

> As, therefore, Jonah passed from the ship to the belly of the whale, so Christ passed from the cross to the sepulchre, or into the abyss of death. And as Jonah suffered this for the sake of those who were endangered by the storm, so Christ suffered for the sake of those who are tossed on the waves of this world. And as the command was given at first that the word of God should be preached to the Ninevites by Jonah, but the preaching of Jonah did not come to them until after the whale had vomited him forth, so prophetic teaching was addressed early to the Gentiles, but did not actually come to the Gentiles until after the resurrection of Christ from the grave.[56]

It is noteworthy that the story of Jonah is interpreted not only in relation to the fate of Jesus, but also the status of Gentiles is discussed in a post-resurrection light. This is a clear sign that the book offers more than the Jonah-Christ typology.

Jerome offers another reading of Jonah that combines Jesus's resurrection and the salvation made available to Gentiles in his brief commentary: "Jonah, fairest of doves, whose shipwreck shews in a figure the passion of the Lord, recalls the world to penitence, and while he preaches to Nineveh, announces salvation to all the heathen."[57] The link between the passion of Christ and the salvation of Gentiles as seen prefigured in Jonah is assumed in this short remark.

Even the above-cited passages give proof of the fact that the significance of the story of Jonah was primarily seen in its relation to

---

[56] Augustine, *The Confessions and Letters of St. Augustine, with a Sketch of His Life and Work*, ed. Philip Schaff, vol. 1, Nicene and Post-Nicene Fathers Series I (Grand Rapids: Christian Classics Ethereal Library, n.d.), 929.

[57] Philip Schaff, ed., *Jerome: The Principal Works of St. Jerome*, trans. W.H. Freemantle, vol. 6, Nicene and Post-Nicene Fathers Series II (Grand Rapids: Chistian Classics Ethereal Library, n.d.), 265.

Christ's suffering and resurrection. Nevertheless, other aspects[58] of the book—particularly the repentance of the Gentiles—were noted and applied to the church. In his commentary on Jonah, John Calvin makes a further step by examining the situation the prophet found himself in as related to that of Peter in Acts 10. Calvin sees the parallel in being sent to Gentiles:

> It was first a new and unusual thing for Prophets to be drawn away from the chosen people, and sent to heathen nations. When Peter was sent to Cornelius, (Acts 10:17) though he had been instructed as to the future call of the Gentiles, he yet doubted, he hesitated until he was driven as it were forcibly by a vision. What then must have come to the mind of Jonah? If only on account of one man the mind of Peter was disquieted, so as to think it an illusion, when he was sent a teacher to Cornelius, what must Jonah have thought, when he was sent to a city so populous?[59]

Calvin sees the resistance of Jonah paralleled in Peter's reluctance to preach to Gentiles. Similar attitudes are evoked by similar situations.

According to my knowledge Charles Williams, a British scholar of the twentieth century, was the first modern commentator to suggest that there might exist a connection between the narrative of the conversion of the Gentiles in Acts and the book of Jonah. In his Acts commentary,[60] Williams somewhat tentatively suggests a typological connection between Peter and Jonah, on the one hand, and the king of Nineveh and King Herod later in Acts 12, on the other.[61] The points of

---

[58] Ben Zvi lists a wide variety of readings of Jonah in the patristic age that go beyond the Jonah-Christ typology and include: deliverance, baptism, the rejection of Jews, salvation of Gentiles—see Ben Zvi, *Signs of Jonah*, 129–54.

[59] John Calvin, *Commentary on Jonah, Micah, Nahum*, trans. John Owen (Grand Rapids: Christian Classics Ethereal Library, n.d.), 16.

[60] C.S.C. Williams, *A Commentary on the Acts of the Apostles*, 2nd rev. ed., BNTC (London: Adam & Charles Black, 1964).

[61] Ibid., 152.

contact with regard to Peter and Jonah are said to be the commission given to both of them to go to Gentiles, the initial reluctance and ultimate obedience that led to the conversion of Gentiles in both Caesarea and Nineveh.

Williams intended to support his argument by the use of several aspects of Jonah in other parts of Luke-Acts in the spirit of circumstantial evidence. The sign of Jonah for instance in Luke's Gospel (Luke 11:29–30), applied in a different way from the Gospel of Matthew (Matt 12:38–42), makes familiarity with the OT book more plausible. The implication is that if Luke went to the trouble of applying the sign of Jonah in a unique way, he might have wanted to use the story in other parts as well. Williams also turns to Peter's Aramaic name—Peter Bar-Jonah[62]—attested in Matt 16:17, to support the typological connection between the prophet and the apostle.[63] The parallels between the king of Nineveh and Herod portrayed in Acts 12 are more detailed but less convincing, as has been shown by Goulder.[64]

The use of the sign of Jonah in the third Gospel appears more promising. After the Pharisees demand for a sign, Jesus is only willing to give them the sign of Jonah (Luke 11:29–32). The third evangelist does not mean the death and resurrection on the third day by the sign in the same sense as it is meant in the Gospel of Matthew (12:40–41). Instead, for Luke Jonah is a sign in the sense that the people should not reject the prophet (Jesus) calling for repentance. By showing an understanding of Jesus being the sign of Jonah different from that of

---

[62] While analyzing the influence of the book of Jonah in Acts both Williams and Goulder attribute significance to Jonah's role in the Gospels, especially in the Gospel of Luke. In the Gospel of Matthew the Aramaic name *Peter son of Jonah* is applied several times. One of the less admirable observations of Williams is that Luke and his readers might have been aware of this name and thus were able to link Jonah with Peter. This suggested awareness does not surface in Luke's writings and therefore it becomes nearly impossible to prove that link.

[63] Williams, *Acts of the Apostles*, 152.

[64] Michael D. Goulder, *Type and History in Acts* (London: SPCK, 1964), 177–78.

Matthew, one is safe to assume that Luke might have more to say on the subject.[65]

The entire question has been taken up and discussed in detail by Robert Wall more recently.[66] As opposed to typology suggested by both Williams and Goulder, Robert Wall proposes conceptual linguistic correspondence as a more accurate description of the parallels found in Acts 10. Wall detected parallels at the level of sequential ordering of catchwords throughout the Cornelius narrative "which go beyond mere coincidence and suggest that it was the intent of the evangelist to place the conversion of Cornelius against the backdrop of Nineveh's conversion."[67] Wall admittedly examined the parallels at the level of words and phrases to propose that at the main turning points of both narratives one can find the same quasi-technical terms.

First, Wall writes of continuity of location, Joppa and the command to go to the Gentiles given to reluctant servants of God.[68] It would have to be added immediately that Joppa plays a different role in both narratives. According to Acts 9:43, while visiting Christian communities along the coast, Peter arrives in Joppa from the South, where he stays at the house of a certain man named Simon. Jonah most likely comes from the same direction to board a ship in the city already in rebellion to God's command which he received earlier. Only Peter receives God's command in Joppa whereas the location of Jonah's encounter with the Lord is not named. Both protagonists are to go to the Gentiles to fulfill their mission.

Second, the objection of both Jonah and Peter comes to an end after God intervenes. In both cases God's intervention is characterized by the number three. One could also strengthen Wall's argument by adding that in both cases animals are involved (fish and the many

---

[65] Ibid., 177.

[66] Robert W. Wall, "Peter, 'Son' of Jonah: The Conversion of Cornelius in the Context of Canon," *JSNT* 29 (1987): 79–90.

[67] Ibid., 80.

[68] Ibid.

creatures in the object) in convincing God's servants. Jonah spends three days in the fish. Peter sees the object filled with animals descending from heaven three times (Jonah 2:1; Acts 10:16). A further link can be seen in the role of Spirit/wind in convincing. According to the book of Jonah, the Lord raised a great wind on the sea (καὶ κύριος ἐξήγειρεν πνεῦμα εἰς τὴν θάλασσαν [Jonah 1:4]). The Spirit has a prominent role in convincing Peter (εἶπεν [αὐτῷ] τὸ πνεῦμα [Acts 10:19]) when it tells him to go with the servants sent for him by Cornelius.

The third parallel is based on verbal correspondence as suggested by Wall. The commands issued to both Jonah and Peter contain the words *arise and go*. God charges his servants to go and preach to the Gentiles using the same words ('Ανάστηθι καὶ πορεύθητι [Jonah 3:2]; ἀναστὰς...καὶ πορεύου [Act 10:20]).

Fourth, in response to the prophetic message, the Gentiles both in Nineveh and Caesarea believed God's word (ἐνεπίστευσαν [Jonah 3:5]; πιστεύοντα εἰς αὐτόν [Acts 10:43]) and were thus forgiven. Wall takes this to be another verbal correspondence.

Fifthly, a thematic parallel is pointed out: the faith of the Gentiles results partly in hostile response. Jonah is angered according to 4:1 that God did not destroy the pagan city as he expected whereas in Acts the brothers in Jerusalem made a hostile response (Acts 11:2) to the inclusion of the Gentiles.

Finally, God convinces the doubters and opponents in a like manner in both stories (Jonah 4:2–11; Acts 11:17–18). After the worm smites the plant that had provided protection to Jonah from the sun, God raises a burning wind (πνεύματι καύσωνος) upon Jonah. As a result, Jonah became so angry that he wanted rather to die than to live (ζῆν). While making a case for receiving the Gentiles in the church, Peter pointed out that the Spirit descended on them: "And as I began to speak, the Holy Spirit fell upon them just as it had upon us at the beginning" (Acts 11:15). At the end, having been convinced, the leaders of the Jerusalem church note that God gave to the Gentiles the repentance that leads to life (εἰς ζωὴν).[69]

Wall notes that quotes from or explicit references to Jonah are absent in the Cornelius episode. It is suggested, nevertheless, that key expressions and motifs from the prophet's book surface in their original sequence. Even more important is the fact, it is argued, that the expressions of turning points from the Jonah narrative were built into one of the core narratives of the early church:

> Luke has not selected incidental catchwords, but decisive "moments" in the Jonah narrative itself: the "place" (*Joppa*) where the story begins; the number three which signifies where Jonah's "conversion" takes place; the "commission" (*arise and go*) to proclaim the Word of God for Gentiles, the "conversion" (*believe*) of the Gentiles, and its "consequences" (anger and God's rebuttal). In our opinion, Luke has rearranged his Cornelius traditions according to the Jonah narrative in order to situate it against the backdrop of the account of Jonah in the Old Testament.[70]

Wall also notes the intent behind using the story of Jonah in the Acts narrative. The aim of telling a story against the backdrop of Jonah is summarized in terms of legitimizing: "Thus, by relating the traditions of Jesus and the early church to the biblical tradition by easily traced catchwords and/or common motifs, the evangelist actually appeals to Scripture to authorize his own contemporizing of God's work in his messiah and church."[71]

Several observations can be made with regard to Wall's proposals. First, there appears to be a dual focus in the way he approaches the text in search for parallels. On the one hand, verbal correspondence is searched for at the level of important words (believe, Spirit, three, etc.)

---

[69] Ibid.

[70] Ibid., 83.

[71] Ibid.

and phrases (arise and go). On the other hand, similar themes (preaching to Gentiles, repentance, resistance to God's initiatives), motifs (God's action characterized by the number three, animals, etc.) are also taken into consideration. Moreover, both verbal and thematic correspondences are searched for in their relative position in both plots. The unspoken assumption appears to be that verbal correspondence is always taken as a sign for larger thematic interaction if its position in the plot makes it justifiable.

Further, thematic correspondence appears to exist without connection at the level of words and phrases. Wall seems to insist on words and phrases where it is possible, but will go without them in case a verbal correspondence cannot be established. For example, the hostile response from Jonah and the Jerusalem brothers is not linked by the use of specific words, but is shown to be purely thematic in nature.

In response to Wall's suggestions, one could point out that some proposed verbal correspondences are not too well founded. The connection of prophetic commission is argued for on the basis of occurrence of the words *arise* and *go*. In still another case the Hebrew word for Gentiles is used to establish a parallel that clearly cannot be a verbal correspondence between two Greek texts. One can also point out that such words as *believe* are used to portray response to God's word in a huge number of cases. The word often occurs in response to God's action; thus, it tends to take a fixed position in the plot of all biblical narratives. An even clearer case can be made with the prophetic commission. There are a great number of commissions in general in the Bible that have one or both words *arise* and *go* at some point.[72] Therefore, the determining factor for establishing connection in this case is not the use of these two words but much rather the *topos* that could be called prophetic commission. One could say that the use of a certain group of particular words is determined by the *topos* and neither allusion nor verbal correspondence should be argued for. This

[72] For example Gen 35:1; Judg 7:9; 2 Sam 19:8 (NRSV 19:7); 2 Kgs 1:3; Luke 17:9; Acts 9:1.

way one could argue for intertextual connection even if instead of the word *believe* another had been used, such as *trust*, or still further it would be circumscribed.

The proposition of this chapter is that the type of textual relation that links the Cornelius narrative and portions of the book of Jonah is to be located at a more implicit and deeper level in Acts than has been suggested by Wall. The term hypertextuality as defined by Genette is the most accurate description of the type that seems to be at work. The hypotext for Acts 10:1–11:18 appears to be the prophetic call of Jonah and the conversion of the Ninevites.

The nature of this type of transtextuality is not reduced to a single point of contact—say a shared motif, or resemblance of a character, or verbal correspondence. The nature of transformation from one text to the other can be viewed as a direct, thematic and diegetic one inasmuch as the action of Jonah is transposed to first century Joppa and Caesarea.[73] Connections at the level of plot play a crucial role. Therefore, questions of sequence and thematic correspondence naturally feature prominently in hypertextuality, whereas verbal correspondence cannot serve as criterion for this type of transtextuality, although it is not excluded either. The transposition thus rests on a close adherence in the hypertext to the plot of Jonah now presented in different spatio-temporal but similar social and religious environments along with characters that resemble one another in significant respects.

A clear parallel between the two narratives is the social and religious attributes of their characters. First, both Jonah the prophet and Peter the apostle are representatives of their religion entrusted with

[73] It would have to be added that indirect transformation or imitation is also at work but at a more general level. Acts, as a whole, imitates not a single book from the OT, but much more the holy history writing present in the LXX. At the same time the Cornelius episode is a direct transformation of the Jonah narrative. Genette points to the possibility of presence of both types of transformation within one text when he writes: "The same hypertext may simultaneously my transform a hypotext and imitate another" (*Palimpsests*, 30).

a task: they are both commissioned by God to deliver his message. In addition, both servants show opposition to God's initiative. Jonah refuses to carry out the mission right away while Peter is reluctant to obey the command to eat the unclean animals—an action that stood for receiving the Gentiles in the church. Peter's religious role and mission resembles that of Jonah, while the apostle departs from the prophet in one respect: he is easier to convince than Jonah. The prophet remains hostile to the end, while Peter stands convinced about God's grace. It must be mentioned here that Jonah's objection is also represented by the circumcised believers of Jerusalem. Once Peter changes from opponent to helper, the role of the former is assumed by the unnamed people in Jerusalem. Both Peter and the people undergo the same development from opponent to helper while Jonah's reluctance remains.

The other main protagonist in the hypertext, Cornelius, closely resembles the king of Nineveh. They are both non-Israelite figures of authority. Naturally, the king is superior to a Roman centurion—a difference in degree. The other important correlation is their surprisingly positive response to God's word. The king repents and orders national fasting. Cornelius received positive religious evaluation from the beginning, yet his coming to faith is still a surprise. In addition, both men of authority stand for larger groups: the king for his people and Cornelius for his household and friends and for the entire Gentile race.

God appears as the one who sends his servant with a message to Gentiles. God's real intentions, however, are not easy to comprehend. First, he appears to will the end of Nineveh but his mercy prevails. The reason Jonah offered for rejecting the first call was God's tendency toward mercy: "That is why I fled…for I knew that you are a gracious God" (Jonah 4:2). God's will is also difficult to understand mainly because he communicates through a vision Peter does not clearly understand. Clarity comes to Peter when he hears about Cornelius's earlier experience: "I truly understand that God shows no partiality, but in every nation anyone who fears him and does what is right is acceptable to him" (Acts 10:34–35). Finally, the outpouring of the Spirit reveals God's acceptance of the Gentiles. Both in the hypotext and in the hypertext God decides to have mercy on Gentiles. In Acts that seems to be his will from the beginning while in Jonah God's initial intention remains hidden. Furthermore, God acts in both narratives to convince his reluctant servants. Convincing Jonah is a major aspect of the narrative. Peter's objection is countered through the vision and through the words of the Spirit. The Jerusalem brothers' opposition is countered by Peter himself who acts like God did with him.

One more character needs to be considered, the Spirit of the Lord. It is not without challenges to present the Spirit as a character either in Acts in general or in the selected narrative within Acts. With regard to the former, William Shepherd argued convincingly for the benefits of considering the Spirit as one of the main protagonists in Acts.[74] It should also be equally justifiable to speak of the role of the Spirit in the hypertext. The Spirit told Peter to go with the messengers without hesitation, according to Acts 10:19–20: "Behold, three men are searching for you. Now get up, go down, and go with them without hesitation; for I have sent them." The Spirit is mentioned again in Peter's address in Acts 10:38 and it is noted in 10:44 by the narrator that the Spirit fell upon the people who heard the message. The outpouring of the Spirit is stated to be the reason for not withholding baptism for the new converts as it is attested in 10:47. Peter therefore stands convinced about the Gentiles by the intervention of the Spirit. Later when the events were recounted in Jerusalem, the group is won over by the outpouring of the Spirit: "If then God gave them the same gift that he gave us when we believed in the Lord Jesus, who was I that I could hinder God?" (Acts 11:17). The Spirit thus plays a crucial role in countering opposition to God's plan to include the Gentiles into his community.

---

[74] William H. Shepherd, Jr., *The Narrative Function of the Holy Spirit as a Character in Luke-Acts* (Atlanta: Society of Biblical Literature, 1994).

The Spirit as character becomes more problematic in Jonah, however. As was pointed out before, the ambiguous Hebrew and Greek word can mean both wind and Spirit. It was the wind that caused the great storm over the sea to prevent Jonah from escaping. It was also the wind that brought the heat over Jonah to make him accept God's mercy toward the Ninevites. In both narratives, thus, the function of the Spirit is to counter opposition raised over God's initiative. In the light of the entire Luke-Acts, the Spirit can be described as a character in the hypotext. In Jonah, however, the wind/Spirit lacks independence and freedom to qualify as a character.

An Israel-Gentile land duality can be observed in both stories. First, as evident from a remark in 4:1, Jonah was commissioned in his own country Judea or, less likely, Israel. In response to the call, the prophet flees to Joppa, an Israelite port city, to flee from God. As part of his visiting tour from Jerusalem along the coast, Peter is said to have stayed in Joppa, the last Jewish city, where he received instruction from the Spirit. Both men are to leave their land. In turn, Jonah flees from God through Joppa, whereas Peter is to obey God's command in the same place.

In addition, in both stories there is a Gentile city in view. As has been noted above, Caesarea was seen as pagan city as opposed to Joppa, which was considered to be the last Jewish place in the North. Crossing from Joppa to Caesarea is of crucial importance in the Acts narrative. Nineveh was seen to be a sinful Gentile city in both Jonah and other prophetic literature. Both cities are destinations for commissioned prophetic figures.

Religion and status are included among social settings. It is rather self-evident that both narratives relate to the problem of Jewish-Gentile relations. More than this, the parallel social setting of the two main characters is rather obvious, too: Jonah is a prophet of God; Peter is an apostle of the church. Both are men of God. The king of Nineveh is a powerful figure in his own world. Cornelius is a centurion, a powerful military official of the Roman army. Jewish and Gentile relations are overreaching themes in both stories. Spacial and social settings thus offer significant points of contact. Not only is there a duality of Jewish land and Gentile land, but also one of the cities—Joppa—is identical in both writings. The epoch of Jonah and of Peter is naturally different, but space offers continuity.

The strongest correlation between the two stories is based on overlapping plots. Events are ordered in corresponding sequences. To begin with, there is a commission in both stories given to the main prophetic characters that involves going to a Gentile community and delivering God's message. In Jonah 1:2 the prophet is sent to Nineveh to cry against it on account of its sin. It is to be remarked here that Jonah's commission is repeated again in 3:2, making it somewhat ambiguous what the content of the message was. Peter also had to go to a Gentile community to give instruction to a man named Cornelius. The commission to Peter is much more complicated than the one given to Jonah.

First, Cornelius the Gentile protagonist plays a role in the very commission. God is said to have sent an angel to the centurion prior to Peter's call. Second, Peter receives a vision whose significance remains obscure before him until arriving in Cornelius's house. It is a complex process: God instructs Cornelius to send for Peter; Peter receives a vision which he does not understand; the Spirit tells Peter to go with the pagan messengers without hesitation; when being told about God's message to Cornelius, Peter understands what God wanted. Peter's commission is more demanding, involving several characters. Nevertheless, both prophetic figures are commissioned to communicate God's message in a Gentile environment.

Next, God's commission is met with resistance from Jonah and reluctance from Peter. Jonah does not respond verbally to God's call, but flees from him instead. Only later does he tell the motivation behind escape. In Jonah 4:2, the prophet names God's graciousness as the cause for not fulfilling the mission the first time. This implies that Jonah did not want the people of Nineveh to be saved. Peter's reluctance is voiced as part of the visionary experience. He did not want to eat unclean animals. The eating of unclean animals stands in parallel with getting into contact with Gentiles and receiving them in the Christian community. In both episodes, thus, God's command is met with rejection or hesitation.

Still another corresponding sequence is seen in countering objections. In response to the objections, God counters the resistance/reluctance of his servants by means that include animals and the Spirit. God raised a great storm on the sea by the wind/Spirit. Jonah's three-day time in the belly of the fish changed his mind as expressed in his prayer. Peter's visionary experience, which centered on creatures, was repeated three times. Still being uncertain about the meaning of the vision, Peter receives instruction from the Spirit not to hesitate to go with the three men. In both stories God convinces his servants to fulfill their mission and in both narratives the Spirit/wind plays a key role.

As a result, the men of God finally agree to carry out the command. Jonah delivers his message after a one-day travel in the city. After hosting the three messengers, Peter agrees to travel with them to Caesarea. Once inside Cornelius's house, Peter delivers a proclamation to them. Both messengers communicate God's message in a pagan setting.

In response to the message, the Gentiles surprisingly believe God. There are prayers and there is a fast in Nineveh. Their religious reaction in the city is led by the king and his noblemen and it involves both people and animals. There is a surprise element in Peter's story as well. The people in Cornelius's house receive the Spirit. Seeing the extraordinary event Peter was unable to deny baptism for his audience. Thus, Gentiles respond to the proclamation with faith.

Finally, the faith of the Gentiles is met by resistance and confusion. Jonah finds it hard to accept that God spared the city. Parallel to that are the brothers in Jerusalem who demand an explanation about baptizing the Gentiles in Caesarea. Jonah's second resistance is embodied not by Peter, but by the leaders of the Jerusalem church. God enters a conversation with Jonah over the value of the great city. God sends an animal again. A worm smites the plant that gave protection against the sun. A hot wind/Spirit makes Jonah sick. The Jerusalem brethren are convinced by Peter who tells them the story, as recounted in Acts 10. The greatest proof of God's acceptance of the Gentiles is said to be the gift of the Spirit. While the Jerusalem brethren are convinced by the outpouring of the Spirit on the Gentiles, the readers will not hear of Jonah's reaction. Both in Acts and in Jonah, God aims to make his servants accept the faith of Gentiles.

In sum, the similar plot entails a prophetic commission to deliver a message to Gentiles, objection raised and then countered by God, the act of delivering the message, surprising repentance of the Gentiles, renewed objection and God's second response to objection. These are the identical sequences in both narratives.

It is to be observed that some sequences of Jonah are over-developed in Acts while others are mentioned only in a passing. Quantitative comparisons can show priorities of the hypertext. Genette's idea of *reduction* and *augmentation* is helpful as long as one bears in mind that Luke was not rewriting the story of Jonah but was telling the story of Peter informed by the former.

First, the prophetic call is very short and simple in Jonah even if the repeated calls are considered together. Peter's experience is more colorful and complex. One would have to bear in mind though that Peter's visionary experience followed by the command of the Spirit involves call, objection and convincing by God. These three elements (call, objection, convincing) are spread throughout in Jonah in chapter 1 and 2. Therefore, the description of Peter's experience remains to be seen as a reduction. But the entire storm experience and the three days spent in the belly of the fish remain uncharted territory for Acts 10.

The speech of the main protagonist in Acts is much more augmented as compared to the speech in Jonah. Peter's speech lasts from 10:28–43, making it a long one while Jonah's address is rendered as an abrupt sentence in 3:4. Beyond the difference of quantity, the content of the speeches stands in even sharper contrast. Jonah announces unconditional destruction while Peter speaks of salvation made available to Gentiles. In Jonah there is a short speech of doom whereas in Acts one can read a long apostolic explanation of salvation through Jesus Christ.

The reaction given to the speeches is that of faith in general. The king of Nineveh along with his nobles ordered a fast and prayer for all—including animals—in hope that God might turn away from fierce anger. When the Lord saw their deeds, he turned away from the evil he plotted against them. Peter's speech was interrupted by the outpouring of the Holy Spirit which was understood as a sign of divine favor. The outpouring of the divine gift was sealed by baptism. In Jonah thus fasting and prayer prove the faith of the Ninevites whereas in Acts the piety of Cornelius was evident from the beginning. The outpouring of the Spirit convinced Peter not to withhold baptism.

Jonah expressed his anger over God's decision to spare the city. The events in Caesarea were reported to the brethren in Jerusalem—probably the leaders of the Jerusalem church. Those of circumcision contended with Peter over eating with the Gentiles. In both stories there is renewed objection to God's decision of grace. Further, in response to the renewed objections, God is said to have brought Jonah into a fragile state by the hot wind/Spirit. In front of the Jerusalem brethren, Peter tells the story of the conversion of the Gentiles with special emphasis on the gift of the Spirit. The community in Jerusalem was convinced while Jonah's reaction is not recorded.

The hypertextual connection in the Cornelius narrative rests on the combination of harmony and contrast with Jonah. Comparability is provided by the parallel plots, spatial and social settings and heroes with similar attributes. There is a strong identity of witness to the Gentiles initiated by God in both stories. God appears to want the same thing in the past and in the time of the apostles. Objection is also present in both passages. It is stronger in Jonah, weaker in Acts, thus the stories begin to move along opposite directions. God makes efforts to convince his servants about fulfilling his will. The convincing is dramatic in Jonah and gentler in Acts. Both servants fulfil the mission but Jonah remains insistent on the destruction of Nineveh whereas both Peter and the Jerusalem brothers embrace God's will in relation the Gentiles. Both prophets go through the same development but only Peter and the Jerusalem brothers embrace what God wants to achieve in the world.

2.3.1.4. Another Reading of Jonah in Acts

Students of the NT are fortunate to find that the shadow of Jonah falls on another great figure of the Acts of the Apostles. Acts 27 tells the story of how the prisoner Paul tried to reach Rome on a ship. Contrary to the advice Paul gave them, the captain and centurion decided to leave their safe harbor and head for Phoenix. Not long after that they found themselves in a storm. The sailors made efforts to guarantee the ship's safety. Next, they threw out the cargo of the ship. The following day the men also threw out the equipment of the ship. At this point the apostle stood forth and, after identifying himself as God's servant, proclaimed deliverance. After a few days the ship was wrecked but all the sailors and passengers were saved.

In the final chapters of Acts, Paul's mission to Rome becomes a dominant theme. One night the Lord stood near him and told him: "For just as you have testified for me in Jerusalem, so you must bear witness also in Rome" (Acts 23:11). This mission is further nuanced by the task of giving testimony in front of Caesar. By being on the ship as a prisoner, therefore, Paul was on his way to fulfill the mission he has been given. An angel stood beside the apostles and spoke to him: "Do not be afraid, Paul; you must stand before the emperor" (Acts 27:24). In Jonah the prophet must appear in Nineveh in the great and sinful city. As a result of the prophet's preaching, the king repents of his sins. Paul in the same way is coming close to the Gentile capital to preach in front of the Emperor.

The two narratives are linked most notably by the identity of words describing the sailor's activity during the storm. Paul, like Jonah, travels together with Gentiles on a ship. In both cases the travellers find themselves in a great storm. The sailors' efforts to save the ship are disappointed. The ship gets into a near hopeless situation. The first clear point of contact is the words describing how the sailors threw away the cargo. Jonah's sailors fear for their lives, cry out to their gods, and throw the cargo into the sea (καὶ ἐκβολὴν ἐποιήσαντο τῶν σκευῶν τῶν ἐν τῷ πλοίῳ εἰς τὴν θάλασσαν [LXX Jonah 1:5]). The sailors in the narrative about Paul first got rid of the cargo and on the third day they also throw out the equipment of the ship (ἐκβολὴν ἐποιοῦντο καὶ τῇ τρίτῃ αὐτόχειρες τὴν σκευὴν τοῦ πλοίου ἔρριψαν [Act 27:18–19]).

The sailors, by casting lots, made efforts to find out who might be the reason for the storm. The lot fell on Jonah. To their question about who Jonah was, he identifies himself and God's servant: "I am a servant of the Lord; and I worship the Lord God of heaven, who made the sea, and the dry land" (Jonah 1:9). Paul identified himself as God's servant voluntarily: "For last night there stood by me an angel of the God to whom I belong and to whom I serve" (Acts 27:23). Jonah declared the reason of the storm to be his running away from God. Following the disclosure, he told them to throw him in the sea to calm it down. Although Paul (and Luke) does not link the storm directly to God's will, nevertheless he proclaims deliverance too. For Paul's sake the whole crew will be spared: "God has granted safety to all those who are sailing with you" (Acts 27:24).

The two narratives examined in Acts are told in comparison with the story of Jonah. Peter and Paul alike continue the mission of the prophets, in general, and of Jonah, in particular. The frame of the book of Jonah shapes both narratives in Acts. Jonah was sent to Nineveh, Peter to Caesarea, Paul to Rome. All these cities were known to be Gentile capitals. As a result of Jonah's preaching, the king of Nineveh repented. As a result of Peter's mission, a high-ranking Roman soldier believed and was baptized. Paul intended to bear witness in front of the Roman Emperor himself.

It is not only the similarities that are striking, but the differences as well. Different parts of the prophet's book influence the portrayal of the apostles. In Acts 10 and 11, the themes from Jonah 1:1–3 and chs. 3 and 4 surface, whereas Acts 27 shows resemblance with the missing part of Jonah 1. One is safe to conclude that Luke saw different parts of the Jonah story fulfilled with each apostle. In Peter's story the author saw the fulfillment of being sent to the Gentiles, of the opposition the sending arose, countering the objections, the conversion of the Gentiles, the new objections and God's action to convince again. In Paul's narrative the motif of travelling on a ship toward a great city and ruler provides the link. Both Jonah and Paul sailed with Gentiles, they were caught in a storm, they identified themselves as God's servants and the crew was saved following their instructions.

The two apostles stand in a slightly different relation to the figure of Jonah. Peter initially followed the path of Jonah whereas Paul stands in sharp contrast to Jonah in several respects. The first apostle showed reluctance in pursuing the actions God commanded him the same way the prophet did. In contrast with this, Paul followed the course God revealed to him without hesitation. Goulder applies the phrase "typology of contrast"[75] in relation to Acts. Jonah must be dragged from the bottom of the ship while Paul comes forth voluntarily. Although both identify themselves as God's servants, Jonah runs from the Lord while Paul, following God's summons, is prepared to stand in front of Caesar. Jonah initially is the cause of the imminent threat to the ship, while Paul is the reason the people on the ship will be saved. The reason for the difference between the portrayal of Peter and Paul in relation to Jonah can be viewed in the apostles' varying situations.

Peter's struggle to accept God's guidance to go to the Gentiles reflects the concerns of the early Jerusalem community. The obstacles lay within the church. By the time Paul was heading for Rome, the reception of the Gentiles into the community was settled; therefore, only circumstances from outside the church could cause harm to the Gentile mission. Such circumstances included imprisonment, natural forces, and growing persecution. In the two stories, only God wants the same thing consequently: he wants to save the Gentiles. Therefore, he sent his servants to Nineveh, Caesarea, and Rome. At times he must

---

[75] Goulder, *Type*, 178.

convince his own servants, while at other times he needs to save them from storms to achieve his goal.

There remains another significant difference between the hypertextuality in Acts 10:1–11:18 and that found in Acts 27. As argued above, the Cornelius episode is a thematic transposition on account of the shared plot, similar characters, and similar settings. Acts 27, however, is best understood as serious thematic imitation of Jonah. Thematic imitation, a term not employed so far, needs explanation, which will be undertaken in the following section.

2.3.2. The Guests of Abraham and the Guests of Peter: A Case of Serious Imitation

The episode of receiving and hosting the messengers sent from Cornelius in Acts 10:9–23 and 11:5–12 is examined in correlation with the narrative of Abraham hosting the three angels of God as depicted in Gen 18:1–8. The nature of this correlation is claimed to be both intertextual and hypertextual. To be more precise, efforts will be made to demonstrate that the intertext denotes the hypotext in this particular case. Added to this, an architextual thrust appears to be at work. The conventional description of hospitality, an ancient Mediterranean *topos*, is utilised in both narratives creating an architextual link. There are thus three transtextual correlations to consider: architextual, hypertextual and intertextual, out of which hypertextual is the most dominant.

Acts 10:9–23 tells of Peter's vision and of his encounter with the three messengers sent from Caesarea. The location of the events is the house of a certain Simon in Joppa, near the sea. At noon Peter went up to the roof of house to pray. He became hungry, and while food was being prepared, he saw a vision. In the vision an object filled with all kinds of animals descended from heaven. An unidentified voice commanded Peter to kill and eat. Peter objected to the command stating that he has not defiled himself with anything "profane or unclean" (Acts 10:14). The voice replied by saying: "What God has made clean, you must not call profane" (Acts 10:15). This happened three times.

While Peter kept thinking about the meaning of the vision, "the men sent by Cornelius" (Acts 10:17) came to Simon's house and stood at the gate asking about him. The apostle, still thinking about the vision, was instructed by the Spirit: "Behold, three men are searching for you. Now get up, go down, and go with them without hesitation; for I have sent them" (Acts 10:20). Peter thus went down and revealed himself to the messengers and asked about the purpose of their coming. The men answered by summing up what the "holy angel" commanded to Cornelius. Peter invited the guests in and hosted them. Next day he got up with them and began his journey to Caesarea. In Acts 10:24 the next episode in Caesarea begins.

Before proceeding to discuss hypertextual connection between the two narratives, some clarification is needed with regard to serious imitation. Imitation as a syntactic phenomenon has already been discussed in relation to the language of Acts. There it was pointed out that turns of phrases, constructions, syntax, morphology, and vocabulary from the LXX are applied throughout the book of Acts. It has also been noted that the effect of such vast imitation of the LXX makes Acts a continuation of the same body of books. Genette, however, extends imitation to further territories, to figure of speech, figure of thought, or characteristic trope—to name a few.[76] He then discusses several types of imitations of playful, satirical, and serious mode. The hypertextual operation at hand clearly is neither playful nor satirical. Serious imitation would have to be a natural choice.

Genette, however, discusses forgery, continuation, and sequel under this heading. None of these describe the correlation of texts examined below. The reason I decided to discuss what follows under serious imitation is that some aspects of the connection proposed stand in harmony with imitation. The hypertextual connection rests on adherence in the hypertext to certain themes, characters, narrative

[76] Genette, *Palimpsests*, 75.

settings, and very often on verbal correspondence, allusions, or even quotations from the hypotext. All these are markers of serious transformation, as in the case of the Cornelius narrative. What distinguishes the type of serious imitation here from serious transformation can be deduced from the lack of shared plot.

It would be more precise to state that the interaction between the texts is too limited in length to establish a shared plot. It is more correct to claim that the connection between the texts rests on an identifiable characteristic theme. Therefore, this could be called—in the spirit of Genette—*thematic imitation*. Characters with comparable attributes or with similar settings also appear to be essential for this kind of operation. Verbal correspondence of some kind makes the connection most identifiable. The close resemblance of temporal, spatial, and social settings also aids the connection. Evoking a certain theme and situation from the OT is one of the most frequent textual connections in Acts 10:1–15:35. Short episodes centering on a shared theme, comparable protagonist, and similar settings evoke their counterparts from the OT. Thematic imitation is suggested to be at work in receiving the three messengers but also in the shipwreck of Paul as explained above, and other episodes in Acts.

2.3.2.1. Genesis 18:1–8

The suggested hypotext for the short episode in the Cornelius narrative is the reception and hosting of the three messengers from Gen 18:1–8. Genesis 18 is part the of the wider Abraham narrative in Gen 12–25, which is dominated by themes of covenant-making and promise. In Gen 18 the Lord is said to have appeared to Abraham at the oak of Mamre. This is a remark by the narrator denoting theophany. Abraham is depicted as one sitting at the entrance of his tent in the heat of the day. The LXX departs from the MT in two respects. The Greek text specifically mentions the *door* of the tent, whereas the MT speaks of the *entrance*. Further, the reference to heat in the Hebrew text is made to reflect more specifically the time of the day—that is midday.

Abraham looked up from the entrance/door of the tent and saw three men who stood by him. Both versions emphasize the patriarch's gestures of greeting the strangers. He ran to meet them and bowed down before them. The greetings are eloquent and detailed, even according to biblical standards: "My Lord, if I find favor with you, do not pass by your servant" (Gen 18:3). The men thus are invited to stay, have their feet washed and rest in the shade. In the LXX the feet of the men are to be washed by Abraham's slaves. In the meantime, Abraham was busy preparing a gracious meal for the guests.

Abraham's hospitality receives emphasis by the repeated reference to speed. He "hurries" to greet the stranger (18:2) and "hurries" Sarah to prepare the meal "quickly" (18:6). Abraham "runs" to get the calf and "hurries" his servants to prepare the beef (18:7). The emphasis on speed, combined with remarkable details of the meal, make Abraham a very eager and generous host.[77]

At this point it is useful to make note of the ambiguity of the text that gave rise to rich interpretations. It is not at all clear whether Abraham recognized the Lord or his messengers in the three men or at what point he did so. The designation, *My Lord* could well be an epithet for God or could simply be read as a courteous gesture to another human being. Another level of rich ambiguity is provided by the back and forth usage of plural to singular in addressing the men.[78] When using the singular form, Abraham could speak to one of them, perhaps a leader, or could speak to the Lord himself as being present through his messengers. What is significant here is that Abraham's eagerness, showed in greeting and hosting the men, could be seen as a mere gesture of hospitality to strangers who only later are found out to be messengers or angels of God.

Following the meal two important revelations are given to Abraham. First, the messengers make a promise about the child who is to be born in a year's time (Gen 18:10). Second, the three messengers

---

[77] Weston W. Fields, *Sodom and Gomorrah: History and Motif in Biblical Narrative*, JSOTSup 231 (Sheffield: Sheffield Academic Press, 1997), 57.

[78] S. Spero, "'But Abraham Stood yet Before the Lord,'" *JBQ* 36 (2008): 12.

set out for Sodom and Gomorrah the next day. Abraham decided to join his guests on the journey. While travelling the messengers repeat the promise that Abraham will be a great nation and that the nations shall be blessed through him. They also reveal to him God's plan to destroy Sodom and Gomorrah, the cities of the plain (Gen 18:20–21). Although Abraham interceded on the behalf of the two cities, there were not enough innocent people to turn away God's anger.

2.3.2.2. Gen 18:1–8 and Other Texts of the OT

The account of Gen 18 is believed by many to stand in close connection with Gen 19 depicting the angels' visit to Sodom. A number of structural, thematic, and verbal parallels point to common design achieved with literary artistry.[79] Both the visit to Abraham and the visit to the inhabitants of Sodom follow a similar plot with contrasting results. As Abraham saw the men from the entrance of the tent, so Lot met the two angels at the gate of Sodom (Gen 19:1). Beyond very similar locations for the meeting, time is also named in both accounts. Moreover, Lot's eagerness to host the two angels compares to that of Abraham—i.e., generous hospitality is offered by both men. However, the dwellers of Sodom intended to violate that hospitality by wanting to be with the strangers. And hosting the messengers in the Abraham story results in the promise of a son, while violating hospitality in the Lot story results in destruction for Sodom.[80]

---

[79] Kenneth Mathews, *Genesis 11:27–50:26*, NAC 1B (Nashville: Holman Reference, 2005), 208–15.

[80] Wenham argues convincingly that Lot stands in parallel with Noah: "But the author does not simply compare Lot with Abraham; he is also interested in comparing the destruction of Sodom with the flood. Clearly the theme is the same: the mass destruction of the world (cities of the plain) and the escape of one righteous man and his family. There are many verbal echoes of the flood story…and the overall structures of the narratives are similar: in both cases the story of the hero's escape and the destruction of the wicked, told in a carefully worked out palistrophe…is follow by his intoxication and shameful treatment by his children" (Gordon J. Wenham, *Genesis 16–50*, WBC 2 [Dallas: Word, 2015], 41).

The degree of hospitality shown by Abraham is unparalleled even within the Bible. Hospitality, however, was a general requirement in ancient Mediterranean cultures. Wild animals, thieves and robbers, cruel climate conditions, and unavailability of food and water made it virtually impossible to survive without assistance from local inhabitants. It was necessary to turn strangers into guests to save them. The right and obligation of strangers[81] in the legal part of the Pentateuch is often emphasized in the context of Israel's nomadic past.[82] Added to this, legal requirements in the Pentateuch are often grounded and exemplified in narratives about patriarchs. Events in the lives of biblical characters become laws to be followed. Narrative motifs contain and reinforce legal principles. Fields names "strangers in your gate" to be a recurring motif reinforced in several biblical stories including Gen 18.[83]

According to Malina "hospitality might be defined as the process by means of which an outsider's status is changed from stranger to guest."[84] The process markedly "differs from entertaining family and friends."[85] Based on several narratives of hospitality,[86] Fields proposed a scheme for portraying hosting guests in the OT:

---

[81] A list of rights and obligations is put together by Fields. The stranger in Israel has the right to eat the Passover meal if circumcised (Exod 12:48); he has the right to flee to the cities of refuge (Num 35:15); he has the right to fair legal procedure (Deut 1:16). Responsibilities include circumcision (Exod 12:48); observance of Shabbat (Exod 20:10); observance of the prohibition against eating blood—see Fields, *Sodom and Gomorrah*, 33.

[82] See especially Exod 22:21; 23:9; Lev 19:33–34; Deut 10:19; 23:8.

[83] Fields, Sodom and Gomorrah, 35.

[84] Bruce J. Malina, "The Received View and What It Cannot Do: III John and Hospitality," *Semeia* 35 (1986): 181.

[85] Ibid.

[86] "Abraham's servant (guest) welcomed by Rebekah (Gen. 24.10–59); Abimelech, his advisor, and his army commander (guests) given hospitality by Isaac (Gen. 26.30, 31); Joseph and his brothers (guests) in Egypt (Gen. 43); Moses in Midian (a guest who becomes a sojourner, Exod. 2.16–22); Boaz and Ruth (sojourner, Ruth 2, 3); David's men (guests) with Nabal's servants (1 Sam. 25.14–16, 21); the man of God from Judah (guest) and the old prophet (1 Kgs 13.18–22);

1. greeting
2. formal offer of hospitality
3. guest's refusal of hospitality and host's reoffer
4. washing the feet
5. rest
6. offering of drink (water, wine, or milk)
7. food
8. sleeping quarters
9. protection
10. care for the travellers' beasts of burden
11. reciprocity (something done for the host by the guest)
12. seeing the guest on his way.[87]

All or some of these actions are found in descriptions of hospitality.

A significant group of biblical narratives, however, portray the destructive results of violating the requirements of hospitality. The destruction of Sodom in Gen 19, the killing of the concubine in Gibeah in Judg 19 and the destruction of Jericho in Josh 2 demonstrate the potential harm in disrespecting the laws of hospitality. Such negative narratives seem to operate on a number of sub-motifs. The liminal aspect of time and space is often in view, and morning or dawn appears to convey safety, whereas night or evening denotes approaching danger. Similarly, space is associated with safety and danger—ranging from home to door, threshold, street/square, gate/wall to field/mountains/desert.

A motif of reversal of safety zones occurs when the home or town is no longer safe and deliverance is available outside.[88] Inimical townspeople appear in negative hospitality narratives when they do not receive guests or even harass them sexually. The negative outcome for

---

Elijah (guest) and the widow of Zarephath (1 Kgs 17.7–24); and Elisha (guest) and the Shunammite woman (2 Kgs 4.8–11)" (Fields, *Sodom and Gomorrah*, 55).

[87] Ibid., 56.

[88] Ibid., 72–86.

the city can be destruction by fire.[89] The negative stories, however, are aimed to reinforce hospitality requirements by emphasizing the destructive outcome of neglecting the obligation.

It could be argued that Gen 18–19 offers a peculiar case since the strangers are angels sent from God. The identity of the messengers is revealed gradually to the characters involved. This could be seen as a sub-category of hosting messengers, a *topos* not alien to Graeco-Roman literature either. In his paper on the theme of hospitality and its use in ethical (right behavior while participating in a feast as in Luke 24:1–24), theological (God visiting his people with salvation in Jesus's coming to the world), ecclesiological (feasts as essential expressions of community in household communities in Acts) and eschatological (foretaste of the eschatological feast as in Luke 13:22–30) contexts in Luke-Acts, Adelbert Denaux suggested that Luke drew on both OT and Graeco-Roman antecedents.[90] Familiarity with the latter can be proven by Luke's use of the *topos* of divine visitors in disguise in a number of passages in Acts. One example comes from Acts 14:8–18. When Paul and Barnabas heal a lame man in Lystra, the people of the city are amazed while shouting "the gods are come down to us in the likeness of men" (Acts 14:11). Moreover, they identify Barnabas as Zeus and Paul as Hermes. Sacrificial animals were brought to the gates to offer sacrifices to divine visitors. Barnabas and Paul made great efforts in pointing out that they were humans like the others.

A similar motif is at work in Acts 28:1–8. After the shipwreck, Paul made his way to the island of Malta where he got bitten by a viper. When the local people saw that the apostles shook off the viper and was not harmed by it, they said that he was a god.

Denaux tentatively suggests that Acts 10:25–26 belongs to the same group as the two texts mentioned above. When Peter was

---

[89] Ibid., 53.

[90] Adelbert Denaux, "The Theme of Divine Visits and Human (In)Hospitality in Luke-Acts: Its Old Testament and Graeco-Roman Antecedents," in *The Unity of Luke-Acts*, ed. Joseph Verheyden, BETL 142 (Leuven: Leuven University Press, 1999), 255–79.

entering the house in Caesarea, Cornelius met him "and falling at his feet, worshipped him." Peter turned away the gesture by stating that he too was a man.[91]

Luke Timothy Johnson, when commenting on Acts 14:12, proposed that the tale of Baucis and Philemon hosting the gods Zeus and Hermes in Ovid's *Metamorphoses* (cf. 8:611–724) stands in close connection with the story of Paul and Barnabas. A clear point of contact can be seen when the two are identified with the two gods. The two gods are said to have looked for lodging for the night in the Phrygian hills in human form just to find out that they were not welcomed by anyone. Finally, Baucis and Philemon, an old couple, hosted the two disguised gods in their humble house and offered them food that was available. As a reward for hospitality, the gods made the aged couple priests of the temple of Zeus.[92] With regard to the tale's connection to Acts 14, Johnson concludes: "It is difficult to avoid the suspicion that Luke's account plays off such a tradition."[93]

Denaux points out that Ovid's tale is informed by a rich tradition of Greek literature and he also suggests that influence from Gen 18–19 cannot be excluded.[94] Establishing a map of influence stands far away from the aim of the discussion here. It is of significance, however, that the literary *topos* of divines visiting in human form is applied in Acts and could well be at work in Acts 10.

In sum, a traditional description of receiving guests with fixed motifs is clearly effective in the Abraham narrative. A more specific form of receiving divine visitors known in both the OT and Graeco-Roman literature is exemplified in Gen 18 and throughout Acts. The reception of the three messengers from Caesarea and the hosting of the three angels in Gen 18 share a common *topos*. This is a silent, archi-

---

[91] Ibid., 264.

[92] Ovid, *Metamorphoses*, trans. David Raeburn, repr. ed. (London: Penguin Classics, 2004).

[93] Luke Timothy Johnson, *The Acts of the Apostles*, SP 5 (Collegeville, MN: Liturgical, 2006), 248.

[94] Denaux, "Theme," 265.

textual connection, where Gen 18 is thought to be the model for the *topos* itself.

2.3.2.3. Gen 18:1–8 as Hypotext for Acts 10:9–23

What follows is an attempt to demonstrate that Gen 18:1–8 is evoked in Acts 10:9–23. Receiving guests, and receiving guests whose identity might be divine, in particular, binds the two narratives. More than that, I will argue that the story of Abraham is evoked beyond the architextual correlation. There exists a hypertextual connection between the two accounts. This situation however presents a particular challenge: with two similar narratives, it is virtually impossible to separate elements that are due to a common *topos*, and elements that are hypertextually evoked. One could easily be misled by claiming a common plot, whereas in reality the *topos* determines the sequence. Allusion and quote, however, cannot come from a common pattern.

The first link is the time settings of the two episodes. The vision and the encounter both take place at noon. Luke uses the expression "the sixth hour" (περὶ ὥραν ἕκτην [Acts 10:9]) to identify the time of events. This time of the day is equivalent to twelve o'clock. The LXX (Gen 18:1) applies a different term: midday (μεσημβρία), referring to the same time of the day. The Hebrew text links the time of that day with heat. The LXX however omits any reference to temperature, thus turning midday into a marker of time. The readers are only told that Abraham in the middle of the day withdrew into his tent. Peter was following the order of Jewish prayer times when ascending to the rooftop. Both events start to take place at the same time of the day.

The second element is the emphasis laid at the entrance of Abraham's gate, on the one hand, and at the gate of Simon's house, on the other. The emphasis on the gate or entrance is characteristic of the *topos*. The LXX text portrays Abraham as sitting at the door of his tent (καθημένου αὐτοῦ ἐπὶ τῆς θύρας τῆς σκηνῆς αὐτοῦ [Gen 18:1]). In the text of Acts the reader is told that after Peter's vision, the three messengers arrived at the gate of the house where the apostle was staying. In verse 17, readers find out that the messengers, while asking about Simon's house, stood at the gate (ἐπέστησαν ἐπὶ τὸν πυλῶνα [Acts 10:17]). In both narratives the encounter has its beginning at the entrance of buildings.[95]

Thirdly, in both Genesis and Acts the narrators reveal a significant detail about the heavenly dimension of events. In the story of Abraham, the voice of the omniscient narrator explains at the beginning that God himself appeared by the oaks of Mamre (Ὤφθη δὲ αὐτῷ ὁ θεὸς). It does not necessarily mean that Abraham was aware of God's coming (cf. Heb 13:2), but readers are given the privilege of knowing. Readers find out in Peter's story that while waiting for food to be prepared and served, the apostle fell into a trance and saw a vision (παρασκευαζόντων δὲ αὐτῶν ἐγένετο ἐπ' αὐτὸν ἔκστασις [Acts 10:10]). He saw the heaven opened and a large object filled with animals descending. While receiving the vision, the apostle conversed with a voice. The unidentified speaker is addressed as *My Lord*. In this context it appears safe to conclude that Peter was speaking to an angel. Finally, at the end of the episode the word *vision* is used (10:19).

Fourthly, identity of words catches one's attention. This is a link of intertextual character. The arrival of the three men is described by the same words in both narratives with minor variation in their order. In the LXX the expression "Behold, three men" (ἰδοὺ τρεῖς ἄνδρες [Gen 18:2]) is used when the narrator draws attention to the three men arriving to Abraham's tent. In Acts 10:19 the order is changed by placing the word *three* at the end (ἰδοὺ ἄνδρες τρεῖς [Acts 10:19]). The Holy Spirit tells Peter with these words to receive the three messengers sent by Cornelius. It is noteworthy that earlier in the Cornelius episode the narrator knew of two servants and one devout soldier (10:7), whereas in the examined passage they are identified as three men having been sent by God himself. The regrouping is justified by the intertext. The parallel account in Acts 11 makes the verbal correspondence even more apparent:

---

[95] The structure of the narrative in Gen 18 proves to be parallel with that of Gen 19. In this later episode two angels visit Lot in the city of Sodom while he was sitting at the gates (Λωτ δὲ ἐκάθητο παρὰ τὴν πύλην Σοδομων [LXX Gen 19:1]).

Gen 18:2	Acts 11:11	Acts 10:19
…behold, three men stood over him.	And behold, immediately three men arrived at the house where they were.	…behold, three men searching for you.
ἰδοὺ τρεῖς ἄνδρες εἱστήκεισαν ἐπάνω αὐτοῦ	Καὶ ἰδοὺ ἐξαυτῆς τρεῖς ἄνδρες ἐπέστησαν ἐπὶ τὴν οἰκίαν ἐν ᾗ ἦμεν	Ἰδοὺ ἄνδρες τρεῖς ζητοῦντές σε

Two further remarks are necessary, as they relate to the verbal correspondence. On the one hand, Acts 11:11 stands closer to Gen 18:2 than Acts 10:19 does. The reason for a closer adherence could well be the lack of supporting narrative context in Acts 11. Whereas in Acts 10 other thematic, temporal and sequential parallels help to establish the connection, in Acts 11 only similar words provide the connection. On the other hand, Acts 11 has a different tense for the Greek verb *to stand.* The change is from perfect tense to aorist. The same change will take place in an allusion in Acts 10:14 and 11:8.

Fifthly, the protagonist in both stories invites the messengers to share a common meal. Owing to its influence on the world of arts, the meal Abraham prepared for the three men is well known beyond biblical scholarship. The vision episode in Acts ends with Peter inviting them into Simon's house.[96] The Greek word used in 10:23 has a wider meaning. The expression "Peter invited them in and gave them lodging" (εἰσκαλεσάμενος οὖν αὐτοὺς ἐξένισεν) involves providing lodging and offering food. Although the words are different in the two

---

[96] Hospitality and table fellowship is a significant phenomenon in the entire NT. For a useful introduction, see János Bolyki, *Jézus asztalközösségei* (Budapest: Református Teológiai Akadémia, 1993).

narratives the meal following the encounter brings them close. The common meal is an unmissable element of the hosting *topos* as well as central to the Abraham narrative.

Finally, the motif of travelling together can be listed among similarities. On the following day Peter, joining the messengers, starts his journey to Caesarea, to the house of Cornelius. Abraham, in a like manner, joins the three men who set out for Sodom. While travelling, the messengers repeat the promise about Abraham becoming a great nation and reveal God's plan to destroy the two sinful cities. Abraham tries to intercede on behalf of the cities. As a result, God shows willingness to spare the people—even for the ten righteous. The attempt to save the Gentiles, however, proves to be unsuccessful. The Lord departs and Abraham returns home. While, seeing the guests on his way is an obligation of the host, Abraham's journey toward a sinful city, however, proves instrumental for the city of Sodom.

In conclusion, Luke built into his narrative several elements of the story about Abraham and the three men. Both stories start at the same time of day. The beginning of the encounter starts at the entrance of buildings—a conventional marker of zones. The narrative time and space speak of the shared *topos* and well as have the potential for bridging the two individual narratives. The frame of vision provides a further link. Finally, the common meal and travelling toward Gentiles strengthen echoes of Gen 18 in Peter's story. The meal fellowship between Peter and the Gentiles is later questioned in Jerusalem. Set in harmony with the obligation of hospitality in general and with the openness to host divine visitors in particular, we see Peter's decision as being in congruity with the law. Peter's interaction thus framed is not an offence but an obligation. The identical words pointing to the arrival of the three men make this point even stronger: the three men are sent by God the way the three men represented God in Gen 18. Obeying them, therefore, is obeying God—the result of which might be a great salvation. On a methodological note, it is to be noted again that this is a short episode relating to one main protagonist and three characters, their encounter, and their feast. This is supported by a nearly identical phrase. Thematic imitation thus appears to be the most accurate term to define the connection.

2.3.2.4. Ezekiel 4:14 as an Intertext for Acts 10:14 and 11:8

The last correlation examined in Acts 10:1–11:18 is a short allusion. The words of Peter's objection in Acts 10:14 to the command given to him during the vision to kill and eat the animals seen in the descending object corresponds to the objection of the prophet Ezekiel in 4:14 to a divine command to eat food prepared in a certain way. The allusion of Acts 10:14 becomes even more evident in 11:8:[97]

Ezek 4:14	Acts 11:8	Acts 10:14
And I said, *Not so, Lord*, God of Israel, surely my soul has not been defiled in *uncleanness* and from my birth until now I have not eaten a carcass or that which was killed by animals, neither has any corrupt flesh *entered into my mouth.*	But I said, *Not so, Lord*: for nothing *common or unclean* has at any time *entered into my mouth.*	But Peter said, *Not so, Lord*; for I have never eaten any thing that is *common or unclean.*
Καὶ εἶπα Μηδαμῶς, κύριε θεὲ τοῦ Ισραηλ· ἰδοὺ ἡ ψυχή μου οὐ μεμίανται ἐν ἀκαθαρσίᾳ, καὶ θνησιμαῖον καὶ	Εἶπον δέ μηδαμῶς, κύριε, ὅτι κοινὸν ἢ ἀκάθαρτον οὐδέποτε εἰσῆλθεν εἰς τὸ στόμα μου.	ὁ δὲ Πέτρος εἶπεν μηδαμῶς, κύριε, ὅτι οὐδέποτε ἔφαγον πᾶν κοινὸν καὶ ἀκάθαρτον.

[97] All of the following translations are my own.

θηριάλωτον οὐ βέβρωκα ἀπὸ γενέσεώς μου ἕως τοῦ νῦν, οὐδὲ εἰσελήλυθεν εἰς τὸ στόμα μου πᾶν κρέας ἕωλον.		

A number of observations can be made about the allusion. In both Acts 10:14 and 11:8 the alluded text is abbreviated. They all start with the identical acclamation, "Not so Lord" followed by the tetragram in the MT, and "God of Israel" in the LXX. Acts leaves out any further names for God. The text in Acts, furthermore, avoids the more general statement about Ezekiel never defiling himself. The rather poetic expression, "from my birth until now" (MT: "from my youth until now") is abbreviated again into a simple word "never" (οὐδέποτε). From this point on the two verses in Acts take a different path. There are two verbs in the perfect tense in Ezek 4:14: *eat* and *enter*. Acts 10:14 therefore makes a general statement about Peter not having eaten anything common or unclean. In Acts 11:8 Peter claims that nothing common or unclean entered his mouth. Both verses in Acts use the aorist tense instead of the perfect. The whole detailed description of carcass and flesh killed by animals, on the one hand, and corrupt flesh, on the other, is replaced by the expression "common or unclean." In sum, common in the two versions of the allusion is that they abbreviate and take the detailed description of unclean food to mean simply "common or unclean." It is noteworthy that the two versions seem to pick up different verbs from the alluded text.

The words of Ezekiel in their original context deserve some examination. The verse is a response by the prophet to a commission given to him by God. Phinney argues for Ezek 4:14 to be seen as a belated objection from the prophet to his call recorded earlier in Ezek

1:2–3:15.[98] The structure of such call accounts in biblical narratives usually can be broken into six elements:[99] (1) divine confrontation, (2) introductory word, (3) commission, (4) objection, (5) reassurance, and (6) sign.[100] Voicing the prophetic objection, following the commission, is usually short, not longer than a sentence, and often introduced by an ejaculatory cry. The objection is related to the specific needs and wants of the would-be prophet. The objection is not merely an expression of the prophet's insufficiency, or humility. It is a response to the difficult task of mediating between God and his people.[101]

However, seeing Ezek 4:14 as an objection to the prophetic call is not without problems. First, the verse lies outside the account of Ezekiel's prophetic call. In Ezek 4 the prophet is entrusted with a particular task. It is also to be noted that there are three further objections in Ezekiel (9:8; 11:13; 21:5/20:49 [NRSV]). It seems to be a better solution to view this episode as a prophetic commission where the prophet is entrusted with a concrete task. The prophetic objection in 4:14 is part of a larger design in Ezekiel containing signs and visions of woe for the people of God (cf. 4:1–11:25). Within the larger section, chapters 4–7 contain messages of doom for Jerusalem and the land.[102] The prophet is compelled to present the fall of Jerusalem and the fate of the people of God through a number of symbolic acts. First, Ezekiel uses bricks to enact the siege (4:1–3). Then Ezekiel is to lie on his left and right side respectively to signify time spent in shame for Israel (4:4–6). A short command follows for the prophet to uncover his arm (4:7) along with a statement about the binding of Ezekiel (4:8). After this, Ezekiel is commanded to eat rationed food and drink

[98] D. Nathan Phinney, "The Prophetic Objection in Ezekiel IV 14 and Its Relation to Ezekiel's Call," *VT* 55 (2005): 75–88.

[99] Examples for prophetic call include among others the call of Gideon (Judg 6:11–17), of Isaiah (Isa 6), and of Moses (Exod 18).

[100] Norman C. Habel, "Form and Significance of the Call Narratives," *ZAW* 77 (1965): 298.

[101] Ibid., 318–19.

[102] Daniel I. Block, *The Book of Ezekiel: Chapters 1–24*, NICOT (Grand Rapids: Eerdmans, 1997), 162.

rationed water (4:9–11) and to prepare cakes from different grain over human waste (4:12–15).[103] Following Ezekiel's protest, God allows his prophet to use cow waste as fuel.

This last episode contains Ezekiel's protest, therefore, deserves attention. Ezekiel is ordered to prepare bread from six different kinds of food: wheat, barley, beans, lentils, millet, and emmer. The prophet is to mix these grains and vegetables to bake bread. Zimmerli notes that Lev 19:19 and Deut 22:9 prohibit Israelites from sowing different kinds of seed in the same field. However, mixing grains in bread is not prohibited in the OT; therefore, it cannot be the issue here.[104] Ezekiel is commanded to eat bread named after only one component, barley. Block suggests that *barley cake* is a reference to the kind of bread only lower classes ate, and composition is not in view.[105]

The issue of food is taken further when Ezekiel is ordered to bake his bread over human excrement. This is to be done to reveal that "Thus shall the people of Israel eat their bread, unclean, among the nations, to which I will drive them" (Ezek 4:13). Gentile land was, by definition, unclean. Thus, living in captivity would entail an unclean life for the sons of Israel.

It should be noted that neither the mixing of grain nor the question of human waste is reflected on directly in Ezekiel's objection. This makes Ezekiel's response something of an enigma. Following his exclamation, Ezekiel begins by saying that his person has never been defiled nor has unclean food entered his mouth. The prophet then names three categories of unclean food.

First, he has never eaten animals that died of disease or exhaustion. Second, he never had the flesh of animals that were killed by other animals. Finally, he kept away from contaminated meat—sacrificial meat that was kept beyond the third day of slaughter. The best, but not entirely satisfying solution is that Ezekiel's response naming concrete

---

[103] Ibid., 167.

[104] Walther Zimmerli, *Ezekiel: A Commentary on the Book of the Prophet Ezekiel*, trans. Klaus Baltzer, vol. 1, Hermeneia (Philadelphia: Fortress, 1979), 169.

[105] Block, *Ezekiel*, 185.

cases of dietary transgressions stands for the entire regulation of food laws: "The prophet's mention of these two elements of purity law should be taken as a metonymy.... His articulation of fastidious observance of one part of purity law is designed to communicate his observance of the entire purity law. This solution, while not wholly satisfactory, probably best explains both the content and apparent tenor of the text."[106] Ezekiel objected to eating what God showed him by stating that he had kept away from all unclean food in his life.[107]

Evoking the objection of Ezekiel in Acts might be driven by the similarity of the situations. Both men are commanded by God to do something they think contrary to dietary laws. Bearing in mind that the action signifies uncleanness caused by Gentiles during the imminent exile in Ezekiel, a further point of correspondence can be established. Both Peter and Ezekiel are concerned with the threat of uncleanness caused by Gentiles. Beyond this, however, no similar plot, or shared motifs bind the two narratives together. This is a purely intertextual correlation that is not part of other transtextual operations. Peter objects to the command with the words of prophet Ezekiel.

2.4. Conclusions

Architextual, hypertextual, and intertextual correlations have been studied in Acts 10:1–11:18. The conversion of Cornelius and the initial reaction by Peter and the church is told by creating a distant connection with narratives about believing pagan men of authority. The vision of Peter and of Cornelius is linked with the previous dual visions in Luke-Acts and other ancient literary works. It has been argued that the overall connection with the story of Jonah is best described as transposition, and thus hypertextual. The story of Jonah sets the narrative on course primarily through common shared plot. Peter is portrayed as driven by God to fulfill God's will to save the Gentiles. The receiving of the three messengers is shown through

[106] Phinney, "The Prophetic Objection," 80–81.

[107] John Calvin, *Ezekiel I: Chapters 1–12*, trans. David Foxgrover, COTC 18 (Grand Rapids: Eerdmans, 1994), 121.

thematic imitation in the light of Abraham's story about hosting the three angels. Feasting with the Gentiles, a major separating issue between Jews and non-Israelites, is thus set into the context of hospitality. Both architextual and hypertextual correlations thus favor the Gentile mission. Objection is made through a loud but not too deep intertextual connection. The words of Ezekiel's objection to the mission are alluded to by Peter, but the objection is countered not least by the more overreaching transtextual operations.

Chapter 3

PETER'S DELIVERANCE AND THE FATE OF HEROD: ACTS 12:1–25

3.1. Introduction

Acts 12 naturally divides into two parts: first, the imprisonment and deliverance of Peter is told in 12:1–17; second, Herod's punishment is recounted in 12:18–23. The chapter closes with a short remark in 12:24–25 about the growth of the church.

Acts 12 begins with the persecution of the church, and of Peter in particular, carried out by the Jewish ruler Herod. This ruler—named Herod Agrippa in historical sources—is the son of Herod the Great. Yet, he is simply called Herod in Acts 12.[1] The killing of James, the brother of John, is summarized in an analeptic fashion in 12:1–2. Peter's arrest was ordered as a result of popularity won by that earlier killing. Next, Peter's deliverance is recounted. The rescue took place on the night of the Jewish feast of Passover. An angel visited the prisoner and led him out miraculously. Following this, the apostle went to the Christian community where he reported the deliverance.

The second part in Acts 12:18–23 depicts Herod as he was punished for hubris. The following morning Herod found out that Peter was gone. The ruler had the guards examined and executed. Following this, the king received negotiators from Tyre and Sidon, whose people depended on Herod for food supply. The king was found guilty by the narrator of receiving praise from the people of Tyre and Sidon that only God should receive. For this act of hubris Herod was punished with a special punishment: an angel struck him and his body was eaten by worms. A final remark is made about the advancement of the word of God in 12:24–25.

---

[1] Witherington, *Acts*, 382.

The narrative, therefore, starts with hostility from a ruler against representatives of the church. In response to the threat, God delivered his servant and punished the evil ruler with an immediate punishment of harsh severity. Finally, the rescue of Peter and the end of Herod contributed to the growth of the church. In the last verse Barnabas and Saul, who will play significant role in the next chapter, are mentioned.

3.2. Hypertextual Correlations

Two hypertextual correlations will be examined in Acts 12. It will be argued first that the deliverance of Peter in Acts 12:1–17 is most appropriately understood as a thematic imitation, mainly of both the exodus account from the book of Exodus and of the passion and resurrection of Jesus from Luke's Gospel. This remark implies that two hypotexts are imitated in one hypertext—a reasonable enough complication. But in fact it gets more complex if one considers that the passion narrative is already shaped after the exodus.[2] One of the hypotexts is thus already the hypertext of the other, and at the same time both remain hypotexts for a third text, Acts 13:1–17. But this is not the end: at least three further exodus-like events are evoked in relation to Peter's deliverance. These alluded texts are the prayer of the Israelites during a threat from Nebuchadnezzar in Jdt 4, the waking of Elijah in the desert in 1 Kgs 19, and the deliverance of Daniel's friends and of Daniel himself in Dan 3 and 6.

Several exodus-like narratives are, therefore, evoked together in the hypertext—some weighing in more significantly than others. It is justified to claim that the topic of divine deliverance, modeled after the exodus narrative and being in interaction with a number of deliverances—particularly Jesus's death and resurrection—constitutes the hypotext for Acts 12:1–17. This is not to claim, however, that our narrative is predominantly shaped by the *topos* of divine rescue. One could argue that, based on the great number of similar stories of divine

---

[2] For an extensive discussion of the correlation between the exodus narrative and passion narrative, see Susan R. Garrett, "Exodus from Bondage: Luke 9:31 and Acts 12:1–24," *CBQ* 52 (1990): 656–80.

deliverance from evil rulers in Acts (see 5:18–20; 16:23–29; 26:17, 22) and in other books of the NT (Matt 2:13–23), an architextual pattern could be established.[3] Moreover, outside the NT, the paradigmatic story of divine rescue is found in the exodus narrative, which tells of the deliverance of Moses and the Israelites from the king of Egypt. The many verbal correspondences and allusions, however, warn against giving precedence to an assumed *topos*. Concrete stories are evoked in Acts 12, which also happen to share a common interest in deliverance for the people of God from evil rulers.

The second thematic imitation is a less complicated hypertextual operation: the cruel fate of Herod in Acts 12:20–23 will be examined in relation to the end of the king of Tyre as portrayed in Ezek 27.

3.2.1. Deliverances from the Hand of Herod, Pilate, and Pharaoh: A (Special) Case of Thematic Imitation

Acts 12:1–4 introduces readers to the critical situation caused by Herod. He is said to have *stretched forth his hand* to harm members of the church: "King Herod stretched forth his hand against some who belonged to the church" (Acts 12:1). Further, Herod killed James and his brother John. Seeing that the aggression was a popular action among the Jews, Herod had Peter arrested and thrown into prison.

Religious and political leaders in Luke-Acts are said to have stretched forth their hands against Jesus and against the disciples on a number of occasions. The same Greek phrase, ἐπέβαλεν τὰς χεῖρας, is used in relation to Jesus in Luke 20:19, to the disciples in a prophecy about their difficult future in Luke 21:12, and to the apostles' arrest in Acts 4:3 and 5:18.[4] The phrase *to stretch forth one's hand against* is used in Luke-Acts to denote hostility from figures of authority against Jesus and his believers.

Further, textual correlations get more concrete than that: the oppression of Pharaoh is evoked in Herod's action. Earlier in Acts in a

---

[3] Witherington, *Acts*, 381.

[4] Robert C. Tannehill, *The Acts of the Apostles*, vol. 2 of *The Narrative Unity of Luke-Acts: A Literary Interpretation* (Philadelphia: Fortress, 1989), 153.

speech Stephen used the phrase *to deal harshly* (κακόω) twice (Acts 7:6, 19) in reference to Pharaoh's aggression against the Israelites. Naturally, the same Greek word is applied in the exodus narrative to depict Pharaoh's cruelty toward the Jews (Exod 1:11; 5:22, 23). The aggression of Herod against the church thus evokes that of the Pharaoh against the Jews in Egypt.

But it is not just Pharaoh whose shadow falls on Herod. The violence against James, John, and Peter is described with the use of the same vocabulary as can be found in relation to Jesus and his followers. The Greek verb for *to kill* (ἀναιρέω) from Acts 12:2 is also used in reference to Jesus in a number of passages (Luke 22:2; 23:32; Acts 2:23; 10:39; 13:28). Added to this, the word for *handing over* (παραδίδωμι) Peter to the soldiers is also used in connection with Jesus being handed over to Pilate and the leaders for death (Luke 9:44; 18:32; 23:25; 24:7, 20). Jesus's followers are also warned about being *handed over* to the authorities (Luke 21:12; Acts 8:3; 22:4). In sum, the critical situation caused by Herod is portrayed in relation to Jesus's arrest and death[5] and in a more distant relation to the affliction Pharaoh caused to the Jews.

The narrative time for the arrest of Peter also creates reverberations with both the passion and the exodus narratives, as it says: "This was during the festival of Unleavened Bread" (Acts 12:3). Passover is specifically mentioned in the following verse. It is useful to recall Conzelmann's point that "in popular usage 'Passover' (on the fourteenth of Nisan) and the 'Feast of Unleavened Bread' (the following week) blend together (cf. Josephus, *Ant.* 14.21)."[6] The time and space of the events in Acts 12:3 create an abrupt syntax that needs explanation. Tannehill, explaining the interruption of the sentence by the insertion of the time for arrest, claims that a connection is created with the time of the arrest of Jesus as told in Luke 22:1–7, which also

---

[5] Ibid.

[6] Hans Conzelmann, *Acts of the Apostles: A Commentary on the Acts of the Apostles*, trans. James Limburg, A. Thomas Kraabel, and Donald H. Juel, Hermeneia (Philadelphia: Fortress, 1987), 93.

happened during the days of Unleavened Bread.[7] Extra-textual evidence further strengthens the significance of the time for the rescue. The night of Passover was viewed by some rabbinic traditions as the time for God to deliver his people: "it was Passover night when Shadrach, Meshach, and Abednego were saved from the fiery furnace, and it was Passover night when Daniel was saved from the lion's den."[8] Passover night links Peter's narrative with the arrest of Jesus but also creates expectation of deliverance.

A further parallel with the passion narrative is found in the action of bringing Peter forward to the people who had no part in the legal process. The remark could be justified on intertextual grounds: Jesus too was brought forward by Pilate in Luke 22:1.[9] Yet another step in Peter's fate is presented in conformity with that of Jesus.

Parallels with the passion go beyond reverberations of arrest on Passover night and being brought forward for judgment. Peter is depicted as one being asleep while chained in prison. In the NT, along with Hellenistic literature, sleep is often a euphemism for death. Being imprisoned and chained between two soldiers while asleep denotes death.[10] The situation is ended by the angelic presence, which brought light, and by the command to get up quickly. The Greek word (ἀνίστημι) used in this verse often refers to God raising Jesus from the dead along with the regular meaning of getting up. In Eph 5:14 an example can be found when *sleep* and *raise* (from the dead) are used in pair:[11] "Sleeper, awake! Rise from the dead, and Christ will shine on you" (Eph 5:14). The sleeping and rising metaphor clearly points to death and resurrection here. Sleep, chains and prison denote death.

From the point of calling to rise up onwards, the narrative employs key motifs of Jesus's resurrection. The first person to meet Peter after his "resurrection" is a woman named Rhoda (Acts 12:13–14), who ran

---

[7] Tannehill, *Acts of the Apostles*, 153.

[8] Garrett, "Exodus from Bondage," 672.

[9] Haenchen, *Acts*, 382.

[10] Garrett, "Exodus from Bondage," 671–72.

[11] Ibid., 673.

to tell the others about deliverance. Jesus, too, was first met by women according to Luke 24:10. Next, we see that Rhoda's report was not believed by the community, just as the women's witness about the resurrection of Jesus was doubted by the disciples (see Luke 24:11). The Christian community of Acts thought it was an angel the woman saw. Then Peter appeared in the community and told them how the Lord had brought him out of the prison (Acts 12:17), just as Jesus appeared to his followers to assure them of his resurrection. During the appearance, the apostle entrusted the members of the gathered community to tell others of his deliverance: "Tell this to James and to the believers" (Acts 12:17). Jesus also entrusted his disciples with the task of witness (Luke 24:48).

Finally, Peter is said to have departed to "another place" (12:17). Garrett takes this to be a reference to Jesus's ascension to heaven.[12] The narrative about Peter's imprisonment and deliverance is presented in conformity with Jesus's arrest, trial, death, resurrection, appearance, and possibly his ascension. The correspondence is not a direct transposition; it mainly rests on similar motifs, similar expression and themes and not on a close adherence to a plot. It is best understood as thematic imitation.

The story of Peter's deliverance shows reminiscence with elements of the exodus narrative not shared by the passion narrative either. Beyond the above noted term *to deal harshly*, other verbal and thematic elements contribute to an intertextual reading. The connection between the exodus narrative and the text at hand can be further strengthened if one considers ancient readers' perspective—a move that goes beyond the limits of the methodology applied in this work. The benefit of such reading, however, only further strengthens the observations made on a structuralist basis; therefore, a crossover will be allowed.

According to one legend, Moses was imprisoned prior to the deliverance from Egypt. Artapanus, a 3rd or 2nd century BCE Jewish

---

[12] Ibid., 673–74.

writer based in Egypt,[13] wrote that the king of Egypt put Moses into prison and that "when night came, all the doors of the prison opened of their own accord (αὐτομάτως), and some of the guards died while others were overcome with sleep."[14] The gate of the prison that held Peter, too, opened of its own accord (ἥτις αὐτομάτη ἠνοίγη αὐτοῖς [Acts 12:10]). Thus, both Moses and Peter were thrown into prison on Passover night and both were delivered by miraculous opening of prison gates.

Passover connections are made stronger by further motifs. It is noteworthy that the angel told Peter him to get up quickly, dress, and put on sandals: "Fasten your belt and put on your sandals" (Acts 12:8). This motif recalls the instruction given to the Israelites how to prepare for exodus: "This is how you shall eat it: your loins girded, your sandals on your feet, and your staff in your hand" (Exod 12:11). Moreover, later Peter claimed that the Lord had rescued him from the hands of Herod: "the Lord has…rescued me from the hand of Herod" (Acts 12:11). Garrett remarks that rescue from Egypt is often described by the use of the verb *to rescue* (ἐξαιρέω). Rescue from the hand of Pharaoh and from the hand of the Egyptians is a recurring expression in the exodus narrative (e.g., Exod 3:8; 18:4, 8, 9, 10). One particular verse in Exodus is very close to how Peter described his deliverance. The verbal correspondence between Acts 12:11 and Exod 18:4 is identical save for the name of the ruler:

Acts 12:11	Exod 18:4
… rescued me from the hand of Herod ...	… rescued me from the hand of Pharaoh ...
ἐξείλατό με ἐκ χειρὸς Ἡρῴδου	ἐξείλατό με ἐκ χειρὸς Φαραω

[13] Carl R. Holladay, *Historians*, vol. 1 of *Fragments from Hellenistic Jewish Authors*, ed. Harold W. Attridge, trans. Carl R. Holladay (Chico, CA: Scholars, 1983), 190.

[14] Ibid., 219.

The exodus parallel is strengthened by another keyword. Later Peter, telling of the deliverance, mentioned being led out (ἐξήγαγεν ἐκ τῆς φυλακῆς [Acts 12:17]) of the prison. There are a number of passages in the Exod (e.g., 6:7, 27; 7:5; 12:42; 13:9) as well as in Acts (e.g., 7:36, 40; 13:17) where that word *to lead out* is used in context of deliverance out of Egypt.[15] It is a quasi-technical word for this particular action of God. Peter's deliverance is thus linked to exodus from the Egyptian bondage by a number of keywords and expressions.

In sum, both the exodus and passion narrative are evoked in the account of Peter's deliverance. Garrett's summary presents the case with clarity: "The early Christian reader would, of course, have recalled the deliverance of Jesus from death at Passover, and would have been cued by such recollection to notice both exodus and resurrection motifs in the subsequent account."[16] Typical expressions of exodus (*to deal harshly*, *to stretch forth one's hand against someone*, *to lead out from*) along with allusions and verbal correspondences point to an exodus connection. Peter and Moses, on the one hand, and Herod and Pharaoh, on the other, resemble one another. The basic pattern of passion narrative is also employed in the narrative of Peter's deliverance. The two narratives therefore, deliverance from Egypt and resurrection from death, provide the hypotext that are being imitated.

Scholars of the NT have noted further verbal correspondences with several other texts of the OT. The challenge again lays not so much in identifying them as it does in showing a probable logic along which these texts are evoked. It will be argued below that the common elements in the allusions and reverberations are the themes of endangered people of God, an evil ruler, and deliverance.

First, a connection was detected by I. Howard Marshall but dismissed as superficial between Acts 12:5 and Jdt 4:9.[17] The Acts

---

[15] Garrett, "Exodus from Bondage," 675.

[16] Ibid., 672.

[17] I. Howard Marshall, "Acts," in *Commentary on the New Testament Use of the Old Testament*, ed. D.A. Carson and G.K. Beale (Grand Rapids: Baker Academic, 2007), 581; Aland et al., *Novum Testamentum Graece*, 355.

verse tells of how the early church prayed for the imprisoned Peter while the verse in Jdt 4 tells of a national prayer during a threat from Nebuchadnezzar and his army:

Acts 12:5	Jdt 4:9
… but *prayer was made fervently* by the church *unto God* for him.[18]	And *cried out* every man of Israel *very fervently to God* and humbled their spirits *very fervently.*[19]
προσευχὴ δὲ ἦν ἐκτενῶς γινομένη ὑπὸ τῆς ἐκκλησίας πρὸς τὸν θεὸν περὶ αὐτοῦ	καὶ ἀνεβόησαν πᾶς ἀνὴρ Ισραηλ πρὸς τὸν θεὸν ἐν ἐκτενείᾳ μεγάλῃ καὶ ἐταπείνωσαν τὰς ψυχὰς αὐτῶν ἐν ἐκτενείᾳ μεγάλῃ

According to the Judith narrative, Nebuchadnezzar wanted to punish the peoples who did not fight with him in an earlier war. In fear for the Temple, the people of Judea determined to attempt to protect their land (Jdt 4:1–3). The high priest ordered a national prayer. Interestingly, this is the only prayer in Judith to which a divine response is recorded: "and the Lord listened to their cry and beheld their distress" (Jdt 4:13). This is not made obvious, however, to the ones who pray. In fact, the rest of the narrative revolves around how the divine favor is realized in the national conflict.

Eynde points out that the language of Jdt 4:9 is particularly reminiscent of two exodus accounts of divine compassion toward the Israelites.[20] First, God responds to the distress of Israel: "And God listened to their groaning, and God remembered his covenant with Abraham and Isaac and Jacob. And God looked upon the sons of

---

[18] My translation.

[19] This translation shows the parallel vocabulary with Acts 12:5.

[20] Sabine van den Eynde, "Crying to God: Prayer and Plot in the Book of Judith," *Bib* 85 (2004): 220.

Israel, and he became known to them" (Exod 2:24–25). Another verbal correspondence is suggested with the following verse: "When I looked, I saw the affliction of my people in Egypt, and I have heard their cry on account of the taskmasters. For I know their pain" (Exod 3:7). The people's cry in national crisis is presented in conformity with God's earlier attentiveness to that cry in Egypt. The receiving of mercy is thus foreshadowed in the wording of the cry.

Ironically, Judea's enemies are more certain about God's help than his own people. The link between Jdt 4 and the exodus narrative is even further strengthened by the account of Nebuchadnezzar's allies. In response to the inquiry of the captain of the army, the neighboring nations recount the history of Israel. Their account emphasizes that God saved the Jews from the Egyptian king and protected them from other nations, smiting their enemies with plagues. The allies claim that as long as Israel does not sin, God will be on their side (Jdt 5:5–21). Based on the many references in Judith to the exodus account,[21] it is reasonable to claim that exodus vocabulary is already evoked in Judith.[22] The prayer of the church in Acts is thus presented with the vocabulary of the prayer of the Israelites in Jdt 4. Both Israel and the church were persecuted by a powerful ruler and both prayed in response. The reference to the potential of prayer in a similar situation endows the prayer in Acts with hope.

A further correlation is suggested between Peter's encounter with the angel and Elijah's experience in the desert:[23]

---

[21] There are many references in Judith to the exodus narrative—see ibid.

[22] While examining connections between the Acts 12 account and Judith, it is to be noted that being eaten by worms, a punishment, is apostrophized in the book: "Woe to the nations who plot against my race; the omnipotent Lord will punish them in the day of judgement, to send fire and worms for their flesh, and they will wail in full consciousness forever" (Jdt 16:17). Herod's punishment for accepting praise from the crowd in Acts 12 is being eaten by worms.

[23] For the following table and the next, see Aland et al., *Novum Testamentum Graece*, 355–56—my translations

Acts 12:7	1 Kgs 19:5
He tapped Peter on the side and woke him, saying, "*Rise up* quickly."	And behold, someone *touched him and said to him*: "*Rise up* and eat."
πατάξας δὲ τὴν πλευρὰν τοῦ Πέτρου ἤγειρεν αὐτὸν λέγων ἀνάστα ἐν τάχει	καὶ ἰδού τις ἥψατο αὐτοῦ καὶ εἶπεν αὐτῷ Ἀνάστηθι καὶ φάγε

Elijah is said to have fled for his life in the wilderness from Ahab and Jezebel in 1 Kgs 19. The queen promised the prophet to take his life for killing the Baal prophets. Elijah escaped to the desert and sat down near a tree, wanting to die. The disillusioned prophet fell asleep. The LXX knows of someone who touched the prophet and commanded him to wake up while the MT text explicitly mentions an angel.

Either way, in both narratives readers find a prophetic figure endangered by a hostile monarch lying asleep and having been awakened by someone. The verbal allusion to the waking of Elijah in Acts 12 thus sets Peter's sleep in a more depressing light. The waking in Acts anticipates a turning point.

Another faint verbal correspondence is noted by the editors of the Greek NT between Acts 12:11 and the Theodotion version of Dan 3:95 and, to a lesser degree, of 6:23. Both narratives in Daniel portray hostility from pagan rulers—first Nebuchadnezzar then Darius—against the men of God.

Acts 12:11	Dan [Theod] 3:95	Dan [Theod] 6:23
...*the Lord has sent his angel and rescued* me from the hands of Herod...	*God…has sent his angel and rescued* his servants, because they trusted in him.	*God has sent his angel* and shut the mouths of the lions.

ἐξαπέστειλεν ὁ κύριος τὸν ἄγγελον αὐτοῦ καὶ ἐξείλατό με ἐκ χειρὸς Ἡρῴδου	ὁ θεὸς...ἀπέστειλεν τὸν ἄγγελον αὐτοῦ καὶ ἐξείλατο τοὺς παῖδας αὐτοῦ ὅτι ἐπεποίθεισαν ἐπ' αὐτῷ	ὁ θεός μου ἀπέστειλεν τὸν ἄγγελον αὐτοῦ καὶ ἐνέφραξεν τὰ στόματα τῶν λεόντων

First, Daniel's friends are put in the fiery furnace as a punishment for not bowing down before the golden image of the king. According to the LXX version, the men sang a hymn of praise in the fire. Upon hearing the hymn from the furnace, the king was amazed. When he looked into the furnace, he noticed a fourth person with them, one having the appearance of one like the son of God. After bringing them out, the king praised God with the words quoted above before the leaders of the empire.

The second passage is found in a similar narrative in Dan 6, where Daniel is cast into the lion's den for praying to God. When early in the morning the kings ran to the den to see if God saved Daniel, the confession about the angel of God shutting the mouth of lions was professed by Daniel. In both Dan 3 and 6, a foreign ruler threatened the Israelite protagonists who were imprisoned in a fiery furnace and in the lion's den (respectively). It is revealed in both cases that an angel was sent by God to save them. As was noted earlier, non-biblical sources suggest that Daniel and his friends were delivered on Passover night—the same time Peter's rescue occurred. Peter's deliverance by the angel is thus set in conformity with the heroes' rescue in Daniel.

The three faint verbal correspondences link elements of Acts 12:1–17 with pre-existing narratives. The prayer of the early church is endowed with hope by a reference to the prayer of Israelites during a threat by a foreign ruler. This parallel, in addition, sets the threatened church and the threatened Israel in parallel. Herod in turn is paired with Nebuchadnezzar. The sleep and waking of Peter is compared to Elijah's depressed sleep in the desert. Elijah, like Peter, was persecuted by an evil ruler. Herod thus by implication ends up in the company of Jezebel, a pagan queen, and Ahab. Finally, the phrasing of the appearance of the angel to Peter creates connections with the deliverance of Daniel and his friends who were also brought into danger by foreign rulers. Again, Nebuchadnezzar and Darius are paired with Herod.

In all three cases the threat comes from foreign rulers, and each case God delivers his people. The rescue is carried out by an angelic figure twice. It is difficult to avoid the impression that the reason behind evoking these particular narratives lies in the common theme.

The opposition between Pilate and Jesus, on the one hand, and Pharaoh and Moses, on the other, portrayed in the two major hypotexts provide the basic pattern of danger and rescue for God's people in Acts. The crisis of the early church and of Peter under Herod is to be seen in connection with those other conflicts. In the light of these connections, the early church, along with Peter, would be viewed as belonging to the threatened and oppressed people of the OT and to Jesus. The role of Herod, a Jewish ruler, is viewed in harmony with kings who meant harm to the people of God.

3.2.2. The Hubris of Herod and of the King of Tyre: Another Thematic Imitation

The Nestle-Aland edition of the Greek NT notes connections with Ezek 27:17, 28:2, 6, 9 in Acts 12:20 and 22 respectively.[24] The former does not qualify as an allusion since it is a contextual pointer to Tyre's dependence on Israel for food, also known from 1 Kgs. It is written in 1 Kgs 5:11: "Solomon in turn gave Hiram twenty thousand cors of wheat as food for his household, and twenty cors of fine oil. Solomon gave this to Hiram year by year."

This statement is in harmony with Ezek 27:17, in particular, which makes mention of the dependence. The verse is part of a lamentation over Tyre. The prophet lists countries with which Tyre traded. The two

[24] Aland et al., *Novum Testamentum Graece*, 356–57.

Jewish states are said to have sold food: "Judea and the land of Israel traded with you; they exchanged for your merchandise wheat from Minnith, millet, honey, oil, and balm" (Ezek 27:17). The economic connection between Herod and the people of Tyre and Sidon assumes the historical precedence known from the OT.

A closer verbal parallel can be detected in Acts 12:20 with the prophecy in Ezek. In Acts, the people's reaction to Herod's oration is reminiscent of an imagined monologue of Tyre:[25]

Acts 12:22	**Ezek 28:2**
The people kept shouting, "The *voice of God, and not of man!*"	And you said "*I am God*"… but *you are man not God.*
ὁ δὲ δῆμος ἐπεφώνει θεοῦ φωνὴ καὶ οὐκ ἀνθρώπου	καὶ εἶπας Θεός εἰμι ἐγώ … σὺ δὲ εἶ ἄνθρωπος καὶ οὐ θεὸς

The king of Tyre claims to be God but his claim is refuted by the prophet. Later the imagined claims of Tyre are taken up repeatedly:

> Since you have rendered your heart as God's heart…
> ('Επειδὴ δέδωκας τὴν καρδίαν σου ὡς καρδίαν θεοῦ [Ezek 28:6])

The prophet passionately refutes the arrogant claims of the ruler:

> When you speak, will you actually say, "*I am God,*" before those that are killing you? But *you are man and not God.*
> (μὴ λέγων ἐρεῖς Θεός εἰμι ἐγώ, ἐνώπιον τῶν ἀναιρούντων σε; σὺ δὲ εἶ ἄνθρωπος καὶ οὐ θεός [Ezek 28:9])

[25] All of the following translations are my own.

Punishment for such boasting is death. Herod's words were praised as the words of God in front of a delegation from Tyre. By accepting the praise, he was found guilty in the same act of hubris as the king of Tyre. The intertextual reading of the Herod incident puts the ruler's acceptance of praise in line with the evil thoughts of the pagan king. In his paper on the topic, Mark Strom argued that verbal parallels are not the only points of contact between Acts 12:20–23 and Ezek 28.[26] In order to view the proposed thematic correspondence, it is beneficial to have a closer look at the oracle in Ezekiel.

Ezekiel's oracle in 26–28 against Tyre follows a path from concrete historical situations (Nebuchadnezzar in 26:1–21 and Tyre's partners in 27:1–36) to archetypal depiction of its hubris (28:1–10 and 28:11–19). The contrast between these two larger units can be seen in the fact that the former is addressed to the city in general, whereas in the latter the entire community stands condemned in its ruler. The glory and sin of Tyre is embodied in its leader. In the final section of 28:11–19 the splendor and sin of Tyre are examined in the light of creation and judgment. Strom summarizes this point by saying that "the effect of these oracles may be summarized as moving from the historical to a timeless and symbolic portrayal of Tyre and its sin."[27] The portrayal of Tyre's aggression transcends the concrete historic situation.

It is to be noted that the MT and LXX differ on the figure of the cherub in the text. While he MT of Ezek 28:14 and 16 is more ambiguous, it nevertheless supports the reading that the king and the cherub are identical. The LXX reading is clear in distinguishing the two figures. The king is said to have been placed on the holy mountain with the cherub in Ezek 28:14. Because of his sin, the ruler is expelled from the mountain: "and the cherub drove you from the midst of the fiery stones" (Ezek 28:16). The king stands in comparison with Adam who too was expelled from Eden.

---

[26] Mark R. Strom, "An Old Testament Background to Acts 12.20–23," *NTS* 32 (1986): 289–92.

[27] Ibid., 298.

Beyond verbal reminiscence, Strom advocates for a number of parallels that could be termed thematic:[28]

Ezek 28	Acts 12
Tyrian king	Tyrian audience
Israel supplies Tyre (27:17)	Tyre depends on Israel
Oppressor of Israel (26:2)	Persecutor of Church
Royal/priestly adornment	Royal robes
Seated on throne	Seated on throne
Utterance of hubris	Acceptance of divine title
Cherub implements judgment	Angel of the Lord implements judgment
Death before onlooker	Death before onlookers
Horrific judgment	Horrific judgment
Pit tradition (26:20?)	Eaten by worms
Judgment is final	Judgment is final
Salvation oracles follow judgment on the nations	Word of God increases and spreads

The number of parallels, however, is not the strongest case for intertextual connections. Strom argues that the general theological purpose of the two texts link them more than verbal or thematic parallels. The larger context of Ezekiel suggests that the sinful ruler along with his nation must be destroyed before God's final purpose is fulfilled. The opponents of the people of God are to be destroyed.

Presenting Herod's death in line the punishment of Tyre adds divine planning to the events. Herod Agrippa is said to be sitting on

---

[28] Ibid., 290.

the throne in royal robes. When the angel smites him, he dies.[29] Thus, the link between the act of hubris and punishment is emphasized. Herod's hubris and punishment is, therefore, presented in connection with the arrogance and doom of the king of Tyre of Ezek 26–28. The connection is strengthened by the reference to the historical dependence of Tyre and Sidon on Israel. Herod's death is an open display of punishment similar to the fall of the king of Tyre.[30]

---

[29] Ibid., 291.

[30] Despite chronological uncertainty, it useful to compare Luke's account of Herod's death with the report by Josephus. While Josephus also writes about a festival, there is no mention of the people from Tyre or Sidon or of food supply (cf. *Ant.* 19.8.2). Instead, principal persons witnessed Herod's actions. Another point of contact with Acts 12 is the description of radiant clothing. Josephus goes into great details on the royal garment. The radiant clothes seem to impress the people, making them claim that Herod was God. Josephus then remarks that Herod "did neither rebuke them, nor reject their impious flattery" (*Ant.* 19.8.2). The king immediately saw an owl, understanding it to bring bad news. He started feeling pain in his belly and realized that death was at hand: "I, who was by you called immortal, am immediately to be hurried away by death" (ibid.). He was carried into his place with the expectation that he would soon die. The people are said to have started mourning and lamentation. But the king died in five days time. Luke's account is considerably shorter (cf. Acts 12:20–23). Nevertheless, Luke also knows of royal robes, of the people's claim that Herod was God, and the immediate punishment. Tyrian audience and the mention of food supply in Acts 12 help to link these events with Ezek 26–28.

Chapter 4
Paul's First Mission Journey: Acts 13:1–14:28

4.1. Introduction

The topic of the Gentile mission in Acts 10:1–15:35 is resumed from Acts 13:1 onwards. Acts 13–14, in particular, concentrates on the theme of Gentile mission as a new element added to the already existing ministry of the church. The two chapters can be broken into three smaller narratives. First, Acts 13:1–12 tells the story of commissioning Paul and Barnabas and their mission in Cyprus. The first notable incident on the trip is the confrontation between Paul and Barnabas with a certain false prophet named Bar-Jesus. Second, the mission in Pisidian Antioch, with strong emphasis on Paul's synagogue speech along with its aftermath, is recounted in Acts 13:13–52. Finally, the short account of missionary trips to Iconium, Lystra, and Derbe with a return to Syrian Antioch is told in Acts 14.[1]

The theme of mission among Gentiles underlies the examined section. Up to this point, mission in Acts mainly concerned Jews. The ethnic and religious lines of Israel were only crossed occasionally. Prior to Paul's missionary journeys, incidents of Gentile conversions were noted in Luke-Acts. The exceptional degree of faith Jesus praised in the centurion from Capernaum (Luke 7:1–7) and the conversion and baptism of the Ethiopian eunuch (Acts 8:26–40) are two examples for the reception of Jesus's proclamation outside the boundaries of Israel. Added to these, earlier missions in synagogues reached the audience with non-Jewish background along with the Jews. All these earlier encounters between pagans and the Christian proclamation, however, are to be seen as preparatory stages for receiving the Gentile Christians

[1] Witherington, *Acts*, 390–91.

in great numbers in the early church. From Acts 13 onwards, the response from non-Jewish converts is planned and counted on. Furthermore, the events recorded in Acts 10:1–11:18 are appealed to as theological justification for accepting pagan converts in the church, whose membership consisted of people with Jewish background. In the realization of the divine plan to convert the Gentiles, as it was initiated by God in the Cornelius's narrative, Paul is portrayed as one playing a key role. It is to be remembered that the apostle was chosen by God to bear witness before "Gentiles, and kings, and the children of Israel" (Acts 9:15). The first missionary journey by Paul and Barnabas shows the first major steps in turning to the Gentiles.

4.2. Architextual Correlations

4.2.1. The Choosing of the Apostles and the Language of Temple Service

The narrative starts and ends in Syrian Antioch in the Christian community, thus providing an introduction and conclusion to the entire first mission journey. The Holy Spirit directed the praying community to separate Barnabas and Paul for the *work* (13:2). When returning to Antioch, the community in the city gave thanks for the *work* (14:26) the two apostles fulfilled. The use of the same word *work* (ἔργον) in both passages to convey the missionary task provides the ideological frame from which the recounted events are to be viewed.[2] Therefore, the connotations of the *work* the apostles were chosen to do are of interpretative significance.

Acts 13:1–4 functions as an introduction to the entire mission trip, and as such a number of thematic elements create anticipation at the outset. Certain named individuals, designated as teachers and prophets, along with Barnabas and Saul, were gathered in the Antioch church where they are said to have ministered to the Lord by fasting (13:2). Following the Holy Spirit's command to separate two of them, namely Barnabas and Paul, for the *work*, the community fasted and prayed again as they laid hands on them (13:3).

---

[2] Tannehill, *Acts of the Apostles*, 159–60.

There are a number of religious actions worth considering in their architextual connotations. First, the conventional description of OT piety characterized by fasting and prayer is clearly detectable in the early church's life in a number of narratives including the one at hand.[3] Further, prayer is frequently mentioned in Acts in the context of revealing God's will.[4] Whenever prayer is mentioned, the potential for revealing God's purpose becomes imminent.

Apart from praying and fasting, two further actions are mentioned. The acts of separating and the laying on of hands were all performed in the context of ministering. The word, *to minister* (λειτουργέω) points to a priestly context of Temple-service.[5] Haenchen goes as far as to claim that, "Luke has borrowed an expression of special solemnity from LXX."[6] Further, laying the hands on someone as a form of dedication for religious service is clearly demonstrated in passages like Num 8:10–12. The verses in Numbers describe the consecration of Levites for service. Marshall notes that the motif of separation along with laying on of hands is present in the passage.[7]

The faint reverberations of holy language related to piety (praying, fasting) and to Temple-service endow the commission of the two apostles with a degree of solemnity and elevation.

---

[3] Marshall, "Acts," 581–82.

[4] The disciples were gathered for prayer when receiving the Holy Spirit at Pentecost (Acts 2:1) and thus were able to testify before the gathering in Jerusalem; the Christian community was praying in response to the threat of the authorities, and after receiving the Spirit they could preach the word with boldness (Acts 4:31); Cornelius was praying when the angel appeared to him and gave instructions to send for Peter (Acts 10:1); Peter was praying while seeing the vision and was sent to preach to the Gentiles (Acts 10:9, 19).

[5] E.g., 2 Chr 5:14, 13:10, 35:3 Jdt 4:14 Joel 1:13, 2:17 Ezek 4:46, 44:16, 45:4. The word is used of Christian service in Did 15:1. Cf. Haenchen, *Acts*, 395.

[6] Ibid.

[7] Marshall, "Acts," 582.

4.2.2. Conflicts with False Prophets and with Magicians

Following a short remark about a stop in Seleucia, the two apostles are said to have arrived in Cyprus. Once on the island, they began preaching the word of God in the synagogues of Salamis. Next, the apostles are found in Paphos where they confront a Jewish magician and false prophet named Bar-Jesus. His role in the political structure is specified by pointing out that he was with the proconsul called Sergius Paulus. Bar-Jesus's position must have been that of a consultant.[8]

Within the narrative world of Acts, conflicts with magicians and with representatives of degenerate religion feature prominently. The conflicts revolve around the themes of magic, money, and hubris.[9] Already in the narrative of Acts 8:9–24 the apostles were said to have encountered a certain magician, Simon of Samaria. He, too, was practicing magic and had great influence on the people. Another encounter with representatives of false religion is recorded later in Acts 19:13–16: the sons of Sceva attempted to exercise authority over evil spirits, the same way the apostles did. A few verses later those who believed are said to have burnt their magic books in response to apostolic preaching (19:18–19). Based on these accounts, it is reasonable to claim that there is a clear interest within Acts in conflicts around degenerate forms of religion.

A thematic connection with the OT is also at work in the portrayal of the conflict between Paul and Bar-Jesus. The designation *false prophet* in Acts 13:6 recalls a number of incidents between OT prophets and their opponents. The struggle between Micah and the opposing prophets recorded in 1 Kgs 22, and the permanent conflict of Jeremiah with the false prophets of his time recounted in Jer 35–36/42–43 are clear examples of such oppositions. The distant architextual relationship aims toward framing the incident in Acts in the light of the OT precedents.[10]

---

[8] Witherington, *Acts*, 398.

[9] Tannehill, *Acts of the Apostles*, 161.

[10] Ibid., 162.

A further connection with false prophets is provided by a parallel with the expression, "the hand of the Lord is against you" from Acts 13:11 in the book of Ezekiel: "and I will stretch out my hand against the prophets who behold falsehoods and utter vanities" (Ezek 13:9). The same divine action of stretching out the hand as in the Acts account is used against false prophets.[11]

Further, the words of denouncement against Bar-Jesus are reminiscent of typical description of arrogant fools in the OT. The expression, *full of all deceit* (πλήρης παντὸς δόλου) in 13:10 can be found in two passages in Ben Sirah—once in Sir 1:30 and once in Sir 19:26. The phrase is part of a stereotypical description of a hypocrite in Sir 1:30 who is of double heart. The consequence of self-exaltation is humiliation in front of the congregation because such person is *full of deceit*. The second example from Sir 19:26 consists of a portrayal of a deceitful person. In addition, the expression *full of all deceit* is used as the opposite of the fear of the Lord in both passages in Sirach. A further instance of the phrase is found in Jer 5:27 in a description of evil men who gain their wealth in dishonest ways. Here, too, such an attitude is contrasted with the fear of the Lord. Still, another example can be found in Ps 10:7/9:28, where the sinner is characterized as one "whose mouth is *full of* cursing and bitterness and *deceit*."

The thematic connection of the Bar-Jesus episode with the conflicts between prophets and false prophets of the OT provides a context of ongoing opposition between the genuine men of God and their false counterparts. The reverberations of the descriptions of arrogant fools tie Bar-Jesus to those who are blind to the power of God. The connections in the Bar-Jesus narrative are to be seen as architextual inasmuch as they relate to the theme of false prophets and to the language of arrogant fools without alluding to any specific texts.

4.3. Metatextual Correlations in Paul's Speech

It is argued here that the intertextual correlations of Paul's speech—allusions, quotes, and verbal correspondences of any kind—are to be

[11] Marshall, "Acts," 582.

seen as part of metatextual operations on certain subtexts. In order to present this case, Genette's notion of metatextuality is to be recalled. Part of the challenge is that one of the least developed types of transtextuality in Genette's map of textual transcendence—i.e., metatextuality—is certainly a significant one in the NT. While not much is offered beyond a strict definition in *Palimpsests*, metatextuality, according to Genette, is a textual transcendence often referred to as commentary. A text speaks of another text sometimes by quoting it and, at times, without even naming it.[12] In accordance with this definition, metatextual relations in Paul's speech are realized through direct quotes and silent evoking as well. Intertexts, therefore, are treated as pointers to metatextual relations.

As I have argued, intertextual connections in Acts 10:1–15:35 are mainly proposed to denote other transtextual correlations. Thus, a quotation, an allusion, or a verbal correspondence of any kind denotes other transtextual strategies like hypertextuality, metatextuality, or even architextuality. This means a quote is hardly ever just a quote. So how does one distinguish between pure intertexts (if they exist) from intertexts that denote other types of transtextuality?

The intertext that denotes metatextuality is distinguished from other intertextual connections simply by the metatext's strong focus on the subtext(s). Instances of metatextuality are assumed when the speaker or narrator shows an invested interest in the subtexts: the subtexts are evaluated, their significance is considered, appealed to, clarity is sought for, etc. A clear orientation toward the subtexts is to be detected to establish metatextuality. Most of the quotes, allusions and silent evoking in Paul's speech will be discussed as part of metatextual correlations. Since metatextuality is significant for the speeches of Acts 13 and 15, methodological clarity and precision will be sought for during the process of interpretation to establish and define metatextual operations relevant for Acts 13 and indeed for the

---

[12] Genette, *Palimpsests*, 4.

entire book. In order to achieve that goal, first an intra-textual study of the speech is to be performed.

4.3.1. Paul's Synagogue Speech and Its Aftermath

The section starting in Acts 13:13 tells the story of the apostles' mission in Pisidian Antioch in two sequences. The apostles travel through Pamphylia and Perga before they arrive in Antioch of Pisidia. The city provides the location for Paul's emblematic synagogue speech (13:14–43) and its aftermath on the following sabbath (13:44–52). Thus, the events of two consequent sabbaths are told in synagogue settings.

4.3.1.1. Paul's Synagogue Speech: Acts 13:13–43

Acts 13 contains stories of Paul's first missionary journey, which are followed by many others later in the book. Paul's mission is initiated by God. Earlier it was declared about him by God that, "he is a chosen vessel unto me, to bear my name before the Gentiles, and kings, and the children of Israel" (Acts 9:15). The mission journey narratives follow up on that promise. It is right to point out that this is not the first mission journey narrative in Acts. Others have traveled from home to distant cities and proclaimed the gospel in synagogues. But these earlier journeys were mainly performed by migrants who had to leave their cities due to persecution, and their focus was on the Jews of the diaspora. Starting in Acts 13, missionary journeys are instrumental in bringing the gospel to the Gentiles.[13]

Arguably, Paul's speech stands at the center of focus in the present narrative. It is useful to remember that throughout Acts there are a great number of speeches, most of which are attributed to Paul but also to Peter and to some other characters including Jesus, Roman officials, and Christian leaders.[14] Some apostolic speeches, nevertheless, have special significance in the design of Acts.

---

[13] Tannehill, *Acts of the Apostles*, 159.

[14] Fitzmyer (*Acts,* 104) identifies the following sections as speeches in Acts: 1. Risen Christ to Apostles and disciples (1:4–5, 7–8); 2. Peter when choosing Matthias (1:16–22); 3. Peter's Pentecost speech in Jerusalem (2:14–39); 4. Peter in the Temple

First, it is to be observed that the Antiochean speech is part of the three Pauline speeches, each addressing different aspects of his mission. Paul spoke in the synagogue to Jews and God-fearers, then in front of a Greek audience in Athens (17:22–31), and finally gave a farewell speech to Christians (20:18–35). This approach focuses on the thematic economy of the sermons of Paul. Tannehill sums up the correlation of speeches by saying: "They are widely distributed in the narrative of Paul's mission journeys, the first and third occurring near the beginning and end of this section of Acts, and each dominates its context."[15]

Furthermore, the speech in Pisidian Antioch gains significance in its relation to other major non-Pauline speeches in Luke-Acts. Most notably, Peter's Pentecost sermon starting in Acts 2:14 and Stephen's defense in Acts 7 provide structural parallels for Paul's speech, each in different ways. In addition, the function of certain speeches is nearly identical with Paul's address. Tannehill makes a point that Peter's Pentecost sermon, while reflecting the function of Jesus's first public address in Luke 4:16–28, initiates certain events. Jesus too started his ministry with a speech while Peter started the ministry of the church

---

on curing the lame man (3:12–26); 5. Peter before the Sanhedrin (4:8–12, 19b–20); 6. Peter before the Sanhedrin again (5:29–32); 7. Gameliel's speech before the Sanhedrin (5:35-39); 8. The twelve on electing the six men for service (6:2–4); 9. Stephen's speech (7:2–53); 10. Peter's speech in Caesarea (10:34–43); 11. Peter to the brothers in Jerusalem (11:5–17); 12. Paul's speech in Antioch (13:16–41); 13. Barnabas and Paul in Lystra (14:15–17), 14. Peter at the Jerusalem Council (15:7–11); 15. James to the assembly in Jerusalem (15:13–21); 16. Paul's Areopagus speech in Athens (17:22–31); 17. Gallio to the Jews in Corinth (18:14–15); 18. Demetrius to the silversmiths in Ephesos (19:25–27); 19. Town clerk in Ephesos (19:35–40); 20. Paul to the Ephesian elders in Miletus (20:18–35); 21. Paul to the crowd in Jerusalem (22:1–31); 23. Paul before Felix, the governor (24:2–8); 24. Tertullus before Felix (24:10–21); 25. Festus before king Agrippa (25:1–27); 26. Paul before Agrippa (26:2–23, 25–27, 29); 27. Paul to the sailors and prisoners on the ship (27:21–26); 28. Paul to the Jews in Rome (28:17–20, 25–28). Following different criteria, others offer a different number—see e.g., Marion L. Soards, *The Speeches in Acts: Their Content, Context, and Concerns* (Louisville: Westminster John Knox, 1994), 21–22.

[15] Tannehill, *Acts of the Apostles*, 164.

after the outpouring of the Spirit. The similar sequences of the narratives in which the speeches are located provide a parallel for Paul's sermon. Both Peter's and Jesus's respective mission were started by a speech, which yielded results at first and later was met with opposition. Further, all three speeches are followed by healing a lame man (cf. Luke 5:17–26; Acts 3:1–10; 14:8–10).[16] Signs from God support the claims of the speeches. Reminders of the beginnings of Peter's and Jesus's missions highlight that Paul's journey initiates a new phase in salvation:

> Like Jesus (Luke 4:18–21) and Peter (Acts 2:14–40), Paul makes a major statement near the beginning of his new mission. His speech resembles that of Jesus in setting (a synagogue service with reading of Scripture) and resembles Peter's in points of content. The three speeches either contain or lead to a Scripture quotation that interprets the mission that is beginning (Luke 4:18–19; Acts 2:17–21; 13:47). They lead immediately (Luke 4:24–30) or in due course (Acts 4:1–3; 13:45–52) to an outbreak of opposition. The inclusion of Gentiles in God's salvation is mentioned and may be part of the provocation (Luke 4:25–28; Acts 2:39; 3:25–26; 13:45–48).[17]

Paul's speech, viewed together with the following opposition, stands in correlation with the similar cycle introduced by Peter's and Jesus's sermons. The new element in Paul's speech is clearly the inclusion of the Gentiles. The emphasis on the Antiochean speech and its correlation with Peter's sermon clearly initiates a new cycle in Acts dominated by the mission to the Gentiles.

Stephen's defense speech provides a parallel in another respect. While both Paul and Stephen recount the holy history of Israel, their priorities in doing so lie elsewhere. There is a strong focus on Abraham and Moses in Acts 7, while Paul focuses more on David.

---

[16] Ibid., 161.

[17] Ibid., 160.

Stephen highlights opposition to God's initiatives in Israel's history, while Paul stresses the stages of God's involvement with Israel through time. Despite differences of focus, both speeches recount certain events from Israel's past to support certain claims. Paul's sermon, therefore, serves the same purpose as the synagogue speech of Jesus and the Pentecost sermon of Peter: they all initiate new events and provide interpretative frames for events; they are all supported by God's miracles; the speeches gain support from the people but later opposition arises. Paul's speech, furthermore, shares a common theme with Stephen's defense speech: the history of Israel.

After reviewing the function of Paul's sermon in its context of Luke-Acts, specifics of the text need to be examined. The spatial and temporal setting of the speech is that of a synagogue on a Sabbath day. Following certain unspecified readings from the law and prophets, both Paul and Barnabas are recognized as brothers in faith and are offered a chance to deliver a *word of exhortation*[18] (λόγος παρακλήσεως). Stylistic parallels of the speech have been investigated in relation to ancient Graeco-Roman rhetoric as well Jewish synagogue homily. On the one hand, Witherington suggested that the apostle's speech follows the pattern of ancient rhetorical performances. According to his proposal, Paul starts with an *exordium* (16), followed by *narratio* (17–25) and *propositio* (26), then turns to *probatio* (27–37), and ends with the final exhortation *peroratio* (38–41).[19] On the other hand, Bowker searched for parallels with ancient Jewish homilies.[20] Due to the lack of Jewish parallels from the time, Witherington rather suggests that Acts 13:13–43 shows signs of typical rabbinic argumentation.[21] Bowker proposed that Paul followed a certain Jewish homily form based on a *seder* text identified as Deut

[18] A sermon on passages of Scripture is called *word of encouragement* in 1 Macc 12:9 and 2 Macc 15:9. Cf. Marshall, "Acts," 582.

[19] Witherington, *Acts*, 407.

[20] J.W. Bowker, "Speeches in Acts: A Study in Proem and Yelammenedu Form," *NTS* 14 (1968): 96–111.

[21] Witherington, *Acts*, 408.

4:25–46 and on a *haftarah* text 2 Sam 7:6–16, bridging the two with a *proem* text of 1 Sam 13:14.[22]

Furthermore, Johnson observed the presence of the method later termed, *gezerah shewa* as being at work in the speech, which, simply put, is a technique of linking different passages together by the occurrence of certain keywords.[23] The challenge of rabbinic parallels rests on the fact that most early Jewish homilies are preserved from rabbis of the 3rd and 4th century CE. The clearest parallels to the speech are other speeches found in Acts. The stylistic elements and structural patterns of Paul's speech borrowed from ancient rhetoric and Jewish ways of argumentation are better to be seen as indicators of the double orientation of both the passage and indeed the whole book of Acts. The general style of the speech reflects both Jewish and Hellenistic ways of public communication, resulting in a particular architextual design.

The greatest challenge in relation to the metatextual nature of the speech is determining the subtext(s) for Paul's sermon. Paul's address is said to follow readings taken from the law and from the prophets. This information gave rise to several endeavors to propose subtexts based on what can be known about synagogue lectionaries. In order to reach this goal, one would have to find out about the liturgy of the synagogue service of the time. In diaspora synagogues the regular procedure seems to be that the *Shema* was recited, which was followed by a prayer, and then readings with possible translation were performed and accompanied by explanation.[24] The challenge of the task, however, is that Jewish lectionaries come from a later time whose origins cannot be traced back to the first century with absolute certainty. Given the lack of information, one would have to look for clues in the speech itself. And the clues are many. There are a great number of OT texts evoked in the sermon. The challenge lies not so much in identifying those texts as much more in proposing a

[22] Bowker, "Speeches."

[23] Johnson, *Acts*, 238.

[24] Witherington, *Acts*, 406.

metatextual economy for recalling, interpreting and arranging them. It will be argued in this chapter that the confusing plurality of intertexts can be best understood as all being part of a metatextual strategy on just two subtexts.

The intertextual reading of the speech suggests a division of the text based on its two subtexts. I propose that the speech can be best viewed as a metatext on the holy history of Israel on the one hand, and on the promise about David's seed as recorded in 2 Sam 7:6–16 on the other. The first part on the holy history of Israel starts in Acts 13:16 with the choosing of the fathers, and ends with the recounting of Jesus's life and resurrection in 13:26–31. The speech then develops into a metatext on the promise of the seed lasting from 13:32 to 13:37. Finally, a warning against disbelief, with the use of Hab 1:5, closes the entire speech.[25] The metatextual relation proposed for linking Paul's speech with the holy history of Israel and the promise concerning the seed will be elaborated on in this order.

Considering the holy history of Israel as a subtext for Acts 13:16–31 may appear more challenging than proposing a certain passage or a number of texts from the OT for the same status. But we can do so for several reasons. One might object, that the section of Paul's speech discussed here is not entirely devoted to the history of Israel. From 13:23 Paul covers the time of John the Baptist and of Jesus. This objection can be easily answered by pointing out that both John and Jesus are discussed in the sermon in their relation to Israel. John is said to have proclaimed the baptism of repentance to the whole nation of Israel in 13:34, whereas it was claimed in 13:23 that Jesus was brought as a savior to Israel. Paul is clearly presenting Jesus and John as human agents in a chain of divine involvements with Israel. This chain started with the fathers, and then included the judges, Saul, David, and finally John and Jesus. This point will be taken up more fully later. It

---

[25] Mark L. Strauss, *The Davidic Messiah in Luke-Acts: The Promise and Its Fulfillment in Lukan Christology*, JSNTSup 110 (Sheffield: Sheffield Academic Press, 1995), 156–57.

is sufficient to point out at this stage that the holy history of Israel was extended to the time of John and Jesus in Paul's speech.

A second objection might be aimed at the proposed hypothetical or perhaps abstract nature of the holy history of Israel. The argument against such a proposal might be made even stronger by pointing out that certain episodes of that history in Paul's sermon are evoked with their very concrete textual expressions from real books of the OT. If it is a hypothetical subtext, why are allusions made to certain passages? Why not claim instead that there are a number of subtexts for the metatext? It appears as though the interpreter is forced to choose one OT allusion out of the many and use it as a hermeneutical key for all the others. On the one hand, an interpreter could emphasize the creative or perhaps arbitrary freedom with which the speaker retells, combines, and evokes episodes of Israel's past without making much of those episodes' intertextual correlations. On the other hand, another choice would be to go after individual intertextual connections of the speech and lose sight of the creative process with which those texts are treated.

It appears more satisfactory, however, to propose that the metatext is not oriented directly toward individual passages from the OT but much more toward the holy history of Israel as a coherent story—one that that contains all the plots, characters, sequences, characterizations, settings, and so on. This history is built on concrete individual narratives and utterances of the OT. Allusions or even quotes remain a key factor in evoking them. The holy history of Israel is to be seen in its *richness* containing all the information of that history irrespective of its relative location within the canon, its genre, or its setting. This brings us to the other characteristic of evoking portions of the holy history of Israel, that is *variability*. Variability is the creative and disciplined freedom with which the speaker or narrator can draw together information related to characters, plots, and events recorded in various locations in the OT to form a new narrative or utterance.

Furthermore, the metatext on the holy history of Israel can reflect the textual, sequential markers of its subtexts resulting in intertextual, or even hypertextual correlations. But it can also avoid verbal or sequential resemblance with the subtext. A summary would be a good example for the latter. Entire narratives can be evoked in a few words of a summary. It is proposed here that viewing the holy history of Israel as the subtext for its metatext, Acts 13:16–31, provides a more satisfactory framework for an intertextual study than considering individual passages in singularity or giving up on intertextual connections. The following study of Acts 13:16–31 is aimed at demonstrating this position.

To begin with, Paul recounts certain events from Israel's past in a particular order with varying emphasis on different events. In the recounting, God remains the actor to the point of bringing Jesus as a savior to Israel in 13:23. Even after that, events are portrayed as fulfillments of God's revealed will. Thus, God is seen as the one who acts and gives, and Israel is seen as the receiver of divine actions. The account starts with reference to the God of the nation Israel. Israel is mentioned again in the context of John's and Jesus's respective ministries. The entire history is viewed in Paul's speech as God's initiatives toward his people. Different events depicted are therefore to be understood as God's involvement with his people Israel.

Events in the history of Israel are presented in periods of time that were characterized by certain acts of God. The earlier part of Paul's sermon is an attempt at periodization. The various epochs share some common elements. Some periods are identified with certain human agents chosen by God. Also, there is a reference to time in relation to most epochs. The time periods ordered this way can be seen as phases of God's engagement with his people.

First, God is said to have chosen the fathers of Israel. Then, God exalted the people in Egypt and brought them out with mighty hands (13:17)—a clear reference to exodus. The next epoch is a period of forty years when God is said to have fed the people in the wilderness (13:18). The fourth epoch is that of inheriting the land following the destruction of the seven nations of Canaan (13:19). The entire time from the fathers to the conquest is said in Acts 13:20 to have lasted for about 450 years.[26] After this, God gave judges to the people up to days of Samuel for an unspecified time period. Apart from the fathers, this is the first epoch where human agents are mentioned through whom God acted in that time (13:20). From here on, chosen human agents will dominate each period.

Next, God gave a king, Saul, to the people for forty years. The human agent in this new phase was requested by the people themselves (13:21). This is the only human initiative in the story. God is said to have removed Saul and raised David. This period receives the longest portrayal where David's positive role is emphasized by a composite quote. Jesus is connected to David in 13:23 as the promised seed. The ministry of John is also described in terms of time: he is said to have proclaimed Jesus *ahead of time*. He spoke of Jesus who was to come *after him*. John's ministry to Israel is the last epoch before Jesus. The epoch of Jesus is introduced in 13:24 and is discussed later in 13:26–31.

A number of remarks are needed about the trajectory of the periods discussed so far. In the first four phases—that is, the election of the fathers along with deliverance, years in the desert, and receiving of the land—God remains the sole actor without emphasis on human agents. The next five epochs are characterized by human agents: judges up to Samuel, Saul and David, John and Jesus. All the agents, nevertheless, were *given* or *raised* by God. Further, the transition from one phase to the next comes at the expense of conflict at two points: God destroyed the nations in Canaan before the Israelites, and God removed Saul before David. The transition from John's epoch to that of Jesus is not marked by conflict. Finally, the portrayal of David as an ideal king and

[26] There are a number of problems with the expression. Most importantly, it is not at all clear what part of the history of Israel is said to have lasted for about 450 years. The most likely solution is that the amount of time is arrived at by adding forty years of wilderness and ten years of conquest (Josh 1–13) to 400 years in Egypt. Haenchen, *Acts*, 408–09. This proposal makes much better sense than to suggest that Paul believed that the judges would have ruled Israel for that period of time. Eugene H Merrill, "Paul's Use of 'About 450 Years' in Acts 13–20," *BSac* 138.551 (1981): 246–57.

of Jesus are the high points and culminations of the epochs. Both David and Jesus are characterized with extensive quotes.

The description of each epoch is in intertextual connections with one or more passages from the OT realized through verbal correspondence, allusions, or reflections of sequence of the same events and occasionally through quotes. At other times, however, Paul simply gives a summary of events that are recorded in entire books or larger narratives without relying on the support of any verbal or circumstantial correlation. Events are evoked, therefore, either in their earlier textual and sequential expressions or simply in the form of summaries.

More than this, a certain logic can be detected in the way elements of the holy history of Israel are activated in the new utterance. First, the holy history of Israel contains all the plots, sequences, characters, and utterances related to all the parts of that history. For instance, the liberation from Egypt is told in the book of Exodus. But the liberation from the house of slavery is also spoken of in various speeches, poems, psalms, hymns, and narratives throughout the OT. These other utterances are either in agreement with the one in Exodus or they add certain new details to it. For instance, information regarding David, which is spread throughout the OT, can be drawn together into a single statement, regardless of their earlier textual location or generic characteristics.

The portrayal of epochs of God's involvement with Israel evokes a confusing number of texts in various ways. To begin with, 13:17–20 covering the election of the fathers, the bringing out from Egypt, time in the desert, destruction of the nations leading to inheriting the land reflects descriptions of deliverance not from Exodus, or of invading Canaan, not from the book of Joshua, but from Deuteronomy. It is useful to compare the text in Acts and the relevant section in Deut 4:37–38:

Acts 13:17–19	Deut 4:37–38
The God of this people Israel *chose our ancestors* and made the people great during their stay in	Because he loved your fathers, he also *chose* their seed after them, and himself *brought you out* of

the land of Egypt, and with uplifted arm he *led them out* of it. For about forty years he *put up with them* in the wilderness. After he *had destroyed seven nations* in the land of Canaan, he *gave them their land as an inheritance*.	Egypt, by his great power, *to destroy* utterly before you great nations, and mightier than yourselves, to bring you in, to *give you their land to inherit*, as you have today.
ὁ θεὸς τοῦ λαοῦ τούτου Ἰσραὴλ ἐξελέξατο τοὺς πατέρας ἡμῶν καὶ τὸν λαὸν ὕψωσεν ἐν τῇ παροικίᾳ ἐν γῇ Αἰγύπτου καὶ μετὰ βραχίονος ὑψηλοῦ ἐξήγαγεν αὐτοὺς ἐξ αὐτῆς, καὶ ὡς τεσσερακονταετῆ χρόνον ἐτροποφόρησεν αὐτοὺς ἐν τῇ ἐρήμῳ καὶ καθελὼν ἔθνη ἑπτὰ ἐν γῇ Χανάαν κατεκληρονόμησεν τὴν γῆν αὐτῶν.	διὰ τὸ ἀγαπῆσαι αὐτὸν τοὺς πατέρας σου καὶ ἐξελέξατο τὸ σπέρμα αὐτῶν μετ' αὐτοὺς ὑμᾶς καὶ ἐξήγαγέν σε αὐτὸς ἐν τῇ ἰσχύι αὐτοῦ τῇ μεγάλῃ ἐξ Αἰγύπτου ἐξολεθρεῦσαι ἔθνη μεγάλα καὶ ἰσχυρότερά σου πρὸ προσώπου σου εἰσαγαγεῖν σε δοῦναί σοι τὴν γῆν αὐτῶν κληρονομεῖν, καθὼς ἔχεις σήμερον.

Deuteronomy 4:37–38 contain four out of the five actions from Acts 13:17–19. The connection is both sequential and verbal.

The two verses in Deut 4 are part of an address by Moses to the people of God. Deuteronomy 4 contains exhortations to observe the law.[27] The subunit in Deut 4:32–40 recalls certain events in the history of Israel to show God's love and care for his people. The holy events of Israel are evoked in an elevated style.[28] In 4:32–35 God's mighty acts of temptations, wonders, and wars are considered. Especially, God's actions

---

[27] Jeffrey H. Tigay, *Deuteronomy*, JPSTC (Philadelphia: The Jewish Publication Society, 1996), 40.

[28] Peter C. Craigie, *The Book of Deuteronomy*, NICOT (London: Hodder and Stoughton, 1976), 142.

with mighty hand and with stretched out arms in Egypt are remembered. Deuteronomy 4:36–39 repeat the themes of 4:32–35 with an emphasis on obeying God's will, revealed through those earlier events.[29] Deuteronomy 4:37–38 emphasize God's love for Israel's ancestors manifested in choosing them and taking them out of Egypt to Israel.

Tigay notes that, "Deuteronomy is the first book in the Torah to speak of God *loving* and *choosing* Israel."[30] This is precisely the combination in Paul's address. Moreover, the sequence of ideas—i.e., loving, choosing, giving inheritance—is claimed to be the process of adoption. It could be compared to a similar sequence of loving, choosing, and inheritance in Jer 3:19. It is to be also noted that in agreement with deuternomistic tendencies, God is said to have delivered his people directly without the involvement of angel.[31] Acts' focus on God as the sole actor in Israel's past is in harmony with the above outlined deuteronomistic tendency.

The sequence of the events, including choosing, bringing out, destruction of nations, and inheriting the land is shared in both passages. Moreover, the Greek terms for choosing (ἐξελέξατο) and leading out (ἐξήγαγεν) are identical both in Acts and in Deuteronomy. Furthermore, the wording of receiving the land as inheritance is similar (δοῦναί σοι τὴν γῆν αὐτῶν κληρονομεῖν [Deut 4:38]; κατεκληρονόμησεν τὴν γῆν αὐτῶν [Acts 13:19]) while the destruction of the nations is portrayed with the use of different words in Deut 4:37–38. It is to be noted that dealing with the nations and receiving the land is spoken of in terms of a promise in Deuteronomy in which events are portrayed as past happenings in the Antiochean speech. Thus, a promise is evoked to portray what already happened.

In sum, the emphasis on fathers and the sequential ordering of election, deliverance from Egypt, destruction of the nations, and inheriting the land points to a correlation. Considering still further possible connections between Deut 4 and Paul's speech, Bowker even

---

[29] Ibid., 144.

[30] Tigay, *Deuteronomy*, 56.

[31] Ibid.

suggested that a portion of the *seder* passage is one of the texts on which the address is based.[32] Although the sequential and verbal correlation between Deut 4:37–38 and Acts 13:17–19 is suggestive, the former passage is treated here as one textual expression of God's love for his people combined with others to form a new utterance on past events.

The speech covering those early years contain other intertextual correspondences. Details of the above-named divine actions are added from other texts. The expelling of the seven nations as expressed by Paul is more clearly spoken of in another passage, in Deut 7:1 in the form of a promise, while the wording of receiving of the land as inheritance points to Josh 14:1.[33] Details on both the nations and the land can be added from other expressions of those themes to form a more complete picture.

A variation of a different kind also needs to be considered. There is an extra sequence in Acts between the exodus and the destruction of the nations as compared to the sequence in Deut 4:37–38: forty years of wilderness in Acts 13:18. This sequence deserves some attention for two very different reasons. First, it is to be observed that the extra sequence is a clear allusion to another passage within Deuteronomy. In Deut 1:31 Moses is quoted saying, "in this wilderness which you saw, how the Lord your God cared for you, as someone would care for his son, along all the way that you went until you came to this place."[34] The sentence is part of a long address on the failures of the wilderness years. The subunit in Deut 1:29–31 revolves around fear from a great enemy. Fear in reaction to the report of the spies of the holy land is recalled. The people are to take courage from the fact that God carried them or cared for them in the desert.[35] The extra sequence in Acts comes from a speech on the desert years.

[32] Bowker, "Speeches," 102.

[33] Marshall, "Acts," 583.

[34] My translation.

[35] Duane L. Christensen, *Deuteronomy 1,1–21,9*, 2nd ed., WBC 6A (Nashville: Thomas Nelson, 2001), 31.

The other reason for considering the verse is that it involves a textual problem not unrelated to questions of intertextuality. The Nestle-Aland edition of the NT has the word, ἐτροποφόρησεν, meaning that God put up with the moods of the people in the wilderness for forty years. The alternate reading, however, has a very similar Greek word: ἐτροφοφόρησεν, which means that God cared for the people. Both readings are well attested in the manuscripts. In addition, the same textual ambiguity exists in Deut 1:31[36] and both readings are possible: "and in this wilderness which you saw, how the Lord your God *cared for/put up with* you, as someone would *care for/put up with* his son, along all the way that you went until you came to this place."[37]

Based on the Hebrew text, both terms could be justified.[38] Gordon suggests that the ἐτροποφόρησεν rendering came to exist due to a recurring Targumic expression used for God's care for his people in the wilderness at times as a mere translation (Deut 2:7; 32:10; Hos 13:5) of and at other times as addition (Zech 9:11) to the Hebrew text circumscribing God's providence in the desert.[39] The implication of the argument is that a typical Targumic expression for God's providence in the wilderness resulted in altered readings in both LXX Deut 1:31 and Acts 13:28. It is to be stressed, however, that this is a likely hypothesis only and does not affect the link between Acts 13:28 and Deut 1:31. In either case, it is noteworthy that the reference to the verse from Deut 1:31 in Paul's speech provides the argument with an extra epoch.

To sum it up, the sequence of themes (choosing, bringing out from Egypt, and giving inheritance) provides the strongest link with Deut 4:37–38. However, the extra added sequence of the desert years from Deut 1:31 and further details related to stereotypical descriptions of

---

[36] Witherington, *Acts*, 409–10.

[37] My translation.

[38] Marshall, "Acts," 583.

[39] Robert P. Gordon, "Targumic Parallels to Acts 13:18 and Didache 14:3," *NovT* 16 (1974): 285–89.

land and of the nations create a combined account of the early portion of the history of Israel.

What follows is a different kind of appropriation of the holy history of Israel—i.e., it is a summary. In these verses one can find very short summaries of larger narratives. In a brief note, God is said to have given judges up to the time of Samuel (Acts 13:20). The period of judges is contained in the book of Judges while the choosing of Samuel is portrayed in 1 Sam 1–2. The assumption appears to be that Samuel was the first prophet, inaugurating a new epoch in God's plan. There is no detectable verbal correlation in the summary. Once again, the emphasis in this new period is on God who gave human agents for the benefit of his people. The 450 years taken to mean the entire period from choosing the fathers up to the conquest of the land might have been informed by a remark in 1 Kgs 6:1, where a similar logic is at work. Again, if the significance of 1 Kgs 6:1 is accepted, it would mean that information gained from a narrative on Solomon is combined with a narrative on the early period of Israel.

The period of judges is followed by another summary on Saul, the first king of Israel (Acts 12:21). The request for a king and choosing of Saul, the first king of Israel is depicted in 1 Sam 8–10. The request for a king is highlighted in the context of warning against such action in the narrative. Later in a speech (1 Sam 12:17, 19), Samuel calls the request a great sin. The forty years of reign of Saul is not mentioned in the OT, although it is suggested by Josephus.[40]

The rejection of Saul is made emphatic in a number of verses in the Samuel narratives. It is particularly articulated in 1 Sam 15:23, 26, and in 16:1, although the language is not similar. The right of God to remove rulers is articulated in other passages. The word *remove* in relation to rulers, but not Saul, is used in the books of the Maccabees (1 Macc 8:13; 11:63; 2 Macc 4:10; 11:23). In Dan 2:21 God is said to have the right to remove kings along with right to change times and seasons. Saul's rise to kingdom and his removal is, therefore, summarized only

---

[40] The MT of 1 Sam 13:1 mentions only two years. Josephus also knows of 40 years—see *Ant.* 6.378. Cf. Haenchen, *Acts*, 409.

with the use of language associated with God's control over rulers. The giving of judges and Saul, followed by the removal of the latter, is therefore presented in a very short account without verbal correlations with those narratives—another example of summary.

Saul is followed by David, an ideal king (Acts 13:22). The figure of David receives great emphasis in the structure of Paul's speech for a number of reasons. In contrast to Saul, who was requested by men, David is given divine credentials. David is said to have been *raised* by God. The use of the word is significant. Both the judges and Saul were said to be *given* to the people earlier.[41] To *raise* must be seen as synonymous with *give* inasmuch as both refer to the type of divine action to call a leader for the future benefit of the people. Moreover, the use of this particular verb will give occasion to link it with the raising of Jesus in Acts 13:30 and 37.

David also stands out because, out of all the human agents discussed so far, only his qualities are mentioned. More than this, the qualities of David are emphasized by a quotation of a specific kind. The quote is signalled with a particular phrase: "In his testimony about him he said" (Acts 13:22). The assumption of the text is that God spoke through the words quoted. The quote is also special because it is a composite quote that is believed to be taken from at least two or possibly three passages. The uncertainty concerns the last phrase in the sentence and will be discussed separately from the first two.

The first part of the quote in Acts 13, underlying the phrase "I have found David," is taken from Ps 89:20/Ps 88:21.[42]

Acts 13:22	**Ps 89:20/88:21**
I have found David of Jesse.	I have found David, my servant
εὗρον Δαυὶδ τὸν τοῦ Ἰεσσαί	εὗρον Δαυιδ τὸν δοῦλόν μου

[41] The verb *to raise* as a reference to God's action to appoint certain people for leadership roles is attested in the book of Judges. God is said to have raised judges as saviors of the people—see Judg 2:16. 18; 3:9, 15; 2:16, 18; 3:9, 15.

[42] All of the translations in the following tables are my own.

Ps 89/88 celebrates the covenant with David and asks for God's mercy after an outbreak of wrath against the dynasty. The immediate context of Ps 89:20/88:21 is that of choosing and anointing David. Psalm 89:19–37/88:20–38 share thoughts and words with the oracle of Nathan in 2 Sam 7:4–17.[43] The one praying says that God spoke in a vision revealing the covenant with David. Help was promised to David against his enemies. A future Davidic king will call God his father and the Davidic king will be made a first-born to God. The seed of David is promised an eternal kingdom.

The designation, *that of Jesse* is not from Ps 89/88, however. There are a number of passages in the OT where that expression occurs (see e.g., 1 Sam 16:1; 1 Chr 10:14; 29:26; Ps 72/71:20). Combining a quote about David with the expression about his father is yet another example of variability at work.

The second part of the quote in Acts 13 referring to David as a "man after my heart" is from 1 Sam 13:14.

Acts 13:22	1 Sam 13:14
a man of my heart	a man of his heart
ἄνδρα κατὰ τὴν καρδίαν μου	ἄνθρωπον κατὰ τὴν καρδίαν αὐτοῦ

The context for the phrase in 1 Sam is that of the rejection of Saul. Samuel, while reproaching Saul for offering a sacrifice to the Lord on his own, told him that his kingdom will not remain and that he will be replaced by a man. The Lord said that he would look for a man according to his heart. Again, the tense in the LXX is future since it is a promise. The context in the quote is past, since the Lord had already found David.

[43] Willem A. VanGemeren, *Psalms*, ed. Tremper Longman III and David E. Garland, rev. ed., EBC 5 (Grand Rapids: Zondervan, 2008), 672.

The last part of the composite quote, "who will fulfill all my wills,"[44] can be seen in two ways. It is either a quote from a third passage, or it is a Targumic paraphrase on "man after my heart" of 1 Sam 13:14, which somehow ended up being mingled with the main text. When we consider the possibility of a quotation, the two texts show remarkable similarity:

Acts 13:22	**Isa 44:28**
who *will do all my wills*	who tells Cyrus to beware and he *will do all my wills*
ὃς ποιήσει πάντα τὰ θελήματά μου	ὁ λέγων Κύρῳ φρονεῖν, καὶ Πάντα τὰ θελήματά μου ποιήσει

As evident, the Isaiah text speaks not of David but of Cyrus. The Persian king is portrayed as the servant of the Lord carrying out his will. In favor of this position it could be pointed out that both David (2 Sam 19:22) and Cyrus (Isa 45:1) have been designated as the Lord's anointed ones.[45] The difficulty with this interpretation is that the attributes of Cyrus are transferred to David. It is questionable whether or not that transfer lies within creative and disciplined appropriation of elements of Israel's holy history. Variability so far concerned statements about the same person, same events, or similar sequences of those events.

As an alternative to this, it has been noted that the Targum on 1 Sam 13:14 regularly paraphrases *a man after my heart* with the expression *a man doing my will*. It might have happened that both the phrase and what were intended to be an explanation of it ended up in

---

[44] My translation.

[45] Fitzmyer, *Acts*, 512; Johnson, *Acts*, 232.

the text.[46] This interpretation is a hypothesis but makes better sense given that David is discussed in the composite quote.

The compilation quote is clearly held together by the common subject, David as an ideal king. The quote is used as coherent testimony from God about David. This is the clearest example of variability in the passage. Information on David in different texts is drawn into a unified statement as a testimony of God.

The metatext on the holy history of Israel could be seen as having ended at the elaboration on the attributes of David. There are reasons, however, for considering the *bringing* of Jesus and the ministry of John in continuity with that history. Both Jesus and John are linked to Israel. Jesus is said to be brought to Israel as savior. The term *brought* is best understood as parallel to *give* and *raise*—the former used in relation to the judges and Saul and later in relation to David. That is to say that at the outset Jesus's ministry is portrayed as yet another epoch in God's history of involvement with Israel. It is to be emphasized that Jesus is linked with Israel. The epoch of Jesus's life is further linked to the history of Israel by the use of the words *promise* and *seed.* Christ is introduced as the *seed* brought to Israel according to the *promise* to be the savior.

The idea of epochs, or periods of time, comes to the fore in relation to John the Baptist as well. Jesus is said to have been proclaimed *ahead of time* by John in Acts 13:24. When "his time was fulfilled," he pointed to the coming of the one who is more worthy than him. John like Jesus is also linked with Israel by the remark that he proclaimed baptism of repentance to the whole of Israel. The periods of John and Jesus are not to be seen as two equals, though. The role of John is seen in the preparation period inasmuch as he was inferior to Jesus. John's saying about Jesus is quoted verbatim. In the relationship of John and Jesus there is a slight implication of conflict and a clear indication of going from the smaller to the greater. They are two human agents who represent two periods, the latter superior to the former. It is of

---

[46] Marshall, "Acts," 583.

significance that John and Jesus are presented as the latest phases of God's involvement with his people.

The section on Israel's history and the life of Jesus is linked along the lines of promise and fulfillment. God is said to have acted according to a promise when bringing the savior to Israel from the seed of David. The promise of a dynasty given to David is most fully portrayed in 2 Sam 7:12–13 (along with its parallel in 1 Chr 17:11–12) and in Ps 89/88, as was discussed above. The promise in 2 Sam 7:12–13 is worth considering:

> And it will be if your days are fulfilled and you lie down with your fathers, that I will raise up your offspring after you who shall be from your belly, and I will prepare his kingdom; he shall build me a house for my name, and I will restore his throne forever.
> (καὶ ἔσται ἐὰν πληρωθῶσιν αἱ ἡμέραι σου καὶ κοιμηθήσῃ μετὰ τῶν πατέρων σου, καὶ ἀναστήσω τὸ σπέρμα σου μετὰ σέ, ὃς ἔσται ἐκ τῆς κοιλίας σου, καὶ ἑτοιμάσω τὴν βασιλείαν αὐτοῦ αὐτὸς οἰκοδομήσει μοι οἶκον τῷ ὀνόματί μου, καὶ ἀνορθώσω τὸν θρόνον αὐτοῦ ἕως εἰς τὸν αἰῶνα.)

The relevant verse in Ps 89/88 elaborating the same theme might be verse 29:

> And I will establish his seed forever and ever and his throne as the days of the sky.
> (καὶ θήσομαι εἰς τὸν αἰῶνα τοῦ αἰῶνος τὸ σπέρμα αὐτοῦ καὶ τὸν θρόνον αὐτοῦ ὡς τὰς ἡμέρας τοῦ οὐρανοῦ.)

Paul claims in Acts 13:24 that Jesus is the seed of David:

> Of this man's seed according to the promise has God brought to Israel a Saviour, Jesus.[47]

---

[47] My translation.

> (τούτου ὁ θεὸς ἀπὸ τοῦ σπέρματος κατ' ἐπαγγελίαν ἤγαγεν τῷ 'Ισραὴλ σωτῆρα 'Ιησοῦν.)

The promise in 2 Sam 7:12 is uttered by the prophet Nathan to David whereas the version in Psalms is part of the vision given by God. The seed is being raised (ἀναστήσω) in the Nathan oracle whereas the seed is placed (θήσομαι) in the prayer of the psalm. In both 2 Samuel and in thes Psalms, the seed is promised an eternal kingdom.

In addition, the promise of an eternal kingdom is remembered throughout the OT. The grace of God given to David and his seed is praised in 2 Sam 22:51. An oath given to David regarding his seed is also articulated and meditated on in Ps 132/131:11.[48] Fitzmyer points out that within the Bible a shift happened in moving away from Solomon as the sole realization of the promise to a future yet unidentified Davidic figure. The promise of a future David is detectable in passages like Jer 30/37:9 and Ezek 37:24–25. In sum, the promise regarding the seed of David is preserved in the narrative of 1 Sam 7:12 and is remembered and praised in prayers and hymns in the OT. The coming of the new Messiah is often portrayed in the light of the Davidic dynasty, even within biblical literature.[49] The application of the promise to Jesus is emphasized by the word *savior*. The bringing of Jesus as a savior is said to be according to promise. Instead of identifying the words of Paul with one of the utterances of the promise, it appears reasonable to suggest that an allusion is made to an element of Israel's holy history, which has many textual expressions.

Next, the figure of John is remembered as a forerunner to Jesus: "before his coming John had already proclaimed a baptism of repentance to all the people of Israel" (Acts 13:24). The phrase, literally "before the face of his coming" (πρὸ προσώπου τῆς εἰσόδου αὐτοῦ), is grammatically unusual and irregular language. Both Marshall and Fitzmyer suggest that the expression is to be read against the wording of Mal 3:1–2 where both "before my face" (πρὸ

---

48 Marshall, "Acts," 584.

49 Fitzmyer, *Acts*, 513.

προσώπου μου) and the "day of his coming" (ἡμέραν εἰσόδου αὐτοῦ) are used to refer to an eschatological messenger who will prepare the way for the Lord.[50] It is to be pointed out here that the figure of John the Baptist is portrayed in the light of Mal 3:1 in the Gospel of Luke, too.[51] In Luke 1:17, for instance, it is promised that John will "come before" the savior whereas in Luke 7:27, Mal 3:1 is quoted to explain John's role in relation to Jesus. It appears as if John is identified with Mal 3:1, especially through the terms *before the face of* and *coming* which combined in Acts take a temporal meaning.

The message and the figure of John, therefore, are recalled through the words of the prophecy now seen fulfilled in him. John is also identified by the content of his proclamation. The next term strongly identified with John is *baptism of repentance*. The phrase is used in Luke 3:3 as an introduction to what John did. The same phrase is used by Paul in a speech in Acts 19:4. *Baptism of repentance* is a phrase meant to identify the message of Jesus's forerunner.

The conclusion of John's epoch is marked by a reference to fulfilling his course in Acts 13:24. A structural pattern of the speech is revealed at this point. Just as discussion on David was finished with a quote, so the message of John is summed up by one in Acts 13:24:

> What do you suppose that I am? I am not he. No, but one is coming after me; I am not worthy to untie the thong of the sandals on his feet.
> (τί ἐμὲ ὑπονοεῖτε εἶναι; οὐκ εἰμὶ ἐγώ ἀλλ' ἰδοὺ ἔρχεται μετ' ἐμὲ οὗ οὐκ εἰμὶ ἄξιος τὸ ὑπόδημα τῶν ποδῶν λῦσαι)

The content of John's proclamation now quoted by Paul is also known from Luke 3:16–17; John 1:20, 27; Mark 1:7; and from Matt 3:11. One would expect a very close resemblance between Paul's words on John and the version in Luke but in fact different parts of the quote stand close to various wordings found in all four Gospels.

---

[50] Ibid.; Marshall, "Acts," 584.
[51] Fitzmyer, *Acts*, 513.

The question at the beginning of the quote, for instance, is not recorded in Luke at all. In fact, such questioning only finds distant parallels in John's account. Starting in John 1:20, John the Baptist is questioned by the Jews of Jerusalem about his identity. Even there, it is not John who is asking the questions but the Jews. In Luke's Gospel, nevertheless, the questions regarding the identity of John is said to be in the people's minds surrounding the preacher: "As the people were filled with expectation, and all were questioning in their hearts concerning John, whether he might be the Messiah" (Luke 3:15). Moreover, later Jesus is portrayed asking questions about the identity of his forerunner starting in Luke 7:24. The response to the question points to John 1:20 again where John the Baptist categorically denies that he would be Christ. At the same time, it would have to be added that the same is assumed in the other Gospels. In the various accounts it is recorded that questions surrounded the identity of John and that he denied being Christ. The questions appear to come from different characters but they all relate to who John was in relation to Jesus.

The part of the quote about the coming of Jesus is expressed in a unique way in Acts, somewhat different from the Gospel accounts. Especially the phrase *after me* (μετ' ἐμὲ) is not attested elsewhere. The equivalent in Mark, Matt and John is a spatial phrase: *behind me* (Mark 1:7; Matt 3:11; John 1:27) whereas there is no equivalent term in Luke. In contrast with Matt, Mark and John, the text in Acts places emphasis on chronology: Jesus comes later than John. This is in accordance with the attempt at periodization in Paul's sermon. For Paul John's inferiority is viewed in terms of time.

The last part of the sentence in Acts, for "I am not worthy to untie the thong of the sandals on his feet" is expressed in all four Gospels:

οὐκ εἰμὶ ἄξιος τὸ ὑπόδημα τῶν ποδῶν λῦσαι I am not worthy to untie the thong of the sandals on his feet (Acts 13:25)
οὐκ εἰμὶ ἱκανὸς λῦσαι τὸν ἱμάντα τῶν ὑποδημάτων αὐτοῦ I am not worthy to untie the thong of his sandals (Luke 3:16)

οὐκ εἰμὶ [ἐγὼ] ἄξιος ἵνα λύσω αὐτοῦ τὸν ἱμάντα τοῦ ὑποδήματος I am not worthy to untie the thong of his sandal (John 1:27)
οὐκ εἰμὶ ἱκανὸς κύψας λῦσαι τὸν ἱμάντα τῶν ὑποδημάτων αὐτοῦ I am not worthy to stoop down and untie the thong of his sandals (Mark 1:7)
οὐκ εἰμὶ ἱκανὸς τὰ ὑποδήματα βαστάσαι I am not worthy to carry his sandals (Matt 3:11)

Matthew, with his peculiar expression, appears to follow a different path. The quote in Acts appears to be shorter and simpler than the ones in the Gospels. Nevertheless, basically they are all very similar expressions of the same statement. In sum, the ministry of John is read as a phase in God's involvement with his people Israel. The temporal character of the ministry of John is emphasized both intra-textually and intertextually. John proclaimed Jesus ahead of time and he is said to have fulfilled his task. The periodization is at work in using Mal 3:1 and speaking of John as the one before Jesus.

Following a repeated address to the audience, the condemnation of Jesus, his death and burial, along with the resurrection and appearances, are recited in Acts 13:26–31. The relevance of what has been said before for the audience is stressed by speaking of the word sent by God to both Jews and God-fearers in 13:26. The sending of the *word of salvation* referring to the content of Jesus's proclamation is reminiscent of Acts 10:36 where the content of the Christian message is designated the same way. Jesus's death is claimed in 13:29 to have happened according to what was written about him. Strauss pointed out the events recited in Paul's speech are identical with the ones mentioned by Paul in 1 Cor 15:3–5 where fulfillment of Scriptures is also stressed.[52] The inhabitants of Jerusalem and their leaders are said

[52] Strauss, *Davidic Messiah in Luke-Acts*, 161.

to have condemned Jesus. The context of their action is ignorance of who Jesus was and of the voices of prophets.[53]

The fulfillment of Scripture is especially linked with two points of Jesus's passion: his condemnation and the way he was killed. The condemning is mentioned at the end of 13:27: "they fulfilled those words by condemning him." No particular prophecy or word of Scripture is identified as seen fulfilled in the condemnation of Jesus. The motif of the innocent righteous condemned finds expression in a number of passages in the OT. They include the portrayal of the suffering servant of God who was punished for the sins of others in Isa 53, with judgment mentioned specifically in 53:8.

Another passage in Ps 118/117:22 speaks of the stone being rejected by the builders, possibly a reference to unjust condemnation.[54] It is to be borne in mind, however, that no verbal correspondences link the verse in Acts with other verses in the OT. It is simply stated that the judging of Jesus is a fulfillment of the prophets. This might be seen as a summary of not one prophecy but of a number of utterances on a certain topic—that is the judging and suffering of Christ leading to death.

Jesus is said to have been found innocent by the Jerusalem authorities, yet Pilate was asked by those authorities to kill him. After everything was fulfilled which was written about him, Jesus was taken from the tree and put in the grave. The short summary viewing Jesus's death as fulfillment of the things that were written about him is extremely vague. It assumes that during the course of Jesus's suffering a number of things had to happen to him in accordance with what was written. Identifying concrete events or motifs is neither possible nor necessary. It is sufficient to observe that the way Jesus died was understood in the light of Scripture.

---

[53] The motif of ignorance is a recurring one throughout Luke-Acts (see Luke 24:2; Acts 8:30; 17:23, 30). Cf. Tzvi Novick, "Eschatological Ignorance and the Hafṭarah on Acts 13:27," *NovT* 54 (2012): 170.

[54] Marshall, "Acts," 584.

Finally, Jesus's resurrection and his appearances are recited in 13:30–31. These events are not linked specifically with OT passages although in a few verses later resurrection will become the main focus. Again, the pattern of reciting resurrection after death is the same as the one found in 1 Cor 15:3–6.

The earlier section of Paul's address discussed so far is dominated by a logic that concentrates on divine initiatives toward God's people. Those initiatives provide the basis for periodization of history. God's actions inaugurate new epochs often by working through human agents such as judges, Samuel, Saul, David, John, and finally Jesus. The portrayal of God's actions and of the human agents at times reverberates with or even quotes from concrete texts of the OT and texts also found in the NT. At other times, however, the connection is reduced to summary. Some argue that a great number of combinations of the several intertexts in Paul's speech is best accounted for as a metatext on not the sum of those texts but on the holy history of Israel. Information regarding an epoch or a certain human agent can be drawn together from several writings of the OT and can be combined to form a new utterance on a person or on divine acts.

The second part of the speech explores and evaluates the significance of Jesus's ministry in general and of his resurrection in particular. From 13:32 on a different kind of metatextual operation can be observed. The speech ceases to tell stories and concentrates on evaluating Jesus's ministry.

In 13:32 Paul stresses the relevance for his generation of what had been said. In the following verses Jesus's ministry and his resurrection are expounded in the light of Scriptural citations. At the end Paul calls his audiences to forgiveness of sins and justification, warning them against disbelief in the light of Hab 1:5. Throughout the argument the fulfillment of Scripture receives great emphasis. To begin with, Paul confessed that God had raised Jesus from the dead, an event followed by Jesus's appearances to his followers for many days. Paul claims that the ones to whom Jesus appeared, including himself, bear witness to him. In 13:32 the idea of witness is taken further: the apostles proclaim the good news of the promise given "to the fathers." The promise is said to have been fulfilled in the raising of Jesus. Fathers of course were mentioned earlier in 13:17 as the ones chosen by God—a reference to the patriarchs. This promise, however, is spoken of in relation to David.[55] Bowker's guess is that the fathers are indeed the ones spoken of earlier particularly in the light of Deut 4:37–38. The speaker thus would return to the passage he started his speech with.

In addition, it could be observed that in the Deuteronomy passage God is said to have chosen the seeds of the fathers. Bowker hypothesizes that Paul returned again to the promise regarding the seeds of the fathers.[56] Promise given to the seeds, however, was not mentioned in relation to the fathers. Paul seems to preserve the word *seed* for David's offspring. Another solution could be offered based on different usages of the word *fathers*. It is true that in a great number of cases in Acts the word simply denotes the patriarchs (Acts 7:11) and their generation (Acts 7:39). At other times, however, *fathers* can be used as a reference to the ancestors of Israel during the times of the prophets as in Acts 7:52, or even ancestors in the most general sense. In fact, David is said in Acts 13:36 to have been buried along with his fathers—a reference to his ancestors in general. It is possible, therefore, that the promise given to the fathers in 13:32 simply hints at the previous generations to whom David belonged. This would imply that the raising of his seed is still in view. The immediate context supports this latter reading. The metaphor of family appears to be at work. Paul calls his generation the sons in 13:33, whereas the previous generations are viewed as fathers in general to whom a certain promise was given.

Following the repeated claim of fulfillment, a number of texts from the OT are cited to prove and expound Jesus's resurrection. First, Ps 2:7 is offered to demonstrate the special status of Jesus. Then Isa 55:3 and Ps 16/15:10, linked by a shared word, are claimed to testify to Jesus's resurrection.

---

[55] Johnson, *Acts*, 234.

[56] Bowker, "Speeches," 102.

The text in Acts is clearly invested in interpreting the cited passages and in linking them with Christ and his life. Treating Acts 13:32–38 as a metatext on a selection of quotes would appear to be a justifiable procedure. In this way the metatext would be linked with the individual passages it quotes and interprets. However, I propose a deeper subtext underlying even those very articulate quotes and their interpretation on a metatextual level. The quotes already are comments on an unannounced subtext. The proposed subtext is the oracle of Nathan to David concerning his seed from 2 Sam 7, already alluded to in an earlier part of the speech in Acts 13:23.[57] Attempts will be made to demonstrate that the intertexts in the form of quotes already comment on different aspects of the deeper subtext seen realized in Jesus's ministry. In agreement with Goldsmith,[58] it will be argued here that the citations that are supposed to expound Jesus's resurrection are part of a metatextual activity on the deep subtext of 2 Sam 7. Paul shows that the promises given to David are now fulfilled in Jesus. That is to say that the various intertextual connections are inspired by and subordinated to the promise in 2 Sam 7.

It has long been noted by many scholars that portions of 2 Sam 7 must stand in the background of the entire speech,[59] or at least some section of it.[60] There is no consensus, however, over the precise nature of correlation. Occasionally the words *Pesher*[61] or *Midrash*[62] are used

---

[57] Raymond Brown convincingly demonstrated that the Davidic promise as known from 2 Sam 7:8–16 is interpreted in the annunciation in Luke 1:32–33. Moreover, the promise of the baby Jesus, Brown argues, echoes Ps 2:7 and Ps 89/88:30—see Raymond E. Brown, *The Birth of the Messiah: A Commentary on the Infancy Narratives in the Gospels of Matthew and Luke*, updated ed., ABRL (New York: Doubleday, 1999), 310.

[58] Dale Goldsmith, "Acts 13:33–37: A Pesher on 2 Samuel 7," *JBL* 87 (1968): 321–24.

[59] Strauss, *Davidic Messiah in Luke-Acts*, 150.

[60] Usually for the second part on the raising of Jesus. Cf. Goldsmith, "Acts 13."

[61] Ibid.

[62] Luke Timothy Johnson, *Septuagintal Midrash in the Speeches of Acts* (Milwaukee: Marquette University Press, 2002).

in a more historic vein to demonstrate that Paul's speech is shaped after a proposed model of Jewish interpretation of Scripture, homily or argumentation.

Attempts have been made to prove that Paul's speech is indeed based on 2 Sam 7. Strauss, in an effort to determine the shape of sermons in Acts, used the term c*onceptual framework* to explain the relationship between Paul's speech and the text of 2 Samuel.[63] Unfortunately, the unexplained term does not provide a clear idea of the correlation. It is clear, nevertheless, that Strauss's comparative chart of 2 Sam 7:6–16 and Acts 13:16–38 is based on textual and thematic correlation. He compared themes and similar phrases.[64] This latter approach stands closest to the one assumed in this work since the metatext shades light on the themes of the subtext. Acts 13:33–38 as a metatext explores themes of the subtext of 2 Sam 7 in its connections with other related utterances of the OT and with the raising of Jesus.

It is beneficial to remember now that the promise seen fulfilled in raising Jesus is that in 2 Sam 7:12–16:

> And it will be if your days are fulfilled and you lie down with your fathers, that I will raise up your seed after you who shall be from your belly, and I will prepare his kingdom; he shall build me a house for my name, and I will restore his throne forever. I will be a father to him, and he shall be a son to me, and if his injustice comes, then I will punish him with a rod of men and with attacks of sons of men, but I will not remove my mercy from him, as I removed it from those whom I removed from before me. And his house and his kingdom shall be made sure forever before me, and his throne shall be restored forever. (καὶ ἔσται ἐὰν πληρωθῶσιν αἱ ἡμέραι σου καὶ κοιμηθήσῃ μετὰ τῶν πατέρων σου, καὶ ἀναστήσω τὸ σπέρμα σου μετὰ σέ, ὃς ἔσται ἐκ τῆς κοιλίας σου, καὶ ἑτοιμάσω τὴν βασιλείαν αὐτοῦ· αὐτὸς οἰκοδομήσει μοι οἶκον τῷ

[63] Strauss, *Davidic Messiah in Luke-Acts*, 150.
[64] Ibid., 154–55.

ὀνόματί μου, καὶ ἀνορθώσω τὸν θρόνον αὐτοῦ ἕως εἰς τὸν αἰῶνα. ἐγὼ ἔσομαι αὐτῷ εἰς πατέρα, καὶ αὐτὸς ἔσται μοι εἰς υἱόν· καὶ ἐὰν ἔλθῃ ἡ ἀδικία αὐτοῦ, καὶ ἐλέγξω αὐτὸν ἐν ῥάβδῳ ἀνδρῶν καὶ ἐν ἁφαῖς υἱῶν ἀνθρώπων· τὸ δὲ ἔλεός μου οὐκ ἀποστήσω ἀπ' αὐτοῦ, καθὼς ἀπέστησα ἀφ' ὧν ἀπέστησα ἐκ προσώπου μου. καὶ πιστωθήσεται ὁ οἶκος αὐτοῦ καὶ ἡ βασιλεία αὐτοῦ ἕως αἰῶνος ἐνώπιον ἐμοῦ, καὶ ὁ θρόνος αὐτοῦ ἔσται ἀνωρθωμένος εἰς τὸν αἰῶνα.)

Second Samuel 7 is the highlight of the books of Samuel because it tells of the dynastic promise given to David.[65] The chapter can be divided into two distinct parts: the dynastic promise in 7:1–17 and David's response of prayer in 7:18–29.[66] The prophecy itself easily divides into two parts: the first part in 7:4–7 deals with David's initiative to build a house for God and also the rejection of that offer, while the second part in 7:8–16 contains God's offer to build a house for David. The building of a Temple is picked up in the second part in the form of promise.[67] The promise given to David in fact involves a number of promises with a few conditions.

First, the promise becomes effective upon David's *falling on sleep* with his fathers (πληρωθῶσιν αἱ ἡμέραι σου καὶ κοιμηθήσῃ μετὰ τῶν πατέρων σου [2 Sam 7:12]), that is his death. Related to this is the promise to raise (ἀναστήσω) a seed after him. Next, a kingdom will be established for the seed. There are further qualifications regarding the kingdom. It is made evident that the throne of the heir will last forever. It is also promised that the house of the seed will be made sure (πιστωθήσεται ὁ οἶκος αὐτοῦ [2 Sam 7:13]). This seed will also build the house of the Lord. More than this, God will be a father to the seed, and he will be a son to God. If the seed sins, God

---

[65] The parallel version of the account is preserved in 2 Chr 17:1–5 and the oracle is celebrated in Ps 89/88.

[66] A.A. Anderson, *2 Samuel*, WBC 11 (Dallas: Word, 1989), 112.

[67] William M. Schniedewind, *Society and the Promise to David: The Reception History of 2 Samuel 7:1–17* (New York: Oxford University Press, 1999), 35.

will reproach him, but grace (ἔλεός) will not be removed from the seed as it had been removed from others. As opposed to the MT, the LXX does not mention Saul at this point but speaks of the *ones*. In sum, David received a promise that a seed will be raised to him, who will receive an eternal, sure kingdom, house and throne; he will be God's son; God will punish him for sins but will not withdraw his grace from him; and the seed will build a Temple for God. All this is contingent upon David's death. Paul's Antiochean speech elaborates on all those themes except for the building of the Temple.[68]

Throughout the speech the language of elevation (raising) is dominant. In 13:33 it is claimed that in fulfillment of the promises to the fathers God raised Jesus (ἀνέστησεν). In 13:34 raising Jesus from the dead is mentioned. It is stated in 13:38 that the one God raised (ἤγειρεν) does not see decay. Earlier in 13:30 Jesus was said to have been raised (ἤγειρεν) by God. Even before that the historic appearance of Jesus in accordance with the raising of the seed is described as being brought (ἤγαγεν) to Israel in 13:23. The language of elevation with the use of different words is in resonance with the promise: God promised to raise a seed after David in 2 Sam 7:12. The fulfillment of that promise is seen in the historic appearance and in the resurrection of Jesus. Clearly the former is in view in Acts 13:23, and the resurrection is definitely spoken of in 13:34 and 13:37.

The majority of commentators view the term in 13:33 as referring to Jesus's resurrection.[69] However, a minority view suggests the phrase ἀναστήσας Ἰησοῦν means the appearance of Jesus on the horizon of history.[70] This latter view proposes that 13:32–33 summarize the entire historic appearance of Jesus (the same as bringing in 13:23) using Ps 2:7 as proof from Scripture whereas the following verse speaks of resurrection from the dead. This argument is made possible by the lack of the phrase *from the dead* in 13:33 in contrast with its presence in

---

[68] It is worth pointing out that earlier in Paul's speech (cf. 13:23), an allusion to 2 Sam 7:12 is clearly detectable.

[69] Witherington, *Acts*, 412; Fitzmyer, *Acts*, 516.

[70] Strauss, *Davidic Messiah in Luke-Acts*, 162.

13:34 and 13:30. A further argument for different raising than resurrection is named by Strauss in the use of the term ὅτι δὲ in 13:34 taken to introduce resurrection as a new aspect of the raising of Jesus.

Perhaps the strongest argument is the intertextual connection with the promise of raising up David's seed in 2 Sam 7:12. The fulfillment of that promise might be seen in both the appearance of Jesus and his resurrection. In this sense the verse in Ps 2 proves Jesus's divine sonship in general and not exclusively his resurrection.[71] Strauss's suggestion is more comprehensive because it takes into account both the strong contextual drive for resurrection and the intertextual drive toward appearance in general: "While taking Ps. 2:7 as a prophecy fulfilled at the resurrection…Luke introduces the verse primarily to prove that Jesus is the Son of God, and hence the messiah, who fulfills the promises to David in his whole life, death and resurrection."[72] The raising in 13:33 probably refers to the entire Jesus event culminating in resurrection. Jesus's entire life, ministry, death, and resurrection are collectively the fulfillment of the promise.[73]

This view does better justice to the role of Ps 2:7 in the argument. The wording in Acts 13:33 is identical with that of the LXX verse: "You are my Son; today I have begotten you." Part of the quote ("You are my Son") was used in the narrative of Jesus's baptism in Luke 3:22 and in his transfiguration in 9:35 to express his messianic identity. The trajectory of those earlier uses suggests that Jesus's divine sonship was confirmed with the phrase "You are my Son."

The second part of the quote ("Today I have begotten you") resonates more with Jesus's resurrection for several reasons. The word *today* clearly suggests a point in time when the begetting happened. The begetting itself is probably a reference to new life the Father gave to his son in the resurrection. Strauss lays out the two parts of the quote together with focus on the two aspects of divine sonship with special clarity:

---

[71] Ibid., 162–63.

[72] Ibid., 164.

[73] Ibid.

> If one were to ask Luke when Ps. 2.7 was fulfilled (as a prophetic psalm), he would probably respond "at the resurrection." However, as the allusions to the Ps. 2.7b in Lk. 3.22 and 9.35 confirm, Luke understands the verse in the sense, "because you are my son (and hence, the messiah), I have begotten you to new resurrection life."... As in Lk. 3.22 and 9.35, the statement of sonship is meant first and foremost to confirm Jesus' messianic identity. The allusion thus fits perfectly as scriptural proof of the general "raising up" of Jesus to be the saviour of Israel. Secondarily, it sets up the resurrection argument which follows by confirming that the resurrection marked the climax and culmination of this fulfillment.[74]

A closer look at Ps 2 might shed some light on the use of it in the context of Acts. Psalm 2 is designated as royal coronation psalm.

Based on the account in 2 Kgs 11:12 and clues from the psalm itself, the process of coronation included the setting of the crown upon the king's head, proclamation, and anointing.[75] The psalm shows a number of parallels with the promise in 2 Sam 7:8–16 leading scholars to characterize the psalm as Davidic.[76] The psalm easily divides into four sections. First, the foreign kings and nations rebel against God and against the king (Ps 2:1–3). Second, God laughs at the attempt of the kings and announces his chosen one in Zion (2:4–6). Third, the new king declares the words of God (2:7–9). Finally, rulers are warned to pay tribute to the new king (2:10–12). The change of speakers is a noteworthy attribute of the psalm. The rulers speak first, then the Lord speaks, followed by the king presenting the words of God again, and finally the kings are addressed either by the new king or by a choir.[77]

---

[74] Ibid., 164–65.

[75] Peter C. Craigie and Marvin Tate, *Psalms 1–50*, WBC 19 (Nashville: Thomas Nelson, 2004), 64.

[76] Ibid.

[77] Ibid., 65.

The *today* of which the decree speaks is the day of coronation or possibly the day of the renewal of kingship. Sonship is the heart of the covenant between the king and the Lord. Craigie sees the roots of the king's sonship in that which was given to the people of Israel in the Sinai Covenant. The language of sonship is spoken of in Deut 1:31 when describing God as the father who cares for his son and also in Deut 8:5, where it is said that God disciplines Israel as a father does his son. The focus of the Sinai Covenant is on God and on the people. The covenant with the house of David, it appears, narrows the focus down on God and the king.

Nevertheless, the same concept of close relationship and sonship is at work.[78] The idea of sonship and begetting is expressed by special clarity by Craigie:

> "I have begotten you" is metaphorical language; it means more than simply adoption, which has legal overtones, and implies that a "new birth" of a divine nature took place during the coronation. It is important to stress, nevertheless, that the Davidic king, as son of God, was a human being, not a divine being, as was held in certain Near Eastern civilizations.[79]

The idea of divine sonship finds expression in yet another Psalm. In Ps 89/88:26 the Davidic king is promised to be able to call on God by saying, "You are my father." As it has been noted earlier, Ps 89/88 is to be seen as the poetic reflection on the promise of the seed of David given in 2 Sam 7. With the use of Ps 2:7, Paul expounds on the appearance of Jesus as the son of God. Divine sonship was promised to the Davidic king in 2 Sam 7:14 and was claimed by the king in Ps 2:7. Thus, 2 Sam 7:14 is the promise announced and Ps 2:7 is the realization of the promise. The declaration of Jesus's divine sonship is given at his conception in Luke 1:35, at his baptism in Luke 3:22, at

---

[78] Ibid., 67.

[79] Ibid.

his transfiguration in Luke 9:35, and finally at his resurrection in Acts 13:33, which points to the final realization of the same promise.[80]

The structure of the Psalm suggests a more extensive connection with Paul's speech. Whereas the quote only links the raising of Jesus with the sonship declared by the Davidic king, the context of the quote creates a larger surface of correlation. The decree of sonship is preceded by a conflict with the nations and foreign rulers in Ps 2. The expression of divine sonship of Jesus was also preceded by a conflict with Pilate, a Gentile, and with the leaders of Jerusalem along with the inhabitants of the city. The very explicit quote brings with it the context so that it can interact with the other aspects of its new location. It could be added that David received the promise after ending conflicts with his enemies.

The next quote in the speech is introduced to prove resurrection: "As to his raising him from the dead, no more to return to corruption, he has spoken in this way" (Acts 13:34). A quote from Isa 55:3 follows: "I will give you the holy things of David which are sure."[81] The wording of the quote is almost identical with what is quoted:[82]

Acts 13:34	**Isa 55:3**
I will give you the holy things of David that are sure.	I will make with you an everlasting covenant, the holy things of David that are sure.
δώσω ὑμῖν τὰ ὅσια Δαυὶδ τὰ πιστά	διαθήσομαι ὑμῖν διαθήκην αἰώνιον, τὰ ὅσια Δαυιδ τὰ πιστά

Two observation can be made with regard to the technique of quoting. First, the phrase *eternal covenant for you* is left out in the metatext

[80] Strauss, *Davidic Messiah in Luke-Acts*, 165.

[81] My translation.

[82] The following translations are my own.

perhaps in accordance with the tendency in Luke-Acts to preserve the word *covenant* for the one made with Abraham (see Acts 3:25; 7:8).[83] Second, δώσω is used in place of διαθήσομαι.

The text of Isa 55:3 deserves some attention in its context. Isaiah 55, rich with imagery, speaks of the relief and bounty offered for the people of God. The metaphor of feast is used to encourage the people to heed the word of the Lord. The reliability of the word of God is stressed on a syntactical and structural level as well. Hearing the word is essential in 55:2–3 whereas the efficaciousness of the word is highlighted in 55:10–11. Further, these two statements are elements in parallel structures within the chapter, adding more weight to the importance of the word. The two parts—55:1–5 and 55:6–13—of the chapter open with invitation (55:1, 6–7), proceed to the word of the Lord (55:2–3, 8–11) and to the promise of a new word (55:3–5, 12–13), and ends with a confession about the Lord (55:5, 13). The two sections are thought to complement each other on similar statements.[84]

The passage starts with a call to feast—a metaphor for listening to the word of the Lord, which is followed by explaining the grounds of the promise of richness from 55:3. A blessing of an everlasting covenant is said to be the reason for confidence. The covenant is made with the people but it contains the mercies of David, probably a reference to covenant promises given to the dynasty. The plural form of the word, *mercy* (חסד), rendered as *steadfast loves* or *unfailing kindnesses*, is significant. Motyer argues that the plural use of the word is to be understood in correlation with Ps 89/88. As noted above, Ps 89/88 contemplates the covenant with David and with his seed.

It is to be pointed out here that throughout the psalm the promise to David is repeatedly grounded in God's mercies. The plural word frames the Psalm: in 89/88:3 mercies are announced and in 89/88:50 they are pleaded for. In between mercies is the connection between the covenant with David in 89/88:4 and the endurance of the monarchy in

[83] Strauss, *Davidic Messiah in Luke-Acts*, 166.

[84] J. Alec Motyer, *The Prophecy of Isaiah: An Introduction and Commentary* (Downers Grove, IL: InterVarsity, 1993), 452.

89/88:5. Thus, David is promised dominion over other nations and a continuous dynasty because God's mercy (singular) is with him (see 89/88:25 and 89/88:29). Motyer argues that "These two singulars … together define the plurals … with which the psalm begins and ends: David will have world dominion and occupy an enduring throne."[85]

The covenant in Isa 55:3 is made for the recipients, that is for the people. There is a detectable shift away from the Davidic king to the people itself. The addressees of the Isaiah passage are promised the blessings of the Davidic covenant, that is, world dominion and an enduring throne. The people are called to enjoy the privileges and blessings of that covenant.[86] In the next two verses David is described as a witness to the nations. The result of that witness will be that the peoples shall run to him for refuge and his dominion over them will be recognized.

The translators of the LXX made a rare choice when translating the word חסד (*loving kindness* or *favor*) with the Greek word ὅσιος, which means holy or pious. A more natural choice would have been ἔλεος. There is only one other place in the LXX where the neutral plural form of the word *holy* occurs, and that is Deut 29:18. The rare choice might have been motivated by a misunderstanding of the Hebrew word[87] or by the similar sound of ὅσιος and חסד. Yet another argument suggests that the word was borrowed from Greek religious language to convey expected divine benefits.[88] Despite the differences of the words, this latter interpretation results in a similar meaning to what is found in the MT. If the general meaning of the text is in view, it becomes evident that in both versions divine benefits are promised in covenant settings.

The meaning of the phrase is even more difficult especially when the context of resurrection is taken into account. The holy things of

---

[85] Ibid., 454.

[86] Ibid., 453–54.

[87] It has been suggested that the close connection between חסד and חסיד might have motivated the translators—see Strauss, *Davidic Messiah in Luke-Acts*, 168.

[88] Ibid.

David that are sure are best understood to refer to the content of the Davidic covenant and not David's piety or holiness.[89] The plural is used to express the many elements of the promise of 2 Sam 7. It must involve a number of things: kingdom, throne, dynasty, protection from enemies, and so on. The word πιστά must be a reference to the reliability and endurance of the covenant blessings guaranteed in the promise of 2 Sam 7.[90] This solution is appealing for two reasons. This is in agreement with the context of the Isa 55:3, despite the unusual rendering in the LXX. The promise given to David is in view in both Isa 55:3 and Acts 13:33. The other reason is that this solution fits the purpose of Paul's speech better, which is to show how the promise to David was fulfilled in Jesus. Strauss puts equal emphasis on the context of Isaiah and of Acts when saying:

> In its Old Testament context, Isa. 55.3 is a renewal of the promise to David, emphasizing its enduring quality (an "eternal covenant" concerning "faithful mercies") and its present application to Israel ("I will make a covenant with you"). This is exactly how Luke takes it. He first states that not only did Jesus rise from the dead, but he rose *incorruptible*. This, he points out, is in accord with the nature of the promise to David (τὰ ὅσια Δαυὶδ) which are eternal and absolutely reliable (πιστά). Thus the key emphasis on the adjective πιστός, the reliability and enduring nature of the promise.[91]

There is also some emphasis on the phrase "I will give to you" that connects the Davidic promise with the people especially with later generations. The holy things of David that are sure are for the audience of Paul's speech. As I pointed out earlier, Isa 55:4 speaks of David bearing witness to Gentiles, a somewhat unusual thought within the

---

[89] Tannehill, *Acts of the Apostles*, 171.

[90] Strauss even argues for a verbal correspondence between the phrase πιστωθήσεται ὁ οἶκος αὐτοῦ of 2 Sam 7:16 and the πιστά of Isa 55:3—see Strauss, *Davidic Messiah in Luke-Acts*, 171.

[91] Ibid., 171–72.

OT. Apart from the repeated address to the Gentiles along with the Jews in Paul's speech nothing supports that aspect in the metatext. Nevertheless, a strong emphasis on the context of the utterance in Isa 55 would result in a reading that has the Gentiles in view.

The use of the words from Isa 55:3 in Acts 13:33 sheds light on rich connections between the metatext and the subtexts. The prophetic utterance in Isa 55:3 concerns the renewal of the promise made to David in 2 Sam 7 seen now fulfilled in the resurrection of Jesus. The Isaiah text completes the 2 Samuel text and Jesus's resurrection is a completion of both. The blessings of the covenant with David were renewed and finally fulfilled in Jesus's resurrection. Out of the many elements of the promise, the resurrection stands in closest correlation with the eternal aspects of it. Jesus being free from decay after being raised from the grave is able to mediate other aspects of the promise.

The next quote is taken from Ps 16/15:10. The two verses both state something important about Jesus's resurrection and are linked in turn with catchwords. The short sentence, "You will not let your Holy One experience corruption" in Act 13:34 shares the words *holy* and *will give* with 13:33: οὐ δώσεις τὸν ὅσιόν σου ἰδεῖν διαφθοράν. Psalm 16/15 is said to be a psalm of confidence perhaps reflecting on deliverance from some sort of calamity or crisis. The prayer also has a polemical tone against some other people from whom the psalmist detaches himself. After a short introduction (16/15:1), the words of the enemies are reflected on (16/15:2–4) and finally confidence in beneficial treatment from God is expressed (16/15:5–11).[92] The quoted section of the psalm is part of the expression of assurance about deliverance by God and restoration to the fullness of life. The one praying is confident that God will not leave him in Hades, a death-like situation or death itself. The alternative to death and corruption is knowing the way of life which is expected in the psalm.

Acts 13:33 and 13:34 are linked by a number of catchphrases. *Holy things* in the former and "Holy One" in the latter provide connection as

---

[92] Craigie and Tate, *Psalms 1–50*, 157–58.

well as shift of focus. From the many things of the Davidic covenant a move is made to the one person, Jesus Christ. There are two more antithetical parallels. It is said in 13:33 that God *will give* the covenant blessings of David, whereas it is said that God "will not give" the Holy One to corruption in 13:34. Tannehill suggests that *sure things* and *corruption* function as opposites of one another in another way.[93] Decay has also been hinted at in the introduction part of the first quote in 13:33. Acts 13:34 is a positive argument for the need of covenant blessing to be eternal; it states that Jesus did not see corruption, therefore, he must be the one spoken of in the promise. The assumption behind the quote is that David was the author of Ps 16/15—an idea shared by many NT writers.

The logic of the metatext on Ps 16/15:10 is very similar to that in Acts 2. The metatext expounds that David died (fell on sleep) and therefore saw corruption. This observation renders the prophecy in Ps 16:10 unfulfilled. There has to be another person in whom it stands fulfilled. The language of falling on sleep is not simply an explanation of Ps 16/15:10, but the language of promise is evoked. The oracle in 2 Sam 7:12 stated that the seed will be raised after David falls on sleep. The explanation therefore brings Ps 16/15:10 into connection with what is stated in 2 Sam 7:12. David's falling on sleep is therefore in accordance with the promise given about the seed. What appears to be a crisis, unfulfilled promise at one intertextual level, is actually how it should be on a metatextual level.

The final part of the speech draws conclusions from what has been said before. The idea of ignorance is picked up again from Acts 13:27. There it was emphasized that the killing of Jesus was carried out in ignorance of the prophets' proclamation. After an explanation of the prophetic promise in relation to Jesus, Paul appeals to revealed knowledge in 13:38 by saying, "Let it be known to you." Paul announces forgiveness of sins and justification—making it the message that is hard to believe. Justification is thought to be a

---

[93] Tannehill, *Acts of the Apostles*, 171.

genuinely Pauline proclamation in Acts.[94] The reason justification might be hard to believe is probably because the word *all* includes the Gentiles along with the Jews.

A final warning against potential disbelief is voiced using the words of Hab 1:5. The quote in Acts 13:41 is introduced by an appeal not to let a negative prophecy come true. The text in Acts is nearly identical with that in Hab 1:5 save word order at a few points. The two texts read as follows:[95]

Acts 13:41	**Hab 1:5**
Look, you scoffers! Be amazed and perish, for in your days I am doing a work, a work that you will never believe, even if someone tells you.	Look, you scoffers and watch, and marvel at marvellous things and perish, for in your days I am doing a work that you will not believe, even if someone tells you.
ἴδετε, οἱ καταφρονηταί, καὶ θαυμάσατε καὶ ἀφανίσθητε, ὅτι ἔργον ἐργάζομαι ἐγὼ ἐν ταῖς ἡμέραις ὑμῶν, ἔργον ὃ οὐ μὴ πιστεύσητε ἐάν τις ἐκδιηγῆται ὑμῖν.	ἴδετε, οἱ καταφρονηταί, καὶ ἐπιβλέψατε καὶ θαυμάσατε θαυμάσια καὶ ἀφανίσθητε, διότι ἔργον ἐγὼ ἐργάζομαι ἐν ταῖς ἡμέραις ὑμῶν, ὃ οὐ μὴ πιστεύσητε ἐάν τις ἐκδιηγῆται.

Following a short introduction (Hab 1:1), Hab 1 presents what must be understood as a dialogue between God and his prophet. First, the prophet complains to God in 1:2–4 about the lack of justice and about oppression of the just. Then in 1:5–11 God responds by proclaiming judgment of unknown proportion to Israel through the Babylonians. The coming judgment is so great and overwhelming that the people

---

[94] Witherington, *Acts*, 414; Tannehill, *Acts of the Apostles*, 172; Fitzmyer, *Acts*, 514.

[95] The following translations are my own.

will find it difficult to believe. Robertson claims that the emphasis is on the unprecedented characters of God's action:

> Apparently, these words intend to describe the unbelievable character of this event even though it should be compared to God's saving events of the past. The Israelites customarily recalled wondrous works of God's previous acts of salvation.... But even if this event which now is being prophesied were to be presented as an act of God's power, it would not be believed.[96]

The overwhelming character of the judgment is grounded in its intensity, its speed, and that God himself will execute it. The LXX rendering suggests that the addressees of the warning are the wicked ones among the people of Israel whose fate is to perish, whereas the MT is more ambiguous on this point.[97] God uses the Babylonians to execute judgment over his people.

Apart from the introductory formula in Acts 13:40, which is not very specific, and the context of the speech of Paul, nothing helps to determine the nature of the correlation between the two texts. The quote itself is supposed to support the claim that it should be known that forgiveness of sins and justification is preached through Jesus Christ. Forgiveness of sins and justification by Jesus is the message which some might be hard to believe. It has been proven that Jesus is the fulfillment of God's covenant promise; therefore, ignorance is no longer an excuse for not accepting the proclamation.[98] The greatness and vastness of the proclamation might be hard to believe.

---

[96] O. Palmer Robertson, *The Books of Nahum, Habakkuk, and Zephaniah*, 2nd ed. (Grand Rapids: Eerdmans, 1990), 146.

[97] Ibid., 143–44.

[98] In a short paper, Novick argued that reading the Torah and giving instruction on it was often argued for to shatter ignorance. Moreover, the same ignorance could be spoken of in relation to the teaching of the prophets as well. He argues that Hab 1:5 was used especially to warn against that ignorance. For further details see Novick, "Eschatological Ignorance."

The nature of intertextual correlation, however, is that of uncertainty. Driven by the lack of interpretive cues, commentators and scholars argue for a more extensive correlation. It could be pointed out for example that Gentiles are in view in both passages. There are Gentiles among Paul's audience and the Babylonians are instrumental in carrying out God's judgment. Based on this observation, Robertson argues for a more extensive correlation:

> It is most instructive to note that this very statement concerning the unbelievable character of the coming judgement of God was employed by Paul to forewarn the Jews that they were hardening themselves against his proclamation of the saving acts of God found in the death and resurrection of Jesus the Messiah (see Acts 13:3ff.). Far from simply taking up a mode of expression found in Habakkuk, Paul capture the heartthrob of the prophet's message and applies its awesome insights into the ways of God with people in his own day.[99]

Robertson is able to correlate judgment on Israel in Habakkuk and turning to the Gentiles in Acts 13:47, forgiveness of sins by Jesus and the general sinfulness spoken of in Habakkuk, and violence in Hab 2:1 (violence is not mentioned in the LXX) and the killing of Jesus.[100] Bowker argues that the unparalleled nature of a divine action in Acts 13:41 links Hab 1:5 with Deut 4:32, where the same phenomenon is described.[101]

Further, Wall argues for certain functions of Hab 1:5 in its new context. The use of the word *work* twice as opposed to just once in the quoted section is thought to correlate with the work of Acts 13:2 and 14:26. Wall argues that the work, therefore, must be Gentile mission. The quote from Habakkuk is also thought to foreshadow the lack of

---

[99] Robertson, *Books of Nahum, Habakkuk, and Zephaniah*, 146–47.

[100] Ibid., 147–48.

[101] Bowker, "Speeches," 102.

faith from Israel.[102] It is possible to read the quote in Acts 13:41 in relation to Gentiles, Gentiles mission, God's judgment on Israel, and the fate of Israel. All these readings depend on interpretative decisions. Limiting the intertextual correlation to the potential of disbelief in spite of an overwhelming divine action is preferred in this dissertation. There are two reasons for the limitation.

First, the quote is contained in a final exhortation against disbelief in general. Naturally, the envisioned lack of faith stands in relation to what has been demonstrated about Jesus. But the warning is more general than specific. It could be used to refer to a great number of divine acts as apparently happened in the Qumran community.[103] Second, the purpose of the quote is to close the speech and not to further the argument; therefore, it should be self-evident what it speaks about. God is said to do a work, which, once told, might be hard to believe by the scoffers.

4.3.1.2. The Aftermath of Paul's Speech: Acts 13:44–52

The two apostles were invited back the following Sabbath to speak again. Many of the Jews and the fearers further specified by the word proselyte followed the two who encouraged them to remain in the grace of God. The next Sabbath the whole city is said to have gathered in the synagogue to hear the apostles. A split is said to have occurred among the Jews and the rest of the gathering. The former, filled with jealousy, contradicted Paul. In reaction the two apostles proclaimed that it was necessary to speak the word first to them, but seeing that they did not consider themselves worthy of eternal life, now they turn to the Gentiles. This latter point is justified by the command of the Lord quoted in:[104]

---

[102] Robert W. Wall, "The Function of LXX Habakkuk 1:5 in the Book of Acts," *BBR* 10 (2000): 247–58.

[103] Novick, "Eschatological Ignorance," 171–75.

[104] The following translations are my own.

Acts 13:47	Isa 49:6
I have set you to be a light for the Gentiles, so that you may bring salvation to the ends of the earth.	I have made you the covenant for a race, a light for the Gentiles, so that you may bring salvation to the ends of the earth.
τέθεικά σε εἰς φῶς ἐθνῶν τοῦ εἶναί σε εἰς σωτηρίαν ἕως ἐσχάτου τῆς γῆς	τέθεικά σε εἰς διαθήκην γένους εἰς φῶς ἐθνῶν τοῦ εἶναί σε εἰς σωτηρίαν ἕως ἐσχάτου τῆς γῆς

Isaiah 49:1–6 contains commands to the servant of the Lord in relation to both Israel and the nations. The section breaks into two parallel testimonies, each containing words of the servant and of the Lord. The despondent servant is reminded that the Lord made him for the very task of restoring the right relationship between God and Israel.[105] Isaiah 49:6 is a divine utterance concerning the task of the servant: he brings salvation not only to Israel but also to the nations of the world.

The use of the quote in Acts is ambiguous for several reasons, not least of which because the introductory formula, "so the Lord has commanded us" raises some questions. Commentators are not in agreement on the identity of the "Lord" mentioned in the verse. Johnson, Fitzmyer, and Haenchen point to Jesus as the "Lord," although the connection they establish is based of different grounds, while Witherington assumes that the Lord in the verse at hand is God himself.[106]

---

[105] Motyer, *Prophecy of Isaiah*, 388.

[106] The quote can be linked with Jesus either by looking at the words *command* and *to command*, or by searching for utterances related to Jesus about mission to the Gentiles. Johnson claims that *the command of the Lord* is reminiscent of the same language in Acts 1:8. The task to bear witness to the nations is voiced in Acts 1:8: "and you will be my witnesseses…to the ends of the earth" (Johnson, *Acts*, 241). Fitzmyer links the command with that given about Paul to Ananias in Acts 9:15: "he is an instrument whom I have chosen to bring my name before Gentiles and kings and before the people of Israel" (Fitzmyer, *Acts*, 521). Haenchen also identifies the Lord as Jesus based on the content of the quote. Jesus is promised to be a light to the

The other question concerns the source of the quote. Acts 13:47 appears to follow the MT. The phrase "a covenant for the nation" used in the LXX is missing from Acts. This could be due to abbreviation, a tendency in Acts' treatment of quotes for reasons of brevity. Or it could be that the phrase was omitted in Acts because the speaker wanted the citation to refer to Gentiles only.[107] Marshall raises the possibility that Acts follows the MT on this verse, where the extra phrase is also missing.[108] Whatever the motivation, the result is a clearer focus on the Gentiles.

Attempts at identifying the Lord in the introductory phrase are indeed more challenging. If Jesus is to be seen as the Lord, the giver of the command, then a number of new questions emerge. For example, an OT passage appears to be quoted as the words of Jesus. Or better, Isa 49:6 can be used to summarize what Jesus said about mission to the Gentiles. If this interpretation is correct, then Jesus is the light of the Gentiles, and he is also the salvation. This position could be held by pointing out that Jesus was designated as "savior brought to Israel" earlier in Acts 13:23. If God is seen as the giver of the command, then the possibility opens up to identify Paul or Barnabas as the servant who are the light and bring salvation as it was promised in Isa 49:47.

It is clear that there are at least two addressees related to the quote. On the one hand, the "we" of the introductory formula is a reference to the apostles, including Paul and Barnabas. They received instructions from the Lord to go to the Gentiles. On the other hand, the "you" of the quote is a reference to the servant, understood to be Jesus in Luke-Acts and in most of the NT literature. Jesus was made to be the light for the Gentiles by God. Thus, it appears that in Acts 13:47 that three horizons are mixed: that of the servant in relation to God as described

---

nations in Luke 2:32. Although it is not a command by Jesus—see Haenchen, *Acts*, 414. Witherington, however, assumes that the Lord is God. The effect of such reading is the identification of Paul and Barnabas with the Servant, the addressee of the command in Isa 49—see Witherington, *Acts*, 416.

[107] Fitzmyer, *Acts*, 521.

[108] Marshall, "Acts," 588.

in Isa 49, that of Jesus in relation to the Father, and that of the apostles in relation to Jesus. That God made Jesus the light of the nations is well communicated throughout Luke-Acts and other writings of the NT.[109] He was understood to be the servant of the Lord bringing salvation to the ends of the earth.[110] Added to this, the task of bringing light to Gentiles was transferred to the apostles as seen in Acts 1:8 and to Paul in particular in Acts 9:15. The command, therefore, is a reference to Jesus commanding the apostles to go to the nations.

The mixing of horizons is inspired by a clear chain of carrying out God's mission, a mission that includes the Gentiles. The quote in Acts 13:47 is a fulfillment and transfer at the same time. The bringing of light to the nations was fulfilled in Jesus and transferred to the apostles. I realize that this interpretation is arrived at through an extra-textual investigation inasmuch as various interpretative tendencies throughout the NT are detected and a trajectory is established. Nevertheless, the ambiguity of both the giver of the command and of the recipient(s) of the command is best understood as a result of three mixed horizons.

The Gentiles' response to hearing about eternal life is that of gladness. It is followed by a remark about the word of the Lord spreading in that area. The Jews of the city stirred up some conflict against the apostles so that they had to leave for Iconium. The two apostles shook off the dust of their feet against their enemies.

4.4. Architextual Correlations in Acts 14:1–28

The rest of the missionary journey takes place in three further cities: Iconium, Lystra, and Derbe. The mission narrative is concluded in 14:21–28 by the return of the two apostles to Syrian Antioch. The

---

[109] The light metaphor is used to describe Jesus's mission in general in Luke 1:78–79 and in relation to Gentiles in Luke 2:32. Jesus's enlightening ministry is discussed with reference to Isa 49:6 in 2 Cor 4:3–6.

[110] The servant of Isa 41:1–4 is evoked in Matt 12:7–21. The servant of Isa 53 is evoked in Luke 22:37 and Acts 8:32–35 to portray Jesus—see Darrell L. Bock, *Acts*, BECNT (Grand Rapids: Baker Academic, 2007), 464.

narrative thus breaks into a section on apostolic activity in Iconium in 14:1–7 and later in Lystra and Derbe in 14:8–20.

4.4.1. Preaching, Miracle, Growth, and Persecution

The summary of the Iconium mission (Acts 14:1–7) follows the usual account of the church's mission with some variations. The apostles went to the synagogue the same way as they did before in other cities. It appears to be assumed that they spoke there and it is stated that many of the Jews and the Greeks believed as a result. Opposition to the apostolic activity also arose. The people were encouraged by the signs and wonders to speak boldly of God, the same way as it happened earlier in Jerusalem and elsewhere.[111] So far, the account shows a very close adherence to how apostolic mission is portrayed in Acts. Variations only concern the shared efforts of the Gentiles of the city and the Jews, along with their leaders, in persecuting the apostles.

Up to this point in Acts, Jews were portrayed as playing a leading role in igniting hostility against the proclamation of the missionaries. A common effort of both races, or even Gentile dominance in persecuting the apostles (Acts 18–19), occurs throughout Acts.[112] The Iconium account speaks of hostility not based on ethnic or religious lines. The other variation concerns the degree of hostility shown toward the apostles. The intention of those who did not believe was that of killing the missionaries. The plot was revealed to the apostles who escaped to Lystra and Derbe. The killing of Stephen as recounted in Acts 7 already introduced the killing of the leaders of the church as a response to preaching. Therefore, the summary of the Iconium mission follows the pattern of missionary activity established in Acts. In sum, a pattern of preaching supported by signs, acceptance, and hostility continues to shape the apostolic mission.

The account of the mission in Lystra in 14:8–20 follows the same pattern as the one in Iconium and indeed in other places. The pattern is

---

[111] Miracles in Acts support apostolic preaching: e.g., Acts 2:19, 22, 43; 4:16, 22, 30; 5:12; 6:8; 7:36; 8:6, 13; 13:22; 15:8; 20:23—see Witherington, *Acts*, 419.

[112] Bock, *Acts*, 471.

based on the recurrence of certain events. The apostles preach and sometimes one or more miracles happen. There is a positive response to the message-miracle pair or to either one of them. Finally, there is hostility around the apostles. The apostles were evangelizing in both Lystra and Derbe. Their message was followed by a miracle, the healing of the lame man in Lystra. Hostility arose leading to stoning Paul. The visit to Derbe is simply summarized with a short remark. Finally, on their way back the apostles encouraged those who converted. The new episodes of the Pauline mission thus follow the pattern of missionary activity.

Clearly, the miracle element is the most emphasized one in the Lystra episode. The healing of the lame man and the reaction of the people to it leading to a speech on clarifying what happened takes up most of the narrative. The architextual correlation of the healing followed by a clarifying speech and the misunderstanding of the apostles' identity deserve some attention. With regard to the first, it is to be pointed out that the miracle narrative shows structural parallels with another healing recorded in Acts 3. Both narratives begin with a near-identical portrayal of the lame man, emphasizing that he was ill from his mother's womb in 3:2 and 14:8. Furthermore, the healing is achieved while the apostles Peter and John (in Acts 3) and Paul and Barnabas (in Acts 14) looked intently at the lame man. Finally, the healed state of both men is described with the words *leap* and *walk*.[113]

More than this, it could be observed that the healings themselves are one element in a larger cycle in both narratives. Prior to the healing, both apostles delivered a major programmatic speech. Peter's Pentecost sermon and Paul's synagogue speech signal the beginning of their mission. Following the miracle, both apostles point to God as the source of healing. Peter explained to those gathered at the Temple that it was not the apostle's power that healed the man, rather it was God's power. Paul, too, pointed out in the speech that they are men and that the living God is the one to be praised for what happened.

---

[113] Witherington, *Acts*, 422–23.

Therefore, the pattern appears to be a major speech, followed by a miracle, and an explanation on the miracle in both narratives. The structural design of Acts thus suggests a Petrine cycle followed by a Pauline one. The most notable difference between the beginnings of the cycle is that of the audience. Peter's lame man was Jewish and the explanation took place in a Temple setting, while Paul's lame man was pagan and the speech took place in a Gentiles setting. This corresponds to the focus of Paul's mission on the Gentiles.

4.4.2. Hosting Divine Visitors

The other correlation of architextual character is detectable in the reception of the apostles as gods by the people of Lystra in Acts 14:8–18. Earlier, when discussing the receiving of three messengers by Peter in Caesarea, the *topos* of receiving guests was explored. Denaux identified both an OT *topos* of receiving divine messengers as guests based on Gen 18–19 and a more Hellenistic realization of the same *topos*. Denaux argued along the lines of possible antecedents which influenced the Lukan theme of hospitality.[114]

The account of Acts 14:11–14 gives the reaction of the people of Lystra to the miracle of healing the lame man. The narrator tells the readers that the people upon witnessing the miracle shouted in Lycaonian: "The gods have come down to us in human form" (Acts 14:11). The inhabitants of Lystra identified Barnabas as Zeus and Paul as Hermes. The reason for identifying Paul as Hermes is given in the fact that he was the main speaker. The priest of Zeus brought animals to offer sacrifices to the gods at the city gate. When the apostles heard about what was planned, tearing their clothes, explained that they were men and not gods.

---

[114] Denaux, "Theme," 255–79.

The episode's connection with Ovid's *Metamorphoses* has been somewhat tentatively suggested by NT scholars.[115] Denaux, however, located the reception of the apostles as gods in the wider Graeco-Roman tradition.[116] Furthermore, Witherington listed external evidence that links Lystra with Zeus and Hermes. His suggestion is that Luke, being aware of the place's strong sentiments for those two gods, showed how they would be received in the pagan context of the region.[117] It is to be remembered at this point that the narrator portrays the attitude of Gentiles in the region towards the apostles. The Gentile character of the people is stressed throughout: it is said that they were speaking their native tongue; attention is paid to the details of the sacrifice they were preparing to offer.

The strong familiarity with either the *topos* of disguised divine visits in general or with the tale in the *Metamorphoses* is used to portray Gentile perceptions early Christian missionaries faced. The reaction of the people can be seen in accordance with that of Cornelius, who bowed down before Peter. The gesture was understood as an expression of respect to a divine being as evident in Peter's warning. The same way people in Lystra had to be warned against such misunderstanding. In sum, the *topos* is put to use to present the Gentiles' attitudes toward miracles and toward early apostolic mission.

4.4.3. Septuagintal Phrases

The misunderstanding of locals gave occasion to Paul to lay out theological truths on idols and the living God. The challenge of idolatry as an act of ignorance was met by a longer explanation in Acts 14:14–17. First, the apostles protested against the sacrifice by the dramatic action of tearing their clothes. The two signaled with their hands and shouted loudly to stop the crowd from offering sacrifice.

---

[115] Witherington, *Acts*, 421–22; Johnson, *Acts*, 248–49; Denaux, "Theme," 264–65.

[116] Denaux, "Theme," 265.

[117] Witherington, *Acts*, 422.

What follows is characterized as *good news* the apostles brought to the city. The speech summary follows a similar logic with the earlier address in the synagogue. There Paul set out how God interacted with Israel his people in the past leading up to Jesus. Here Paul first points out that God let the nations walk in their own ways in the past but did not leave them entirely without witness. The witness to the Gentiles in the past was rain and fruitful seasons resulting in food and gladness. This was God's initiative toward the nations before the coming of Jesus.

The speech begins in 14:15 by stating that the apostles are *men of like passions* (ὁμοιοπαθεῖς). The rare word occurs only twice in the OT Apocrypha (4 Macc 12:13; Wis 7:3), and one other time in the NT (James 5:17), in the context of stressing humanity in each instance. The apostles deny the divine identity that was attributed to them. Instead, they proclaim the good news "to turn away from those vain things" (Acts 14:15). The Greek word for *vain things* (μάταιος) is used in a number of passages discussing idols in the OT (e.g., Lev 17:7; 2 Chr 11:15; Jer 2:5).[118] The phrase *to turn away from idols* is also found in 1 Thess 1:9 as a summary of the Gentiles' conversion. Witherington suggests that early Christian vocabulary is at work.[119]

The turning away is followed by turning to the living God. The word *living* as an epithet for God is a common in the OT especially when comparing him with idols (Deut 5:26; Josh 3:10; 2 Kgs 19:4; Hos 1:10).[120] Paul continues with what is generally recognized as a quote[121] or allusion[122] about the living God. The suggested source can either be a verse from what is commonly called the Decalogue in Exod 20:11 or a prayer in Ps 146/145:6:[123]

---

[118] Marshall, "Acts," 588.
[119] Witherington, *Acts*, 426.
[120] Marshall, "Acts," 588.
[121] Ibid.
[122] Fitzmyer, *Acts*, 532.
[123] The following translations are my own.

Acts 14:15	Exod 20:11	Ps 146/145:6
who made the heaven and the earth and the sea and all that is in them.	in six days the Lord made the heaven and the earth and the sea and all that is in them.	who made the heaven and the earth and the sea and all that is in them.

Nevertheless, Johnson is right in pointing out that similar wording can be found in Neh 9:6 and Isa 37:16.[124] Thus such characterization could simply be seen as a general Septuagintal expression.

Further, God is said to have allowed the previous generations of the nations to follow their own ways, a reference to the conduct of life. God, however, did not leave them without witness. Time is clearly divided for the Gentiles into a former time and present time. The past witness to the nations is further specified as doing good. God's benevolence to the nations is portrayed as a witness. The giving of rain and fruitful seasons are realizations of the witness resulting in food and gladness in the Gentiles' heart. Johnson draws into attention that "The blessings enumerated (rain, harvest, food, gladness of heart) recall passages such as LXX Ps 144:13–17; 146:8–11."[125] Added to this, Fitzmyer links the terminology of natural blessing with Ps 147/146:8 and Jer 5:24.[126] As mentioned earlier, Ps 146/145:6 is one candidate for the source of the quote in the apostles' address. But there is more that links Ps 146/145 to Ps 145/144 and 147/146–147.

For example, Ps 146/145:7 also speaks of food as a divine gift like 145/144:16 and 147/146:9. There are thus three subsequent psalms that speak of food as a divine gift to the world, the same way the apostles do in their speech to the Gentiles. It is argued here that there is more that links these three psalms and the speech with one another. There appears to be a progress of thought at work in the psalms as well as in the speech. The progress of thought seems to move from not trusting

[124] Johnson, *Acts*, 249.

[125] Ibid.

[126] Fitzmyer, *Acts*, 532.

in humans to hoping in the Lord and ending in the portrayal of divine gifts of nature.

Psalm 146/145 also shares a near identical language with the speech. Following a call to praise the Lord, Ps 146/145 starts with a warning against putting trust in leaders and the sons of men: "Do not put your trust in rulers and in sons of men, who have no deliverance" (Ps 146/145:3). The reason for not trusting them is portrayed along the lines of their transience. The leaders and humans are perishable and their plans come to nothing. Instead, the one whose help is in the God of Jacob and whose hope is the Lord God is said to be blessed. God is characterized as the one who created heaven and earth and everything in it, keeping justice, doing righteousness to the wronged, giving food to the hungry (Ps 146/145:7). Other actions of God directed toward the disadvantaged are named. The thought of the psalms thus starts with warning against putting trust in humans; instead, hope in the Lord is recommended; then God's credibility is demonstrated by his creative activity; finally, the realization of God's power among the disadvantaged is shown.

Two of these elements (i.e., natural blessings and warning against trust in humans) can be found in the following psalm, although in reverse order. Psalm 147:1–11/146 is a praise of the Lord for building up Jerusalem and gathering the sons of Israel. God is also praised for healing, ruling the stars, lifting up the meek, and bringing down the sinners. In 147/146:8 and 147/146:9 God is praised in particular for natural blessings. God is said to cloak the skies with clouds, to prepare rain for the land, to make grass grown on the mountains, and to give food to animals. The Greek words for rain (ὑετός) and food (τροφή) are used for divine blessings. Both food and rain are listed in Paul's sermon and food is said to be a divine blessing in Ps 147/146:8–9. Psalm 147:1–11/146 ends with a declaration that contrasts the physical strength of horses and men with those who are fearers and hopers in the Lord. Psalm 147:1–11/146, therefore, contains the divine blessings of rain and food, along with a declaration of God's displeasure in the physical strength of horses and men. Finally, the giving of food is also mentioned in Ps 145/144:15. The Lord is said to give food in due time to all who hope in him.

All three psalms portray God as giving food. The food is given to the hungry (146/145:7), to animals (147/146:9), and to all living things (145/144:16). Furthermore, Ps 147/146:8 puts the giving of food into the context of rain that causes grass to grow. Added to this, in Ps 146/145 and 147:1–11/146 God's providence is contrasted with human strength. Moreover, Ps 146/145 shares the words of characterizing God as the creator with the apostles' speech. The thought pattern of Ps 146/145 is close to that of Acts 14:14–17. The apostles point out that they are only humans implying that the healing should not be attributed to them. The psalm warns against putting trust in leaders and in humans. Both the psalm and the apostles point to God as the creator with identical words. Finally, God's providence is evoked in both passages, with emphasis on giving of food. The language of God's providence is also reminiscent of that in the two other Psalms.

4.5. Conclusions

It was argued in this chapter that the separation of the apostles for missionary work is presented by using Temple service language. The conflict with Bar-Jesus recalls the long struggle between prophets and false-prophets and also the confrontations of the apostles with degenerate forms of religion in Acts. These architextual connections endow the narrative with a larger perspective and possible outcome. In like manner, architextual connections of Acts 14 were investigated. The results of apostolic activity are presented in conformity with earlier efforts. Change occurs at two points: Hostility is intensified while the mission finds new direction toward the Gentiles. The attempt to worship the two apostles as gods and the response the apostles give testifies again to the use of the *topos* of receiving divine visitors. Finally, the thought progress of Ps 145/144–147:1–11/146 is clearly evoked in the apostolic message to the Gentiles.

The most significant intertextual connection, however, is that of metatextuality in Paul's synagogue speech. Efforts were made to propose that the complex ways of appropriating Scripture citations in the speech are best understood as being a metatext on just two subtexts. First, the earlier part of the speech is a metatext on the holy history of Israel while the second part is on the dynastic promise to David. The history of Israel is presented by echoing certain texts but at the same time by submitting them to the logic of a new utterance. The most outstanding characteristic of intertextuality is a combination of several utterances in a new context. The promise is connected with further expressions of it within the OT and also with events in Jesus's life. To my knowledge, neither of these proposals has been made before. I believe my proposal has the benefit of accounting for both the meaning of the subtexts and the meaning of the metatext. Further clarity on metatextuality will be achieved in the next chapter that focuses on speeches again.

Chapter 5

THE JERUSALEM COUNCIL:
ACTS 15:1–35

5.1. Introduction

Acts 15:1–35 tells of the meeting of the apostles in Jerusalem to settle the growing unrest the conversion of the Gentiles caused in the church. The purpose of the discussion was to define who constitute the people of God to put an end to disputes within the communities. The account of the Jerusalem Council reflects on a number of themes raised earlier in the book to settle uncertainties posed by earlier events. The chapter also presents a turning point in Acts in two senses. First, from here on Peter will disappear and Paul will take the center stage. Second, the issues of the Jerusalem meeting are not brought up later. The decree of the Council is assumed to have been accepted and is never raised again in Acts.

The section begins with presenting events leading to the Council. The conflict in the Antioch church and the trip of Paul and Barnabas to Jerusalem are depicted in 15:1–5. The Council itself is recounted in 15:6–29, resulting in the issuance of a decree. The implementation of the Council's decision in Antioch is told in 15:30–35.

Some individuals "from Judea" (15:1) are said to have arrived in Antioch. These teachers were proclaiming that unless the Christians in Antioch get "circumcised according to the custom of Moses," they cannot be saved. A dispute arose between the teachers, on the one hand, and Barnabas and Paul, on the other, leading to a journey to Jerusalem to settle the issue. While on the way, the two apostles reported the conversion of the Gentiles in the churches who received the news with gladness.

The Council of "the elders and the apostles" (15:6) begins with Peter's speech in 15:7–11, followed by a summary of Paul's and

Barnabas's account in 15:12. The last speaker is James, who recommends that the Gentiles be received without circumcision but that they should observe certain laws. James's lengthy speech is contained in 15:13–21. The Council agreed to issue a decree which was to be sent by Paul and Barnabas to Antioch. The words of the decree are quoted in 15:23–29. Finally, a letter is carried to Antioch and it is received with joy according to 15:30–35.

The narrative about the Council in Jerusalem stands in comparison and in contrast with the two other meetings in Acts. The Sanhedrin in Acts 4–5, too, was gathered to settle a conflict. There were witnesses in both narratives who were investigated by the members at the meeting. The words of Gamaliel, like the words of James, led to a solution that was implemented. The Sanhedrin, however, did not settle the issue and practiced violence whereas the issuing of the letter of the Jerusalem Council resulted in gladness in Antioch.[1]

The role of violence in Paul's trial in Acts 22:30–23:10 is even more prominent: the apostle was smitten, the Pharisees and the Sadducees were divided, and the meeting resulted in turmoil. The role of the leader of the meeting, Ananias, is reduced to giving commands to smite Paul. All three meetings—the Sanhedrin, the Jerusalem Council, and Paul's trial—were meant to deal with conflict; they were all led by a leader, but only the Jerusalem Council yielded peace.

5.2. Metatextual Correlations

The conflict that was faced in Acts 15 concerns circumcision of the Gentiles as it is prescribed in the law of Moses. Certain unnamed individuals stirred up some conflict in Antioch by teaching that the Gentiles need to be circumcised to be saved. The proclamation of the teachers is quoted in 15:1: "Unless you are circumcised according to the custom of Moses, you cannot be saved." This view later finds support from among the Pharisees. They are quoted saying in 15:5 that the Gentiles "be circumcised and ordered to keep the law of Moses." Circumcision therefore is tied to keeping the law or custom of Moses.

[1] Witherington, *Acts*, 450.

Circumcision and complete or some form of Torah-observance appears to have been propagated by certain groups of the church leading to conflict. Circumcision was the traditional form of inclusion in the people of God from the time of Abraham (Gen 17:9–27). Circumcision is also prescribed in the exodus narrative, in Exod 12:43–44, for non-Israelites wishing to take part in the Passover meal.[2] It is entirely logical from a Jewish perspective that the newly converted Gentiles would have to submit to the same process as foreigners wishing to live among Israelites. The Council's focus on law-observance rather than circumcision reveals that the latter is seen as the entry point for the former.

5.2.1. Peter's Address on the Holy History of the Church: Acts 15:7–11

The gathering of the apostles and elders is said to be on "this matter," namely the circumcision and Torah observance of the Gentiles. After much disputing, Peter stood up to speak (Acts 15:7–11). The intertextual character of Peter's address is best understood as being a metatext on the holy history of the church, particularly on the conversion of the Gentiles as recorded in Acts 10:1–11:18. Just as Paul was commenting on and evaluating events from the history of Israel in Acts 13, so does Peter evaluate events related to the conversion of the Gentiles. In both cases events that took place earlier are seen as normative for the present. What happened in the house of Cornelius is seen as God's normative act equal to the choosing of the fathers or of David, for instance. This implies that the early events in the church were seen as being part of the history of God's initiatives with his people. Those events, once properly evaluated in the light of Scripture, reveal God's will in dealing with the world in the days of the apostles.

It is clear that events recounted in the Cornelius episode are alluded to and summarized in Peter's words in front of the Council. But there is something more at work. Peter evaluates certain elements of the Cornelius narrative in a new light as compared to his earlier recounting in Acts 11. Whereas in Acts 11 the purpose of the debate

---

[2] Marshall, "Acts," 589.

was whether to accept the conversion of those particular Gentiles, this time the apostle draws general conclusions from singular events relevant for a new situation at hand. Peter clearly reads what happened earlier with a certain hermeneutic.

The apostle begins by presenting his ministry to the Gentiles from the beginning as being part of common knowledge: "My brothers, you know that in the early days God made a choice among you, that I should be the one through whom the Gentiles would hear the message of the good news and become believers" (Acts 15:7). Commentaries agree that the events around the conversion of Cornelius in Acts 10 constitute the *choosing* of Peter for the Gentiles to believe.[3] Peter thus presents the events of Acts 10 leading to the conversion of Gentiles as *choosing* initiated by God. The "early days" mentioned in 15:7 are therefore seen as the beginnings of Gentiles mission for which Peter was chosen. It is very likely that the entire chain of events leading to the outpouring of the Spirit constitutes choosing.

The purpose of Peter's choosing is that the Gentiles might hear the gospel and believe in God. Clearly Peter's task was to give instructions to Cornelius as it stands attested in Acts 10:22. His message was that God forgives the sins of all those who believe in him (Acts 10:43). It is made clear that Peter's experience in Joppa and in Caesarea is not to be seen as a singular event related to just Cornelius and to his household but much rather general implications are highlighted. A singular event of Gentile conversion is presented as God's will for other Gentiles through Peter. Further, God is said to have "testified" in 15:8 to the Gentiles by giving them the Holy Spirit—an event recorded in Acts 10:44. The Cornelius episode is a *choosing* for Peter and at the same time a *testimony* to the Gentiles.

Additionally, the Spirit event is compared to the Pentecost experience of the disciples: "God…testified to them by giving them the Holy Spirit, just as he did to us" (Acts 15:8). The outpouring of the Spirit on the Gentiles is seen in parallel with the outpouring the Spirit on the disciples in Acts 2. This is remarkable for several reasons. The

---

[3] Johnson, *Acts*, 261; Fitzmyer, *Acts*, 546; Marshall, "Acts," 589.

outpouring of the Spirit on the Gentiles is compared to an earlier event in the history of the church. The same status is claimed for the latter apparently the former already had. This is an evaluative activity. The outpouring of the Spirit on Cornelius's household is to be understood as a Gentile Pentecost. Added to this, the structural link between the various outpourings of the Spirit in the cycles of Acts achieved by the narrator is made explicit by one of the characters. Peter states that the two events are of the same status.

Finally, the singular event of the giving of the Spirit is thought to have general significance. The Spirit experience in Cornelius's house is relevant for making general claims. The testimony of God, manifest in the giving of the Spirit, is understood by Peter to mean that God does not discriminate between the Jews and the Gentiles in the church. The language of discrimination is a reference to the voice of the Spirit telling Peter not to discriminate in Acts 10:20, namely to follow the messengers to Joppa. Just as the voice was telling him not to discriminate against Cornelius, so too the Spirit tells that God did not discriminate against the Gentiles, cleansing their hearts because of their faith.

While the cleansing of hearts is never mentioned explicitly in the Cornelius episode, cleansing features prominently in Peter's vision. In response to Peter's objection to eating the creatures in the object, the voice from heaven in Acts 10:13 declared that he should not call profane "what God has cleansed" (Acts 15:9). The vision is never explained later. A metatextual correlation of Acts 10 and 15 suggests that the cleansing in the vision is equivalent of the cleansing of the hearts of the Gentiles.

Finally, Peter appeals to the participants of the Council. It is noteworthy that he equates burdening the Gentiles with the law with tempting God. The tempting or testing of God is a recurring phenomenon in the exodus narrative.[4] Testing God is an attitude that disregards divine initiative and divine acts. The threat of testing could

---

[4] Exod 15:22–27; 17:2, 7; Num 14:22; Isa 7:12; Ps 77/76:18. Cf. Fitzmyer, *Acts*, 547.

be realized by not recognizing the gifts of God through Peter among the Gentiles. Peter calls for recognizing God's initiative among the Gentiles. A new form of solidarity is stressed between the two groups: it is emphasized that Jews and Gentiles are in solidarity by being saved through the grace of Jesus. By implication, unity between the two entities is possible by grace and not by law.

Following Peter's address, the words of Barnabas and Paul are summarized in just a single verse (see 15:12). The two are said to have reported the signs and wonders God did through them among the Gentiles. The function of the summary is to show that Peter's experience among the Gentiles was continued by God, therefore, a trajectory can be established.

5.2.2. James's Address on the Booth of David: Acts 15:13–18

Following Peter and the two apostles, James delivered an address. The speech is the most significant one out of the three on several accounts. First, the nine verses make it the longest one. Second, James is the last one to have spoken drawing on what was said before. Undoubtedly, James was in position to say the final word in the debate. In addition, James proceeded to make concrete suggestions which turned out to be the decree for the Gentile Christians. His speech concludes the meeting itself.

James's proposal reflects on both the pro-Gentile suggestion of Peter and the sensitivities of the pro-circumcision party. The two aspects of the proposal coincide with the two major intertextual correlations of the speech. The pro-Gentile aspect is quite evident. To begin with, the relevance of Peter's account is accepted by James. The lengthy quote from the OT in Acts 15:16–18 is introduced by saying that it agrees with the divine favors bestowed earlier upon the Gentiles. It is stated that the Gentiles converts are not to be troubled.

The other part of the speech in 15:19–21, however, prescribes a number of regulations to be observed by the Gentiles. Pro-circumcision sentiment was given even more attention when pointing to synagogues where the law of Moses continues to be available.

James first summarizes what Peter has told before: "Simeon has related how God first looked favorably on the Gentiles, to take from among them a people for his name" (Acts 15:14). The word, *first* (πρῶτον) used by James must be seen as an equivalent to the phrase, *from the early days* (ἀφ' ἡμερῶν ἀρχαίων) in Peter's account in Acts 15:7.[5] It appears that the Cornelius's episode is understood as a *beginning* of Gentile mission, offering normative guidance not just for Peter but also for James and indeed for the entire community.

It is useful to recall that earlier the outpouring of the Spirit upon the Gentiles was compared to the Pentecost event which was also said to have happened at the *beginning*. When earlier questioned in Jerusalem, Peter proclaimed: "And as I began to speak, the Holy Spirit fell upon them just as it had upon us at the *beginning*" (Acts 11:15—emphasis added). The gift of the Spirit to the Gentiles is presented in conformity with the Pentecost event at the beginning. James confirms that the Cornelius narrative is indeed a new beginning for the church.

The language James uses in his own evaluation of the events shows a remarkable intertextual tendency. James states that, "God first visited the Gentiles, to take from among them a people for his name" (Acts 15:14).[6] The language of visitation is used throughout Luke-Acts to portray exceptional divine intervention in the world.[7] The expression of *taking* or *choosing* a people is Septuagintal language detectable in a number of passages in the LXX.[8] One example from Deut 7:6 should suffice to illustrate the election language at work in both the LXX and the Acts:

---

[5] Van de Sandt rightly emphasizes the presence of temporal expressions in James's speech (Acts 15:7, 14, 18, 21)—see "An Explanation of Acts 15.6–21 in the Light of Deuteronomy 4.29–35 (LXX)," *JSNT* 46 (1992): 74.

[6] My translation, reflecting Johnson's evaluation—see Johnson, *Acts*, 264.

[7] E.g., Luke 1:68, 78; 7:16; 19:44; Acts 7:23—see ibid.

[8] Deut 14:2; 7:6; 26:18–19; Exod 19:5; 23:22. Fitzmyer, *Acts*, 554.

Deut 7:6	Acts 15:14
For you are a people holy to the Lord your God, and the Lord your God *has chosen you to be for him an exceptional people*, more than all the nations on the face of the earth.	God first visited the Gentiles, *to take* from among them *a people for his name.*

It is to be noted that the election language in the OT is applied in relation to Israel. In Acts 15, however, the language is redirected toward the Gentiles. God is said to have taken a people from among the Gentiles the same way he chose Israel. Applying election language to non-Israelites, however, does not obscure a notable difference between the two nations—i.e., Jews and Gentiles. God does not elect Gentiles *en bloc,* but rather takes a people for himself from among the Gentiles. James applies election language to describe what began to happen in the events around the conversion of Cornelius.

James further specifies the status of the nation from among the Gentiles by the phrase "a nation for his name," yet another Septuagintal phrase. Fitzmyer even suggests that there is a direct link with a prophecy from Zechariah.[9] Indeed in Zech 2:11/2:15 Gentiles are spoken of as a nation of God—a significant diversion from major trends within the OT. It is worth quoting Zech 2:10–11/2:14–15 together: "Rejoice, and be glad, O daughter Zion. For behold, I am coming and will tent in your midst, says the Lord. And *many nations* shall flee to the Lord for refuge on that day and *shall become a people to him*, and they will tent in your midst" (emphasis added).

Gentiles are called a people of God while James calls them a people for his name. Bock however looks at the wider picture and argues for a specific language at work rather than an allusion in Acts 15:14. He proposes that the idea of incorporating Gentiles in the

[9] Ibid.

people of God is not alien within the OT. There are a great number of passages in the prophetic literature where the same idea is expressed. James, in this sense, evokes tradition and not a passage.[10]

The last phrase in James's summary of Peter's account, *a nation for his name*, might be illuminating at this point. The expression finds no exact parallel in the LXX. Fitzmyer points to Targum in general where the phrase, *a nation for my name* is often used as a substitute for *a nation of God*.[11] Moreover, Marshall points to the identical targumic expression on this exact verse (MT Zech 2:11).[12] It appears that *a nation of God* is interpreted in the Targum as, *a nation for his name*. The identical targumic expression on Zech 2:11/2:15 makes an allusion in Acts 15:14 to Zech 2:11/2:15 more plausible.

After finishing the reflection on Peter's account (and leaving out any comment on the two apostles' account), James makes a transition to a quote in 15:15: "This agrees with the words of the prophets, as it is written." The word *this* is clearly a reference to what has been said before, that is God visiting to take from among the Gentiles a nation for his name. James claims that the words of the prophets that follow *are in agreement* (συμφωνοῦσιν) with what has been said before. The plural use of the word *prophet* gives rise to an expectation that more than one prophetic utterance will be quoted or at least what follows stands for more than just one prophetic word.

The Greek word for *to be in agreement* is a rare one in the Bible and in most cases conveys practical unity, harmony or even conspiracy between people.[13] It is never used however to express correspondence between events and Scripture. The emphatic word introduces

---

[10] Bock argues that James refers to the entire corpus of Prophets where many passages can be found on Gentiles. In particular he proposes connections with Zech 2:11; 8:22; Isa 2:2; 45:20–23; Hos 3:4–5; Jer 12:15–16—see Bock, *Acts*, 503.

[11] Fitzmyer, *Acts*, 554.

[12] Marshall, "Acts," 589.

[13] The word is used for joining of forces (Gen 14:3), complete cooperation (4 Macc 14:6) and agreement between peoples (Isa 7:2). Cf. Walter Bauer, *A Greek-English Lexicon of the New Testament and Other Early Christian Literature*, 2nd ed. (Chicago: University of Chicago Press, 1979), 788.

justification or scriptural basis from the Prophets for the events. A complex intertextual correlation is to be observed: events related to the Cornelius episode are evoked through an allusion to Zech 2:11/2:15 and are said to be in agreement with the words of further prophets. Thus, at the outset of the quote two expectations are created. First, the theme of the quote will be God's involvement with the Gentiles. Second, more that one prophetic word will be evoked.

The following quote is not without challenge. It is certainly not simply a quote from Amos 9:11–12 with minor alterations. It will be argued here that Acts 15:16–18 is composite thematic citation of Amos 9:11–12, of verses from Zech 8, from Hos 3 and from Isa 45. Further, it will be argued that the evoked texts elaborate mainly on the promise of the Temple expressed in 2 Sam 7. Thus, the composite quote itself is already a comment on the Davidic promise the same way Paul elaborated on certain aspects of the same promise in Acts 13. The three passages evoked are used to elaborate on the promise of the Temple.

The Greek word συμφωνοῦσιν, *to be in agreement*, could be well used to describe the intertextual activity in the metatext. The background of the word is that of acoustics. Sounding together, being in musical harmony would be a naive but at the moment a useful rendering. Multiple voices are shown to be in conformity with the situation James was describing. The many voices of the prophets are evoked in agreement with one another and with the conversion of the Gentiles.[14] The quoted texts share common themes and common character: they are all future salvation oracles with special focus on restoration.

---

[14] When discussing James's speech, Bowker points out that "It is most improbable that a halakic decision of such far-reaching effect would have been established on the basis of a prophetic book alone" (Bowker, "Speeches," 108). He then claims that reference to the Torah must have been involved in the decision making (ibid.). This is of course a claim about what must have happened in the Jerusalem Council. It is noteworthy however that a halakic decision making usually involved the evoking of several scriptures.

Beyond this, three of them—Amos 9, Zech 8, and Hos 3—share common vocabulary. Each text, however, offers details that others do not have. Biblical scholarship most often saw the significance of Zech 8, Hos 3, and Isa 45 in those limited and distinct details and the rest of the metatext was simply seen as taken from Amos 9:11–12. I do not intend to deny the central role of the Amos text. Nevertheless, it is argued in this work that the significance of Hos 3, Zech 8, and Isa 45 is not limited to their distinct phrases in the metatext, but much rather it involves what they share with Amos 9:11–12.

The metatext is the result of a complex exegetical work based on several texts. This view is presented as a more plausible reading based on the LXX rather than the MT. It is to be mentioned here, that the intertextual interpretation has the potential of deciding whether the restoration of Davidic dynasty or the restoration of the Temple is in view in Acts 15:16–18. A strong alternative in biblical scholarship to the Temple view is the restoration of the Davidic dynasty which is also spoken of in 2 Sam 7. If the quote is understood as a composite quote from Amos 9:11–12, Hos 3:5, Zech 8, and Isa 45, then the Temple reading becomes more plausible. This point will be taken up later.

To begin with, the introductory phrase, "After this I will return" and closing phrase, "known from long ago" have been noted to be allusion to other passages distinct from the one found in the book of Amos. Possible candidates are named in Jer 12:15, Hos 3:5, and Zech 8:3 for the first one. The last phrase is often connected with Isa 45:21.[15] The central section of the quote is usually understood to be taken from Amos 9:11–12. In an effort to see where the metatext differs from what is suggested to be one of its subtexts, the chart below is designed to show harmony, resemblance, and contrast between Acts 15:16–18 and Amos 9:11–12:

[15] Fitzmyer claims that the Jeremiah verse as the source for the introductory phrase and the one in Isaiah for the last phrase—see Fitzmyer, *Acts*, 555. Johnson agrees with him—see Johnson, *Acts*, 265. Bock, however, simply lists possible candidates—see Bock, *Acts*, 502.

Acts 15:16-19	Amos 9:11-12
μετὰ ταῦτα ἀναστρέψω After this I will return	ἐν τῇ ἡμέρᾳ ἐκείνῃ On that day
καὶ ἀνοικοδομήσω τὴν σκηνὴν Δαυὶδ τὴν πεπτωκυῖαν I will rebuild the tent of David that has fallen	ἀναστήσω **τὴν σκηνὴν Δαυιδ τὴν πεπτωκυῖαν** I will raise the tent of David that has fallen
	καὶ ἀνοικοδομήσω τὰ πεπτωκότα αὐτῆς and will rebuild it ruins
καὶ τὰ κατεσκαμμένα αὐτῆς ἀνοικοδομήσω καὶ ἀνορθώσω **αὐτήν** and its ruins I will rebuild, and I will set it up	**καὶ τὰ κατεσκαμμένα αὐτῆς** ἀναστήσω καὶ **ἀνοικοδομήσω αὐτὴν** and its ruins I will raise, and I will rebuild it (καθὼς αἱ ἡμέραι τοῦ αἰῶνος,) as the days of old
ὅπωσ ἂν **ἐκζητήσωσιν οἱ κατάλοιποι τῶν ἀνθρώπων** τὸν κύριον in order that all other peoples may seek the Lord	**ὅπως ἐκζητήσωσιν οἱ κατάλοιποι τῶν ἀνθρώπων** in order that all other peoples may seek
καὶ πάντα τὰ ἔθνη ἐφ' οὓς ἐπικέκληται τὸ ὄνομά μου ἐπ' αὐτούς and all the Gentiles over whom my name has been called.	**καὶ πάντα τὰ ἔθνη ἐφ' οὓς ἐπικέκληται τὸ ὄνομά μου ἐπ' αὐτούς,** and all the Gentiles over whom my name has been called.
λέγει κύριος ποιῶν ταῦτα Thus says the Lord, who does these things	**λέγει κύριος** (ὁ θεὸς ὁ) **ποιῶν ταῦτα.** Thus says the Lord, God who does these things.
γνωστὰ ἀπ' αἰῶνος known from long ago.	

The temporal marker *on that day* of Amos 9:11 has been replaced with *after this* in Acts 15:16. The word for *I will return* is also added in the introduction which has no parallel in Amos. The final phrase *known from long ago* in 15:18 is also an addition without parallel in Amos.

At first sight adherence to Amos 9:11–12 appears dominant in Acts 15:16–18. There are a number of disturbing differences, however. Most of them are omissions (or alterations), but there is also one addition in the Acts text. The phrase *as the days of old* from the Amos text is completely left out in Acts. The reference to the Lord is also made shorter in Acts 15:17 by leaving out the word *God*, which is present in the prophecy. Abbreviating complex expressions is a tendency in Acts as could be seen for instance in the allusion to Ezek 4:14 in Acts 10:14. On the opposite side there is an extra phrase in the metatext. The phrase *the Lord* in Acts 15:17 as the object of the verb *to seek* was added for some reason.

The use of the word *to rebuild* in the metatext as opposed *to raise*, as found in Amos 9:11, is neither the result of addition nor of omission. Bauckham argues that the word ἀναστήσω from Amos 9:11 is twice replaced with ἀνοικοδομήσω in Acts 15:16a and 15:16b. Further, the only ἀνοικοδομήσω in Amos would have been replaced with ἀνορθώσω later in the same verse. Bauckham understands the replacements as alternate translations of the Hebrew words אקים for *rebuilding/raising* and ובניתיה for *setting up*.[16] This assumes that the exegesis at work in James's address relies on the use of the MT at this point. Another equally possible solution would be the rearranging of the Greek thought parallels of the LXX version. There are two thought parallels in the Amos 9:11:

> I will *raise* the tent of David that has fallen / and will *rebuild* it ruins
> and its ruins I will *raise*, / and I will *rebuild* it.

---

[16] Richard Bauckham, "James and the Gentiles (Acts 15.13–21)," in *History, Literature, and Society in the Book of Acts*, ed. Ben Witherington (Cambridge: Cambridge University Press, 1996), 157.

Each parallel has for the first verb *to raise* and for the second *to rebuild* resulting in an ABA'B' form. The metatext only has three verbs from the Amos subtext: *to rebuild* twice and *to set up*. The metatext does not follow strictly the thought parallel of the subtext. It is plausible that the verbs of the second part of the parallels would have replaced the verbs in the first part: the verb to rebuild moved to the first position and the remaining part of the first parts of the parallels were preserved. The only challenge to this view could be the use of the verb *to set up* in the second half of the second parallel where the word *to rebuild* was used in Amos. The use of verb *to set up* might have been due to 2 Sam 7:13 where the same word is used for establishing a kingdom for David in proximity with the word *to build*:

> He will *build* me a house for my name, and I will *set up* his throne forever.[17]
> αὐτὸς οἰκοδομήσει μοι οἶκον τῷ ὀνόματί μου, καὶ ἀνορθώσω τὸν θρόνον αὐτοῦ ἕως εἰς τὸν αἰῶνα.

The single verse contains both the promise that the seed of David will build the temple and that god will set up the seed's throne. *Setting up* the booth of David could have been preferred because of the prominence of the word in the dynastic promise.

Rearranging the thought parallels of the Greek subtext is a more plausible suggestion than the one according to which a combination of both an alternate translation of the Hebrew text and the LXX version would have taken place—an assumption on which Bauckham builds his argument. The predominance of the LXX in Acts as the text of the OT has not been challenged so far and thus it proves difficult to bypass the LXX in this particular instance. Despite different explanations for the changes in Acts 15:16–18 in comparison with Amos 9:11–12, both interpretations point out that *building* is preferred over *raising* in Acts. Whether it is viewed as alternate but legitimate rendering of the MT or as a swapping maneuver in the LXX thought parallels, the metatext is

[17] My translation, with added emphasis.

clearly oriented toward a building of some kind. In sum, based on the additions and omissions along with alterations it is clear that very definite exegetical maneuvers are present in the metatext which result in a focus on building.

Extra phrases that cannot come from Amos 9:11–12 are also to be observed in the metatext. Most notable of them are the first words of the quote in Acts 15:16:

> After these things I will return
> μετὰ ταῦτα ἀναστρέψω

These words present a dual challenge to interpreters. First, Amos 9:11 contains a different temporal marker ("On that day") than the one found in Acts[18] and it does not have any corresponding word for *I will return*. One would be compelled to search for other OT texts as possible sources of the quote. This endeavor, however, leads to the second challenge, namely that no single verse in the LXX contains these exact three words (μετὰ ταῦτα ἀναστρέψω) as they stand together in the metatext—leaving interpreters in a difficult position.

Alternatively, one would have to search for the phrases μετὰ ταῦτα and ἀναστρέψω either in separate passages or in passages where they occur in reasonable proximity. The phrase *after these things* can be found in a little less than one hundred verses in LXX whereas the word *I will return* occurs only three times (Gen 18:14; 2 Sam 22:38; Job 10:21), none of which seem relevant. Methodological challenges are highlighted here to show that a more comprehensive approach is needed to determine the inter-textual correlation between the relevant parts of James's speech and OT passages. The approach has to be based on more than just the occurrence of phrases and words.

---

[18] A reverse exchange of the expressions can be observed in Acts 2:17. The words *after this* from Joel 2:28/3:1 have been replaced with *in the last days*—see Bauckham, "James," 163. One would need more instances of such exchange to assume interchangeability however.

Beyond shared words, common themes, and further shared vocabulary are to be sought to establish a relevant intertextual correlation.

Hosea 3:5 has been suggested by scholars as one possible source of the phrase *after these things*.[19] It is worth considering the verse together with 3:4:

> For the sons of Israel shall sit many days without king and without ruler and without sacrifice and without altar and without priestly office and without Urim. And *after these things*, the sons of Israel shall *return* and shall *seek the Lord* their God and David their king, and they shall stand in awe at the Lord and his good things in the last days.

The passage from Hosea speaks of judgment and restoration of the cultic system and of David's rule. The turn from judgment to salvation is marked by the phrase *after these things*. The phrase and its context are a very clear thematic and verbal point of contact between Hos 3:4–5 and Acts 15:16–18. But connections run deeper than a common theme. Further resonance with Acts 15:16–18 and 15:19 is created through shared words. It is said in the suggested subtext that the "sons of Israel shall return" (ἐπιστρέψουσιν) and "seek the Lord their God" (ἐπιζητήσουσιν κύριον τὸν θεὸν). The seeking of the Lord is yet another clear point of contact. James too speaks of seeking the Lord in Acts 15:17: "so that all other peoples may seek the Lord—even the Gentiles." Both the Hosea and Amos text speak of seeking. Amos does not mention the object of seeking whereas Hosea names the Lord. The addition of the word *Lord* in the metatext to the quote from Amos is usually explained to be a grammatical correction. It could well be, however, that the reason behind the addition is the presence of the word in Hos 3:5.

The relevance of the Hosea text gains further support from the presence of the word *to return* in Acts. The *return* mentioned in Hos

[19] Ibid.; cf. Witherington, *Acts*, 459; W. Edward Glenny, "The Septuagint and Apostolic Hermeneutics: Amos 9 in Acts 15," *BBR* 22 (2012): 12.

3:5 is clearly that of the Israelites as opposed to the return of the Lord spoken of in Acts. Bauckham however is right in pointing out that the return of the human beings is also spoken of in the metatext, in Acts 15:19: "Therefore I have reached the decision that we should not trouble those Gentiles who are turning (ἐπιστρέφουσιν) to God."[20] The metatext has two turnings: one of the Lord in 15:16 and one of the Gentiles in 15:19. The latter is in harmony with the promise of Hos 3. Hos 3 thus surfaces in the metatext through the expression *after these things*, the *seeking* of the Lord and the *return* of the people to God. The addition of the word *Lord* and the temporal phrase *after these things* are distinct contributions of the subtext to the metatext whereas the seeking language is shared by both the Amos and Zechariah text.[21]

Added to the connection with Hosea, a further correlation with Zechariah was suggested by scholars. It has been proposed that the source for the Greek word for *I will return* in Acts 15:16 is indeed Zech 8:3.[22] Zechariah 8:3, like Hos 3 and Amos 9, contains a promise of salvation:

> This is what the Lord says: And *I will return* [ἐπιστρέψω} to Zion, and I will tent in the midst of Jerusalem, and Jerusalem shall be called a city that is true, and the mountain of the Lord Almighty, a holy mountain.

---

[20] See Bauckham, "James," 163 n.27.

[21] Bauckham, too, understands the insertion of the word *Lord* as an attempt to evoke more passage that share the same theme. The common theme shared by both Amos 9 and Zech 8 is the seeking of the Lord. He suggests however the word comes from the MT of Zech 8:22 instead of the LXX. In the latter the nations seek the *face of the Lord* (ἐκζητῆσαι τὸ πρόσωπον κυρίου) whereas in the former they *seek the Lord* (לבקש את־יהוה צבאות). Bauckham thus argues that the insertion of the word *Lord* without the word *face* is a result of influence from the MT of Zech 8:22—see ibid., 162. If we accept however that Hos 3:5 is evoked in James's speech along with Amos 9 and Zech 8, then the need to involve the MT is made unnecessary.

[22] Glenny, "Septuagint," 12–13; Bauckham, "James," 163–64.

The surface of interaction between Zech 8 and Acts 15:16–18 is wider than just a word. Later in 8:22 the seeking of the Lord by nations is portrayed:

> And many peoples and many *nations* shall come *to seek* the face of the *Lord* [ἔθνη πολλὰ ἐκζητῆσαι τὸ πρόσωπον κυρίου] Almighty in Jerusalem and to appease the face of the Lord.

The correlation is not just seeking of the Lord, but seeking by Gentiles. In Zech 8, therefore, beyond a shared theme of restoration, metatextuality involves the word for God's *return* and the *seeking* of the Lord by the Gentiles.[23]

The last sentence of the metatext—"thus says the lord, who has been making these things known from long ago"—is more difficult to account for. Both Acts 15:18 and Amos 9:12 share the expression "thus says the Lord." The Acts text omits the following word, *god* and the definite article before the phrase, *doing these things*. These changes can be seen as abbreviations.

What follows, however, in the metatext is an addition not from Amos. It is said that these things are "known from long ago." Part of the challenge is that the Greek phrase γνωστὰ ἀπ᾽ αἰῶνος finds no exact match in the LXX. Biblical scholars point to Isa 45:21 where a similar expression can be found.[24] In a context of return from captivity it is asked, "who made these heard from the beginning?" The Greek phrases—τίς ἀκουστὰ ἐποίησεν ταῦτα ἀπ᾽ ἀρχῆς and γνωστὰ ἀπ᾽ αἰῶνος—are very distinct even if abbreviation is considered as an option. What they share is that they speak of God's actions as something ancient or old. When considering the two verses in relation to one another, Bauckham pointed to the wider context in Isa 45 and

---

[23] The use of ἀναστρέψω in the metatext instead of ἐπιστρέψω might be due to an attempt to harmonize the word with the twice used words of ἀνοικοδομήσω and with ἀνορθώσω—see Bauckham, "James," 164.

[24] Ibid., 165; Glenny, "Septuagint," 14; Earl Richard, "The Creative Use of Amos by the Author of Acts," *NovT* 24 (1982): 47.

suggested that James alludes to the Isaiah verse.[25] The context of Isa 45 is worth considering.

The passage starting in Isa 45:20 speaks of those who are "saved from the nations." The expression is most naturally understood to be a reference to the Israelites scattered throughout the world although it is possible to take it to mean Gentiles who are saved, as Bauckham implies. In addition, in 45:22 those from "the ends of the earth" are summoned to God. A distant thematic resemblance can be established with James's speech: they share the restoration setting. The question remains, however, concerning the reason for the strong alteration of the suggested subtext in the metatext. Bauckham suggests that in the metatext the "exegete was using not the LXX but the Hebrew of Isa. 45.21."[26]

Another equally plausible interpretation is offered by Earl Richard. Richard too proposes that an allusion in Acts 15:18 is made to Isa 45:21. Then, however, he claims that the alteration of the LXX subtext occurred due to a larger literary strategy employed in Acts and not because of the use of the Hebrew text. Richard points out that the word *beginning* of the subtext "has a very particular connotation"[27] in the design of Acts, therefore a substitution occurred. The significance of the temporal marker in question was dealt with earlier in this chapter. The phrase "as in the days of old" (καθὼς αἱ ἡμέραι τοῦ αἰῶνος) of Isa 45:21 was eliminated and the word αἰῶνος was substituted for ἀρχῆς in the metatext.[28] Although Richard does not discuss the substitution of ἀκουστὰ for γνωστὰ, a similar point can be made. The word *known* is a catchphrase in the apostolic preaching. It is often claimed by the apostles that their proclamation *be known* to Gentiles and Jews alike.[29]

---

[25] Bauckham, "James," 165.
[26] Ibid.
[27] Richard, "Creative Use," 47.
[28] Ibid.
[29] Acts 2:14; 4:10, 16; 13:38; 28:28.

It has been argued so far that Acts 15:16–18 (along with 15:19) is best understood as being a metatext of not just Amos 9:11–12 but also Hos 3, Zech 8, and Isa 45 together. While verbal connection is most prominent with the Amos text, other prophetic oracles are also evoked. The significance of these other texts is most detectable in but not limited to the extra words and phrases of the introduction and ending of the metatext. Hos 3, Zech 8, and Isa 45, like Amos 9, also speak of future salvation in the context of restoration. Seeking of God is also mentioned in Hos 3, Zech 8, and Amos 9. Gentiles are mentioned explicitly in relation to restoration in Amos 9 and Zech 8, whereas Isa 45:22 is ambiguous enough to include them. All three texts speak of seeking of the Lord and of returning. James was showing that the conversion of the Gentiles indeed agrees with words of the prophets, not just one prophet. Several prophecies are evoked together on a certain theme, the restoration of Israel and the conversion of the Gentiles.

After establishing the structural characteristics of metatextuality in James's speech, an attempt will now be made to determine the meaning of the composite quote in Acts 15:16–18. This task is assumed in order to demonstrate hermeneutical potential of intertextual investigation. More precisely, it is the purpose of this study to link intertextual considerations with intra-textual concerns.

Given its eminent role in the metatext, the use of Amos 9:11–12 appears to be a good starting point. Since connections with the MT as well as with the LXX have been proposed, it is beneficial to give an overview of both versions. First, a closer look at MT text of Amos 9:11–12 in its context might shed some light on its use in Acts:

> On that day I will raise up the booth of David that is fallen, and repair its breaches, and raise up its ruins, and rebuild it as in the days of old; in order that they may possess the remnant of Edom and all the nations who are called by my name, says the LORD who does this.

The oracle is part of a series of salvation oracles in Amos 9:11–15. These verses function as a conclusion to the entire book of Amos.[30] Following a vivid description of doom in the context of captivity, the prophet finally announces restoration, rebuilding, and bounty. The shift from judgment to salvation is abrupt and seems unconditional. At last, restoration is promised in the distant future, "on that day." First, David's booth will be raised and the walls will be rebuilt. This will lead to the possession of Edom's remnant and eventually to domination over all the nations. Next, idyllic conditions are promised in 9:13 with the use of agricultural imagery. Finally, a return from the exile for the Israelites is promised in 9:14–15 along with the rebuilding of the cities. Israel will be rooted in the land and no one will be able to uproot them.[31]

A restoration of some sort is envisioned in Amos 9:11. The raising of the booth of David and building imagery in the rest of the verse creates tension: a booth does not have walls or does not have breachers on it. This tension can be resolved either by taking the booth as a metaphor for a building of some kind (Jerusalem, city, Temple) or by viewing the entire verse as metaphorical language referring to some abstract entity (dynasty, kingdom).

This basic dilemma is clearly expressed by Niehaus when saying "the walls here are not, however, the walls of the hut.... For the Old Testament never speaks of repairing the broken walls of huts."[32] The Hebrew word for *booth* in the OT usually means a temporary shelter built from branches or other material. The Hebrew word for booth—סכה—is used in relation to the festival of booths in the Pentateuch (Lev 23:42; Deut 16:13).[33] The other significant use of the word in the

[30] Jeffrey Niehaus, "Amos," in *Minor Prophets: Hosea, Joel and Amos. An Exegetical and Expository Commentary*, ed. Thomas Edward McComiskey, vol. 1 (Grand Rapids: Baker, 1992), 490.

[31] Douglas Stuart, *Hosea-Jonah*, WBC 31 (Nashville: Thomas Nelson, 1987), 397.

[32] Niehaus, "Amos," 1:490.

[33] William Gesenius, *Gesenius' Hebrew and Chaldee Lexicon to the Old Testament Scriptures: A Dictionary Numerically Coded to Strong's Exhaustive*

MT of the OT is related to the presence of god, however. In the Psalms, the word can refer to God's heavenly abode or pavilion (Pss 18:12; 31:21), whereas in Isa 4:5–6 the term conveys the canopy through which god provides protection for his people on Zion. Dunne points out that the verbal form of the word is used to picture the Temple in Jerusalem in Ps 27/26:4–5. The exact word *booth*, however, together with David is not attested in the OT.[34]

Most commentators conclude that the *booth of David* in Amos either stands for royal dynasty or davidic rule in general.[35] The booth in this interpretation can be synonymous with the house of David promised in 2 Sam 7. The booth is said to be falling thus conveying the fragile state of the dynasty either in the present or in the future. Therefore, restoration spoken of in Amos must be that of the kingdom.

In contrast with this, identifying the booth as the Temple gained support among OT scholars recently. Dunne, for instance, devoted an entire study focusing on just this question.[36] He begins by noting his frustration that a great number of NT scholars simply assume that the booth stands for Temple in James's speech—a conclusion in the end he shares with them—without dealing with its meaning in the MT. It is proposed then by Dunne that understanding the role of Amos 9:11 in its context of the entire book will help to determine its meaning. First, he understands the link between the assumed rebuilding the Temple in 9:11 and 9:12 and agricultural fertility described in 9:13–15 to be causal: "the rebuilding of the tent of David leads to an abundance of

---

Concordance with an English Index, trans. Samuel Prideaux Tregelles, 7th ed. (Grand Rapids: Baker, 1979), 585.

[34] The closest to pairing those words is attested in Isa 16:5 where another word for tent (אהל) is used in the construct *David's tent*. The meaning of the phrase appears to be related to Jerusalem—see John Anthony Dunne, "David's Tent as Temple in Amos 9:11–15: Understanding the Epilogue of Amos and Considering Implications for the Unity of the Book," *WTJ* 73 (2011): 363–74 (esp. 367).

[35] Dunne gives an exhaustive list in note 17 of scholars arguing for dynastic or royal interpretation of the booth—see ibid., 366.

[36] Ibid.

fertility in the land."[37] The connection between the Temple and natural blessings is a well-known one in the OT.[38] Thus according to this argument since the rebuilding of the tent of the David results in agricultural blessing, the tent could well be the Temple.

Second, in response to the objection that David did not build the Temple, Dunne argues that the promise of the two houses, that is a house for David (i.e., a dynasty) and house for the lord (i.e., a Temple) in 2 Sam 7, are inseparable parts of the davidic covenant. Even though David himself did not build the Temple, the promise remains attached to his name even if it will be carried out in the future, after his death.[39]

Thirdly, Dunne refines his argument by claiming that "the temple is functioning as a synecdoche for all of Jerusalem."[40] The Temple is envisioned as part of the entire politico-religious establishment of Jerusalem. By implication, the renewal of the Temple spoken of in Amos is connected to the restoration of the entire political and religious establishment in Jerusalem. One stands for the other.

Finally, the correspondence between the final verses and the rest of the book of Amos make a Temple reading more plausible for Dunne. The final verses of the book, understood as an epilogue, must stand in correlation with the judgment announced in the previous section. Dunne's argument is very simple at this point. Sin and judgment are realized in a cultic context throughout the book.[41] Restoration, therefore, must involve the renewal of the temple cult: "the restoration of the cultic system of Israel, typified by 'David's tent,' provides the most natural connection to the preceding material in the book of Amos where cultic concerns are prevalent."[42] The restoration of the tent as

---

[37] Ibid., 364–65.

[38] Blessings were given when the Temple cult functioned well (cf. Isa 51:3; Ezek 47:1–12; Hos 2:21–23; 6:11; 14:4–8; Joel 2:18–27; 3:17–18; Zech 8:9, 11–12) whereas the opposite leads to devastation (cf. Hos 1:6, 10-11; Joel 1:9–13, 16; Hag 2:15–19; Zech 14:17)—see ibid., 365.

[39] Ibid.

[40] Ibid., 367.

[41] E.g., Amos 2:6–8; 3:9–10; 6:1–7; 4:1—see ibid., 370–71.

[42] Ibid., 371.

temple also corresponds to the first words of Amos. In 1:2 the prophet says: "the LORD roars from Zion." This is most likely a reference to the Temple. The restoration of the cultic system therefore is an appropriate closure of the book.[43]

The immediate context of Amos 9:11–12 further strengthens this structural argument. In 9:1 the Lord appears standing beside the altar announcing destitution upon it. In 9:5–6 the Lord is said to build a sanctuary in heaven thus abandoning the earthly temple. The promise of the restoration of that Temple in the future is a logical move from the announced judgment.[44]

Dunne demonstrates well that in the light of the whole book of Amos understanding the tent to be the Temple is a plausible reading of the Hebrew text. It does not contradict the general tendencies and patterns of the book and makes as much sense as viewing the tent as dynasty. From our point of view, the most significant observation by Dunne is that the Temple is envisioned together with is surrounding in Jerusalem. The visions concern a complete restoration of Jerusalem with special focus on the temple. The Temple is envisioned as the center of the cultic life, of Israel and of the renewed world.

The purpose of the restoration is given in Amos 9:12. The Lord will restore the collapsing booth of David so the people of the world might come under the rule of God. The people will possess the remnant of Edom and other nations. Niehaus suggests that "the nations alluded to are those conquered long before by David"[45] as listed in 2 Sam 8:1–14. Implicitly, however, the promise includes all the nations under the restored rule.

The nations are designated as the ones on whom God's name is called. The phrase, *to call God's name over someone* most likely expresses ownership. The connotations of ownership can be different, however. On the one hand, it is said about Israel in 2 Chr 7:14 that they are a people for God's name. The same kind of covenantal

---

[43] Ibid.

[44] Ibid., 372.

[45] Niehaus, "Amos," 1:491.

ownership is expressed in passages like Deut 28:10 and Jer 14:9. On the other hand, the phrase can be used in connection with Gentiles. A remark in 2 Sam 12:28 is significant in this respect. There it is said that Joab, the military commander of Israel, threatened David with overtaking a city and calling it by his own name and not by the name of David.[46] Possessing the Gentiles is clearly in view in Amos 9. The concept of ownership remains open to a military dominance as well as a covenantal relationship. Both can be in view in Acts.

The LXX version of Amos 9:11–12 shows some remarkable difference when compared with the MT. These alterations are followed by the text of Acts. The most notable of them are found in 9:12. Instead of the phrase "in order that they may possess the remnant of Edom" we have "in order that they may seek those remaining of humans" in the LXX. No available Hebrew manuscript supports the LXX rendering. Scholars therefore are left to speculate about the reason for the alterations. It has been suggested that the LXX translator must have either followed a different Hebrew manuscript from the one that is available to contemporary scholars,[47] or that the translator of the tradition preserved in Acts followed an alternate exegesis. Bauckham has demonstrated convincingly that, although the two versions of Amos 9:12 appear to have very different meaning, the LXX version can very well be a legitimate rendering of the MT.[48]

The LXX text of Amos 9:11–12 makes a reading of the tent of David as a reference to the Temple more perceivable. Whereas the phrases the *tabernacle of Moses* or the *tabernacle of witness* on the one hand, and the tent/booth of David contain two different words in the MT, the LXX uses the same word for both. In Exod 26, for instance, where instructions are given about the tent, the same word, σκηνή, is used several times. The tent of Moses is not the tent of David. Using the same word for both, however, helps connecting the two. Association of this kind is possible only in the LXX.

---

[46] Ibid., 1:492.

[47] Glenny, "Septuagint," 4–5.

[48] Bauckham, "James," 157–58.

There is another tent/booth whose possible connection with the tent of David is overlooked or does not receive emphasis in biblical scholarship. Psalm 132/131 is thought to be a meditation on the promise given to David in 2 Sam 7. Both Davidic dynasty and Temple feature prominently in the Psalm with more emphasis on the latter. The Psalm uses the word σκήνωμα (a cognate of σκηνή) three times in the context of recounting David's meeknesses. In the first instance, in 132/131:3, the phrase *the tent of my house* refers to David's house and stands in parallel with his bed, that is a place of rest. Second, David refuses to go into his house until he finds "a place for the Lord, a tent for the God of Jacob" as stated in 132/131:5. This is clearly a reference to God's dwelling. At last in 132/131:7, the one praying calls the worshippers to enter the tent of the God and worship in his place. This must be a reference to God's dwelling. Ps 132/131 appears to use the word tent in reference to both God's tent and David's tent.

In addition, the Psalm appears to be a text of liturgical re-enactment of the bringing of the ark into Jerusalem by David. The story itself it told in 2 Sam 6. David decided to bring the ark from house of Obed-Edom to Jerusalem. The undertaking was performed in a procession led by the king himself. Second Sam 6:17 is noteworthy: "And they brought the ark of the Lord and set it in its place *into the midst of the tent* [εἰς μέσον τῆς σκηνῆς] that David pitched for it" (emphasis added). Very little is known about this particular tent David set up for the ark. It is significant, however, that Ps 132/131 seems to connect the tent David built for the ark with the Temple Solomon—the former being the core of the later. Huwiler further clarifies the issue stating that it is not the Temple, but God's dwelling place that is in focus: "Psalm 132 does not specify that place as Temple but allows the designation to remain the more general Zion. David's virtue, then, lies not in intending to build a Temple, but in finding out that Zion is

Yahweh's chosen resting place."[49] Later, however, Huwiler admits that the Temple and Zion are integrally connected:

> This focus on Zion rather than on Temple, on site rather than on structure, is not to be overemphasized. Surely the presence of Yahweh in Jerusalem and the existence of the Temple were integrally related. To the worshippers who used the psalm in the Jerusalem Temple, the acclamation of Zion as holy place must have implied the necessity of the Temple.[50]

A look at the use of the word for tent in Acts might prove useful. Both the words σκηνή and σκήνωμα are employed in Stephen's speech in Acts. The former (σκηνή) is used in Acts 7:42–43 to speak of the tent of Moloch in a quote from Amos 5:25–27. This tent is contrasted with that of Moses in Acts 7:44. The term σκήνωμα is also used in the same speech in 7:45–46. These verses are noted to be an allusion to Ps 132/131:5.[51] It is said that "David, who found grace before God and asked to find a dwelling [σκήνωμα] to the house of Jacob" (Acts 7:46). There is, however, a textual problem in 7:46.

The house of Jacob is substituted with the God of Jacob in significant manuscripts. A dwelling/tent for the God of Jacob, as a clear reference to the Temple, makes more sense but it is not as well attested as the alternate reading. Witherington proves convincingly that the phrase "house of Jacob" is also a reference to the Temple.[52] Whatever textual decision one favors, the context of 7:46 clearly suggests that the Temple is in view. It is stated that David asked to build a dwelling/tent whereas Solomon built a house for God.

Lenski makes a case to link the tent of David with the interim sanctuary set up by the king for the ark. Lenski excludes that the word

---

[49] Elizabeth F. Huwiler, "Patterns and Problems in Psalm 132," in *The Listening Heart: Essays in Wisdom and the Psalms in Honour of Roland E. Murphy*, ed. Kenneth G. Hoglund et al., JSOTSup 58 (Sheffield: JSOT Press, 1987), 208.

[50] Ibid., 208–09.

[51] Aland et al., *Novum Testamentum Graece*, 341.

[52] Witherington, *Acts*, 273.

σκηνή would be a reference to the dynasty of David by pointing out that the word is never used in that context. The tabernacle of David was a place of worship where the king honored God with Israel before the Temple was built.[53] A similar position is held by Mauro.[54]

I hope to have established that Amos 9:11–12 can be read as a promise about the restoration of the Temple. The LXX context makes this reading more plausible than the MT, although there exists an opinion within OT scholarship that holds the same view with regard to the Hebrew text too. The metatextual approach that is utilized in this work can potentially further the discussion.

First, if one considers seriously that Acts 15:16–18 is not just a quote from Amos 9:11–12, but also from other prophetic oracles then those other prophecies might potentially confirm or disapprove if James's speech envisioned the restoration of the Temple in the early church. The question to be asked is this: Do Hos 3, Zech 8, and Isa 45 speak of cultic or of dynastic restoration? Hosea 3:4–5 speaks of both:

> For the sons of Israel shall sit many days without *king* and without *ruler* and without sacrifice and without altar and without priestly office and without Urim. And after these things, the sons of Israel shall return and shall seek the Lord their God and *David their king*, and they shall stand in awe at the Lord and his good things in the last days.

The italicized words refer to judgment and restoration of the dynasty whereas the underlined words have cultic connotation. Judgment involves living without a *king* and a *ruler* whereas political restoration involves the seeking of *David their king*.

On the other side, judgment related to the Temple involves living without *sacrifice*, *altar*, *priestly office* and *Urim*. Seeking God in Hos

---

[53] R. C. H. Lenski, *The Interpretation of the Acts of the Apostles 15–28* (Minneapolis: Augsburg Fortress, 2008), 609–10.

[54] Philip Mauro, *The Hope of Israel: What Is It?* (Swengel, PA: Reiner, 1970), 212–14.

3:5 must be related to the restoration of the Temple. Hosea 3 envisions both dynastic and cultic judgment and restoration with more emphasis on the latter. The political and religious aspect of restoration in Hos 3 is in accordance with the promise of the two houses from 2 Sam 7. They appear to go hand in hand.

Zechariah 8, however, speaks of the restoration of the Temple without mentioning political rule. The chapter first speaks of God's compassion for Jerusalem and Zion: "I have been jealous for Jerusalem and Zion with great jealousy, and I have been jealous for her with great wrath" (Zech 8:2). The statement of grief over Zion is followed by the promise of God's return and the restoration of his presence: "And I will return to Zion, and I will tent in the midst of Jerusalem, and Jerusalem shall be called a city that is true, and the mountain of the Lord Almighty, a holy mountain" (Zech 8:3). The Temple is explicitly mentioned in 8:9. In the remaining verses the return of the sons of Israel and agricultural blessings are promised—an idea that is traditionally linked with Temple service.

In the last section from Zech 8, the nations are said to join the people of Israel in seeking God's presence: "And many peoples and many nations shall come to seek the face of the Lord Almighty in Jerusalem and to appease the face of the Lord" (Zech 8:22). Finally, the interaction between the Israelites and the nations is envisioned: "In those days if ten men from all the languages of the nations take hold, then let them take hold of them of a Judean man, saying, 'We shall go with you, for we have heard that God is with you'" (Zech 8:23). Zechariah 8, therefore, clearly speaks of God's return to Zion in cultic terms: God's presence will be available even to the Gentiles who will seek him. The return of God and seeking God by the Gentiles are evoked in Acts 15:16–18. Isaiah 45:20–22 belongs to the groups of texts that speak of the eschatological conversion of the Gentiles only without reference to political or cultic realities.[55]

---

[55] Richard Bauckham, "James and the Jerusalem Church," in *The Book of Acts in Its Palestinian Setting*, vol. 4 of *The Book of Acts in Its First Century Setting*, ed. Richard Bauckham (Grand Rapids: Eerdmans, 1995), 456.

The significance of the promise of the Temple from 2 Sam 7 was raised earlier. It is a logical deduction that just as the deep subtext of Paul's sermon was the dynastic part of the promise from 2 Sam 7, in a similar way the subtext of the quote in Acts 15:16–18 is the part of the promise which focuses on the Temple.

In sum, Amos 9 most likely refers to the restoration of the Temple when speaking of David's booth; Hos 3 speaks for both cultic and political restoration with more emphasis on the former, whereas Zech 8 only speaks of restoring God's presence in Jerusalem and Zion. The composite quote, especially with Zech 8 in it, strongly suggests that James was speaking about the restoration of the Temple in the early Christian community where both Jews and Gentiles will live together.

5.2.3. Gentiles Christian and the Aliens Dwelling Among Israel: Acts 15:19–20

Finally, the apostolic decree will be considered in relation to Lev 17–19. At the end of his speech James concluded by suggesting that the "Gentiles who are turning to God should abstain only from things polluted by idols and from fornication and from whatever has been strangled and from blood" (Acts 15:20).[56] Literature on the apostolic decree apart from commentaries is enormous.[57] Discussion here will be limited to questions of intertextual relevance.

James speaks of pollution of ritual nature.[58] Four specific instances of pollution are mentioned: idols, fornication, things strangled, and blood. The intertextual challenge lies in identifying passages from the

---

[56] The decree is repeated later with some variation later in Acts 15:20 and in 21:29.

[57] Some useful works on the subject include: Bauckham, "James"; idem, "James and the Jerusalem Church"; Terrance Callan, "The Background of the Apostolic Decree (Acts 15:20, 29, 21:25)," *CBQ* 55 (1993): 284–97; Clayton N Jefford, "An Ancient Witness to the Apostolic Decree of Acts 15," *Proceedings* 10 (1990): 204–13; A.J.M. Wedderburn, "The 'Apostolic Decree': Tradition and Redaction," *NovT* 35 (1993): 362–89. Witherington offers an exhaustive and helpful treatment of the decree—see Witherington, *Acts*, 460–66.

[58] Bauer, *Greek-English Lexicon*, 37.

OT that contain specifically these four prohibitions. The Noahic commandments from Gen 9:3–4 can be excluded on these grounds: neither idolatry, nor fornication is mentioned there.[59] The other more likely candidate is the list of prohibitions in Lev 17–18. There are a number of commands that are addressed to the residents who live among the Israelites. Bauckham presents a convincing argument about how the prohibitions of Lev 17–18 and of Acts correspond.

He starts by pointing out that the Hebrew phrase for *the alien who sojourns in your/their midst* occurs five times in Lev 17–18, namely 17:8, 10, 12, 13; and 18:26. Since the second commandment repeats the first, there are in fact four commandments said to be observed by the aliens and not just the Israelites. These four are claimed to correspond to the prohibitions propagated by James. Leviticus 17:8–9 deals with burnt offerings and sacrifices whose meat could be eaten by the worshippers. This argument is based on the assumption that sacrifices not brought to the Tabernacle were considered as being offered to idols (Lev 17:7). Second, the consumption of blood is prohibited in Lev 17:10, 12. Third, Lev 17:13 prescribes the proper procedure for killing sacrificial animals with special attention on letting their blood out. This is a positive command which seems to be reflected in the negative prohibition of not eating strangled things. Fourth, all forms sexual immorality are prohibited in Lev 18:6–26. The word πορνεία used in the decree covers these all.[60]

Bauckham's argument is convincing in pointing to an OT background for the prohibitions in Acts 15:20. Even he admits though that the text of Acts does not provide further clues about the process of how these prohibitions were reached. It remains uncertain why only these commandments were prescribed for the Gentiles. There were other commandments in the OT that were prescribed for the aliens living in Israel. The observance of Sabbath (Exod 20:10; Deut 5:14) for instance is not brought up in Acts. Bauckham imagines that

---

59 Witherington, *Acts*, 464; Bauckham, "James and the Jerusalem Church," 4:465.

60 Bauckham, "James and the Jerusalem Church," 4:459–60.

perhaps the letter sent to the Gentile Christian contained a more detailed exegesis of Lev 17–18.[61] But there are more problems with this intertextual connection.

Witherington points out that blood is the only clear point of contact between the Lev prohibitions and the apostolic decree. The Greek term for idolatry does not occur in Lev 17–18. Strangling is only implied at best whereas the sexual offensives of Lev 18 are of different nature from the ones covered by the fornication of Acts. Both Witherington and Bauckham search for other factors that must have given rise to four prohibitions in Acts.[62]

This is a point of intertextual investigation where the precise nature of the subtext and metatext cannot be determined. The exegetical process that resulted in the first part of James's speech was clear enough: a number of texts were evoked to a certain effect. An argument was made that the conversion of the Gentiles is the fulfillment of God's promise to build and eschatological community as the new Temple. The second part of the exegetical process, however, remains hidden. It appears clear that the decree is based on Lev 17–18 but even more remains obscure. Why only these prohibitions were derived from the OT? Why not others? How is the situation of aliens living in the Holy Land comparable to the mix of Gentiles and Christians in diaspora settings?

Answering these questions would involve studying the history of interpretation of the Lev 17–18, early Christian understanding of pagan cults, and other related historical questions. All these questions, however necessary they may be, are outside the limits of the approach taken in this study. One must be content with pointing out that the prohibitions are based on Lev 17–18, but the precise nature of these texts would have to include other approaches to intertextuality and even extratextual study.

---

[61] Ibid., 4:462.

[62] Ibid., 4:460; Witherington, *Acts*, 465.

Chapter 6

CONCLUSIONS

6.1. Introduction

When studying the rich intertextual connectedness of the text of Acts, one may find the sharp remark made by post-structuralist literary theorist Roland Barthes especially appropriate: "the Text might indeed take for its motto the words of the man possessed by devils: 'My name is legion, for we are many' (Mark 5:9)."[1] The voices in Acts 10:1–15:35 are indeed many. A significant portion of these voices—intertextual connections mainly but not exclusively with the Holy Scriptures—were examined in line with Genette's types of textual transcendence. The choice of a structuralist approach was motivated not by the desire to reduce or even to manage plurality but rather to discover and define patterns of evoking texts in the narratives of the early church. Types of transtextuality were observed in isolation in the text to arrive at a more precise and fuller understanding of dialogue, polyphony, and symphony of voices in the text.

6.2. Transtextuality and Echo

I hope to have demonstrated that distinguishing among different types of intertextuality (transtextuality) can result in greater precision and a more comprehensive approach to textual correlations. Two narratives can seem "similar" either because they both follow a fixed form of telling stories or because one evokes the other. Architextuality reveals culture at work whereas hypertextuality points to a more explicit

[1] Roland Barthes, "From Work to Text," in *The Rustle of Language*, trans. Richard Howard (Berkeley: University of California Press, 1989), 61.

correlation of two texts.[2] These are two very different intertextual practices yet they both remain within the field of intertextuality. Added to these, when speakers comment on certain texts, that is yet another very different intertextual practice—i.e., metatextuality. These types of intertextuality (transtextuality) need to be distinguished to avoid confusion.

A great number of biblical scholars appear to assume that one unified notion of intertextual correlation can be established and applied throughout the NT, or at least in a certain group of texts within the NT. Ever since Richard Hays introduced the concept of *echo* for the Pauline epistles,[3] other scholars appear to offer a modified version of it so that it fits the Gospels, Acts, or other writings of the NT.[4] Hays derived his notion of echo partly from the works of Harold Bloom[5] and to a greater extent from the work of John Hollander.[6] In *The Figure of Echo,* Hollander dealt with "a way of alluding that is inherently poetic,

---

[2] For a useful distinction between "culture at work" and intertextual correlation see Umberto Eco, "Borges and My Anxiety of Influence," in *On Literature* (San Diego: Harcourt, 2005), 118–35.

[3] Richard B. Hays, *Echoes of Scripture in the Letters of Paul* (New Haven: Yale University Press, 1989); Richard B. Hays, Stefan Alkier, and Leroy A. Huizenga, eds., *Reading the Bible Intertextually* (Waco: Baylor University Press, 2009).

[4] A few titles should suffice to illustrate the influence of Hays's concept of echo: Gary T. Manning, *Echoes of a Prophet: The Use of Ezekiel in the Gospel of John and in Literature of the Second Temple Period*, LNTS 270 (London: T&T Clark, 2004); Mark Allan Powell, "Echoes of Jonah in the New Testament," *WW* 27 (2007): 157; Kenneth D. Litwak, *Echoes of Scripture in Luke-Acts: Telling the History of God's People Intertextually* (London: T&T Clark, 2005); Christopher A. Beetham, *Echoes of Scripture in the Letter of Paul to the Colossians* (Leiden: Brill, 2008); James Todd Hibbard and Hyun Chul Paul Kim, eds., *Formation and Intertextuality in Isaiah 24–27*, AIL 17 (Atlanta: Society of Biblical Literature, 2013); Ryan P. Juza, "Intertextuality and Tradition in 2 Peter 3:7–13," *BBR* 24 (2014): 227–45.

[5] Harold Bloom, *The Anxiety of Influence: A Theory of Poetry* (New York: Oxford University Press, 1997).

[6] John Hollander, *The Figure of Echo: A Mode of Allusion in Milton and After* (Berkeley: University of California Press, 1981).

rather than expository"[7] present in the works of Milton. Hays particularly utilized what Hollander wrote about metalepsis.[8]

My remarks are not meant to give a full account of either Hollander or Hays's treatment of Hollander. It is only pointed out here that Hays offered sensitivity more than methodology, as he called it,[9] to interpret a certain type of intertextual connections based on a segment of Hollander's work. Hays was after a certain kind of intertextual connection and many scholars seem to assume that there is only one kind. Genette's notion of transtextuality, in contrast, has the benefit of incorporating many dimensions of intertextuality. Utilizing his map of textual transcendence provides the basis for a more precise and nuanced picture of textual relations.

It is by no way implied, however, that other biblical scholars did not probe various other concepts of intertextuality from the field of literary theory. Richard Lawson Brawley is one good example for building mainly on Bloom's theory, but he also included ideas from several literary theorists.[10] Added to this, Huizenga's latest work offers strong readings of intertextuality in the Gospel of Matthew based on Umberto Eco's theory of intertextuality.[11] The method applied in this work based on Genette's approach is yet a further attempt to search better ways of understanding textual connections in the NT.

6.3. Transtextual Economy in Acts 10:1–15:35

The most implicit of textual connections is that of architextuality. It is of special relevance to examine modes, figures, styles, forms, themes, and literary techniques dominant in Acts 10:1–15:35. Certain themes within the LXX appear to have their own style. Creation, exodus, and Temple service, for instance, have their own distinct vocabulary as

---

[7] Ibid., ix.

[8] Hays, *Echoes*, 20.

[9] Ibid., 21.

[10] Robert L. Brawley, *Text to Text Pours Forth Speech: Voices of Scripture in Luke-Acts* (Bloomington: Indiana University Press, 1995), 10–13.

[11] Huizenga, *New Isaac*; cf. idem, "The Akedah in Matthew" (Ph.D. diss., Duke University, 2006).

well as syntax. Additionally, narratives of receiving guests, of healing, of pagans coming to God, for example, follow certain fixed narrative patterns. Narratives and utterances in Acts evoke themes and forms of the OT through verbal reverberations without making reference to individual passages. This phenomenon is to be taken seriously.

When reading commentaries, especially the ones that pay attention to OT allusions, one can regularly find that a certain proposed allusion is discredited on the grounds that it "just Septuagintal language" and not a conscious allusion.[12] This might be so, but "just Septuagintal language" is also part of intertextuality even if it can be located on a different level than allusions and citations. The architextual tendencies of narratives are just as relevant as the other types.

More than this, observing architextual tendencies can potentially result in establishing an architextual economy. The use of sacrificial expressions in relation to Cornelius's piety and the use of Temple-service language in relation to Gentile mission all point in the same direction: stories about Gentiles are endowed with an atmosphere of holiness. The sacrificial and cultic tone under the words and stories sets the mood of the narrative. This tendency naturally builds on tension: placing Gentiles and cultic holiness together is an odd pairing. The tension is expressed openly in the text: Peter objects to eating unclean animals; the people in Jerusalem question Peter for eating with the Gentiles. The mute architextual dimensions, however, already anticipate a solution. Similarly, reading the portrayal of Cornelius in the light of OT narratives about believing pagan officials, or reading the conflict between Bar-Jesus and Paul in the light of past conflicts between false prophets and true prophets create expectations. The stories of the church are told in a similar fashion to the stories of Israel, thus creating anticipation.

One last question relevant for architextuality in Acts needs to be addressed. The issue of distinguishing between architextuality and hypertextuality (or other types of textual transcendence) in the text was raised more than once. First, it was argued that the receiving of the

---

[12] Marshall often makes this remark—see Marshall, "Acts."

messengers by Peter in Acts 10:9–23 is linked with Gen 18:1–8 by virtue of a shared *topos*—i.e., a hospitality narrative. Further, the two narratives also correlate by thematic imitation—i.e., a hypertextual operation. It was argued that both architextual and hypertextual thrust are detectable in the text. Second, it was decided that in Acts 12:1–11 thematic imitation of the exodus is at work, even though evoking exodus language in general could be recognized. Hypertextuality was given precedence over architextuality. In both cases intertexts and close adherence to some scenes of narratives of the hypotext helped to decide and to clarify the case.[13]

The task is further complicated by the generic influence of OT narratives. Single stories in the OT set the norm for later narratives, both in terms of content and form. The issue of distinguishing architext from the hypotext is related to a methodological challenge: how to determine forms in the Bible. We could, therefore, say building on the result of traditional Form Criticism (*Formgeschichte*) of both the OT and the NT might result in greater precision and clarity architextual investigation needs.[14] In sum, architextuality is a complex issue in Acts that deserves more attention and further study. Clarity regarding categories of architextuality is to be established based on a definition of forms of narratives and of utterance as well as of style and genre. Next, hypertextuality also provides a relevant perspective from which textual connections in Acts are to be studied. Two hypertextual operations have been detected in the text of Acts: transposition and thematic imitation.

I hope to have demonstrated that diegetic transposition, as explained by Genette, provides the most accurate description of

[13] A similar issue of distinguishing type-scene from allusion is raised by Jocelyn McWhirter, *The Bridegroom Messiah and the People of God: Marriage in the Fourth Gospel*, SNTSMS 138 (Cambridge: Cambridge University Press, 2006), 7.

[14] Form criticism was originally introduced by German OT scholar Hermann Gunkel in his commentary on Genesis (Hermann Gunkel, *Genesis: übersetzt und erklärt* [Göttingen: Vandenhoeck & Ruprecht, 1901]) and later developed by many others. For a general introduction, see David L. Petersen, "Hebrew Bible Form Criticism," *RSR* 18 (1992): 29–33.

transtextual correlation between the narrative of Cornelius's conversion in Acts 10:1–11:18 and the story of Jonah. Ancient and modern intertextual readings of the two narratives were cited and evaluated to demonstrate the potential of and the need for the accuracy of hypertextual description of the textual connection in question.

The diegetic transposition of the plot of Jonah is the most extensive transtextual strategy in the selected part of Acts. It covers nearly two chapters: Acts 10 and the bulk of Acts 11. Transposition also allows for other types of transtextuality to take place. Intertexts or even imitation of other texts also have been observed in Acts 10:1–11:18. Yet, adherence to the plot of Jonah in the hypertext has not been interrupted. Transposition is indeed a longer and more extensive literary practice, as Genette remarked.[15] This area, however, needs further study.

In the five chapters of Acts, only one instance of transposition was discovered.[16] While this begs for more probing, Thomas L. Brodie comes closest to describing intertextual correlation that rests on adherence to a shared plot without necessarily relying on intertexts. His approach is too complex to introduce here.[17] In addition, most biblical scholars seem to agree that while Brodie offers interesting ideas, he delivers mixed or even ambiguous results.[18] The orientation of his intertextual approach, nevertheless, points to the need for establishing a kind of intertextuality that involves plot, characters, settings, and other elements of narrativity. Direct transformation with its several operations is a good starting point toward defining this kind of intertextuality.[19]

---

[15] Genette, *Palimpsests*, 46.

[16] The intertextual correlation between Jonah and Acts 27 is of a different nature.

[17] Thomas L. Brodie, *The Birthing of the New Testament: The Intertextual Development of the New Testament Writings* (Sheffield: Sheffield Phoenix, 2006).

[18] For a thoughtful review, see Jozef Verheyden, "The Birthing of the New Testament: The Intertextual Development of the New Testament Writings," *Bib* 87 (2006): 439–42.

[19] Brawley and Litwak equally stress narrative context for establishing intertextual connections in Acts. Their method, however, has a very different

Imitation, the second hypertextual operation, is more frequent in the text of Acts. Thematic imitation, a term introduced in this work to express imitation of a special kind, was defined as a hypertextual operation that rests on the correspondence of identifiable characteristic themes, of one or more characters, and includes some form of verbal reverberations between two or more texts. The correlation of this kind is short, involving few sequences. Allusion or verbal correspondence of some kind helps to link the similar situations of the hypertext and the hypotext. An example not from Acts should suffice to illustrate the point.

In "Lyubka the Cossack", a story by Isaac Babel, a Russian-Jewish novelist of the early 20th century, there was a debate about finances between a middleman, Zudechkis and a wealthy lady, Lyubka. The middleman refused to pay for services and was locked in a room as a result. The narrator depicts Zudechkis's situation with the claim: "'Oy, poor Zudechkis!' the small middleman then said to himself. 'You have fallen into the hands of the Pharaoh himself!'"[20] This acclamation naturally is a reference to the captivity of the Israelites in Egypt. The short episode involves two protagonists, one wealthy and powerful, the other poor and in need. In addition, the weaker person is locked in a room—a captivity-like situation is created. Finally, the open reference to Pharaoh creates a clear point of contact between the scene in Odessa and the captivity in Egypt. One character openly links his state with that of the Jews in Egypt and also the other character with the king of the Egyptians.

Similarly, the hubris and punishment of the king of Tyre of Ezek 27 is thematically imitated in Acts 12:18–23. The two kings are linked by claiming or accepting the claim to be god. The wording of the claim is a clear verbal correspondence. Once this connection is observed, several other points of contact emerge: both men are kings, both wear royal robes, and both are punished for arrogance before onlookers. The

---

theoretical basis from the one assumed here. See Litwak, *Echoes of Scripture in Luke-Acts*; Brawley, *Text*.

[20] Isaac Babel, *The Complete Works of Isaac Babel* (New York: W.W. Norton, 2005), 278.

audience from Tyre and Sidon creates further resonance between the two narratives.

A similar point was made about imitating Jonah's fate on the sea in Paul's voyage in Acts 27. This time, however, imitation is based on contrast rather than conformity—i.e., there is a similar situation on the ship of Jonah and on the ship carrying Paul, but the apostle acts in contrast with Jonah. Both identify themselves as God's servants but with opposite intentions: Paul wants to serve the Lord, whereas Jonah flees from him. The concept of thematic imitation was also used to describe the connection between the hosting of the angels/messengers by Abraham in Gen 18:1–8 and the receiving of the messengers from Caesarea by Peter in Acts 10:9–23. In both cases, the messengers are introduced in near identical words. Once this is observed, other points of contact emerge: similar time (noon), space (gate), comparable protagonists (Abraham, Peter), and similar settings (meal).

A more complex way of thematic imitation was observed in Acts 12:1–17. Several motifs and episodes of the exodus and of the passion of Jesus Christ are imitated throughout the section. The story of Peter's imprisonment and deliverance is told against the background of the narratives of the exodus and of the passion of the Lord. These are the main hypotexts. In addition, short episodes from the stories of Elijah, Judith, and Daniel and his friends are evoked in relation to the early church and to Peter. It is possible to view each thematic imitation separately. However, a thematic coherence can be observed. All the narratives evoked are already imitation of the exodus, or offer very similar settings to the exodus. There is an economy of thematic imitations at work: stories of oppression and deliverance are evoked in Acts in combination with one another. Telling the deliverance of Peter in relation to several deliverances in the Bible is clearly at work.

Richard Hays's notion of an *echo* appears to overlap partly with thematic imitation. It is worth pointing out that the concept of an *echo* was coined to propose intertextuality for the Pauline epistles of the NT. Naturally, verbal correspondence is a criterion for echo. But Hays also claims that writers of the epistles evoke more than just words from the OT. Interference runs deeper than just the correspondence of a few words.[21] Not only the sub-text, but also the sub-context is evoked in the texts.[22] Hays's notion of echo is determined by his reading of the epistles. Narratives settings, characters, plot do not play a significant role in establishing echo. Thematic imitation, in contrast, relies on all these. Evoking words as well as narrative context characterizes thematic imitation.

Owing to the large number of speeches, metatextuality is yet another very important transtextual type in the five chapters of Acts.[23] When examining this type, we discovered that Scripture is most openly quoted and alluded to by the speakers of the narratives.[24] Metatextuality, moreover, also involves evaluating and interpreting subtexts. Metatextuality is strongly determined by both the subtext and the communicative intent and the context of the speeches. Texts from the LXX are more or less openly evoked, cited and interpreted to certain effects.

It is proposed here that, based on the dominance and visibility of the subtext(s) in metatext, three metatextual modes can be observed in the speeches. The first mode appears to be dominated by the logic of the metatext/speech and subtexts are evoked from a distance and only occasionally to support the strong claims of the speaker. This will be

---

[21] Hays, *Echoes*, 1–33.

[22] Samuel Emadi, "Intertextuality in New Testament Scholarship: Significance, Criteria, and the Art of Intertextual Reading," *CBR* 14 (2015): 11.

[23] Apostolic speeches plays a crucial role in the design of Acts. For some useful work, see e.g., Joshua D. Garroway, "'Apostolic Irresistibility' and the Interrupted Speeches in Acts," *CBQ* 74 (2012): 738–52; Bowker, "Speeches"; Johnson, *Septuagintal Midrash*; David Peterson, "The Motif of Fulfilment and the Purpose of Luke-Acts," in *The Book of Acts in Its Ancient Literary Setting*, ed. Bruce W. Winter and Andrew D. Clark (Grand Rapids: Eerdmans, 1993), 83–104; Atef Mehanny Gendy, "Style, Content and Culture: Distinctive Characteristics in the Missionary Speeches in Acts," *SMT* 99 (2011): 247–65; Richard I. Pervo, "Direct Speech in Acts and the Question of Genre," *JSNT* 28 (2006): 285–307; Peterson, "Motif."

[24] In contrast with this, the narrator of Matt frequently quotes the Scripture. In Matt 1:22, for instance, the narrator says: "All this took place to fulfill what had been spoken by the Lord through the prophet: 'Look, the virgin, shall conceive'." In Acts, quoting and interpreting is reserved for the characters.

termed *performative* metatextual mode. The second mode is activated when subtexts are quoted in precision and interpretative conclusions are drawn from them in the metatext. The process of interpretation is manifest. Participation and approval from the audience is expected. This will be called *interpretative* metatextual mode. A third mode can be observed when texts are quoted openly and at length but interpretation does not follow. The subtext is allowed to speak on its own terms; immediacy is achieved. This mode does not lack interpretation, but it is more hidden and implicit. This last strategy will be called *paracletic* mode. In the performative mode the subtexts are used to illustrate and add Scriptural feel to arguments. In the interpretative mode subtexts are cited and the process of interpretation is displayed. In paracletic mode the subtext receives dominance and interpretation is offered by hidden clues—introductory formula, combinations of several texts, changes in the subtexts.

The metatext in Acts 13:16–25 has a very firm logic to which the subtext is subordinated. Performative mode characterizes the relationship. The logic of Paul's speech is determined by telling the story of God's initiatives that culminates in David and in his seed, Jesus Christ. Paul speaks of periods of time, most of which were dominated by human agents. Portrayals of periods and of human agents are supported by allusions, quotes and summaries. The intertexts from various books, chapters and verses of the OT are merged to form unified statements on the selected subject.

A similar tendency can be observed in Peter's speech at the Jerusalem Council in Acts 15:7–11. Peter tells the story of the church when making reference to the outpouring of the Holy Spirit on the Gentiles (Acts 10) and on the disciples at Pentecost (Acts 2). The conversion of the Gentiles is presented with an allusion to Zech 2:10–11/2:14–15. In the speeches of Paul and Peter, the past events of Israel and the church are evoked and evaluated through combining textual expressions of those events. Nevertheless, the communicative context is the most dominant factor.

In contrast with this, a different kind of the metatextual activity can be observed in the second part of Paul's missionary speech: texts are openly quoted and the process of interpretation is revealed. In Acts 13:32–38 several verses from different books are quoted. Each verse is quoted in precisions and interpretation follows. The significance of passages is seen in offering arguments in a chain of arguments. The process of interpretation is revealed. The audience has a role in deciding if the interpretation is appropriate and correct or the opposite is true. This is an instance of interpretative mode.

The third kind of metatextual activity is discernible in James's speech in Acts 15:13–21. Scripture is openly quoted at length. The most notable difference, however, is that interpretation does not happen openly or interpretative gestures are kept to the minimum. Only the introduction formula and changes in the subtexts give clues about meaning drawn from the subtexts. James pointed out that the conversion of the Gentiles agrees with the word of the Prophets. The *words of the Prophets* in the compilation quote imply the restoration of the presence of God that will be available to both Gentiles and Jews.

Similarly, Paul closed two of his speeches with long quotes without adding interpretation. In Acts 13:41 he finished with a quote from Hab 1:5. Only the introductory formula gives clues about the intended meaning: "Beware, therefore, that what the prophets said does not happen to you" (Acts 13:40). Then at the end of his second speech in Antioch, Paul claims that the apostles have to speak first to Jews and then to the Gentiles. Justification for his claim is offered by a quote from Isa 49:6. Earlier I pointed out that several changes were made in the subtext. I argued that the changes are of interpretative motivation and are best described by what is called the mixing of horizons. The presentation of the quote from Isa 49 shows marks of interpretation. It is of significance that interpretation in not done on the surface when paracletic mode is realised.

It is important that individual speeches can realise several modes; speeches can shift modes. Paul, for instance, starts in performative mode when telling the history of Israel in Acts 13, then shifts to interpretative mode when explaining the *raising* of Jesus, and closes in paracletic mode when warning against disbelief. Certain modes dominate certain aspects of the speech. It is to be noted that this categorization of metatextual modes is mainly based on speeches in Acts 10:1–15:35 and the use of this model outside this section demands further testing and clarification.[25] Building on the results of linguistic and literary concepts of metatextuality can further the understanding of the metatextuality of speeches in Acts.[26]

Evoking Scripture in Acts 10:1–15:35 is inherently characterized by relating and combining several utterances to express truth about the reality the early church was living in. Opposition to receiving the Gentiles is expressed with the words of Holy Scriptures: Peter objects to eating unclean animals in Acts 10:14 with the words of Ezekiel, a prophet who experienced oppression by Gentiles. Eating and living with Gentiles as well as circumcising them are all issued discussed by the Torah. In contrast, receiving the Gentiles in the church is also motivated by the words of the Scriptures. The apostles quote and combine utterances from the Prophets to show that the conversion of the Gentiles is a fulfilment of God's will as revealed in the Scriptures. The narrator tells the story of Gentile conversion in harmony with earlier stories about Gentiles coming to faith. The dilemmas the early church faced correspond to the voices of the Holy Scriptures. Both the dangers and the potential of the situation are voiced with the words of Scriptures.

Bakhtin's observation about Dostoevsky's artistry in combining voices of the past with voices of the present and of the future is comparable with work of Luke. Bakhtin writes: "Dostoevsky … heard

---

[25] I realize that David Buttrick offers a similar approach in relation to sermons and texts of the Bible on which sermons are based. Buttrick points out that sermons can either make the audience part of the biblical narratives or they can reveal certain contexts of the Bible relevant for everyday experience. David G. Buttrick, *Homiletic: Moves and Structures* (Philadelphia: Fortress Press, 1987), 319–31.

[26] A good introduction to commentaries as metatext can be found in Balázs Déri et al., eds., *Metafilológia*, Filológia 2 (Budapest: Ráció Kiadó, 2012), 435–538.

resonances of the voice-ideas of the past."[27] More than this, he wrote that "Dostoevsky possessed an extraordinary gift for hearing the dialogue of his epoch, or, more precisely, for hearing his epoch as a great dialogue, for detecting in it not only individual voices, but precisely and predominantly the dialogic relationship among voices, their dialogic interaction."[28] The narrator of Acts provides a more implicit, hypertextual relationship between events of the early church and God's past saving acts recorded in the Holy Scriptures. The speakers of Acts openly propose a relationship between the past of God's people and their own present. Architextual correlations provide a deeper interaction between the LXX and the narratives in Acts. The voices of Scriptures are evoked in implicit and explicit ways in the narratives about the incorporation of the Gentiles in the church.

---

[27] Bakhtin, *Problems*, 90.

[28] Ibid.

BIBLIOGRAPHY

Adams, Sean A. *The Genre of Acts and Collected Biography*. SNTSMS 156. Cambridge: Cambridge University Press, 2013.

Aland, Barbara, Kurt Aland, Johannes Karavidopoulos, Carlo Maria Martini, and Bruce M. Metzger, eds. *Novum Testamentum Graece*. 27th rev. ed. Stuttgart: Deutsche Bibelgesellschaft, 1993.

Alexander, Loveday. *Acts in Its Ancient Literary Context*. LNTS 289. London: T&T Clark, 2007.

Alkier, Stefan. "Intertextuality and the Semiotics of Biblical Texts." Pages 3–21 in *Reading the Bible Intertextually*. Edited by Richard B. Hays, Stefan Alkier, and Leroy A. Huizenga. Waco, TX: Baylor University Press, 2009.

Allen, Graham. *Intertextuality*. London: Routledge, 2000.

Anderson, A.A. *2 Samuel*. WBC 11. Dallas: Word, 1989.

Augustine. *The Confessions and Letters of St. Augustine, with a Sketch of His Life and Work*. Edited by Philip Schaff. Vol. 1. Nicene and Post-Nicene Fathers Series I. Grand Rapids: Christian Classics Ethereal Library, n.d.

Babel, Isaac. *The Complete Works of Isaac Babel*. New York: W.W. Norton & Company Incorporated, 2005.

Bakhtin, Mikhail. *Problems of Dostoevsky's Poetics*. Edited by Caryl Emerson. Translated by Caryl Emerson. Minneapolis: University of Minnesota Press, 1984.

Barrett, C.K. *The Acts of the Apostles*. Vol. 1. ICC. Edinburgh: T&T Clark, 1994.

Barthes, Roland. "From Work to Text." Pages 56–64 in *The Rustle of Language*. Translated by Richard Howard. Berkeley: University of California Press, 1989.

Bauckham, Richard. "James and the Jerusalem Church." Pages 415–80 in *The Book of Acts in Its Palestinian Setting*. Vol. 4 of *The Book of Acts in Its First Century Setting*. Edited by Richard Bauckham. Grand Rapids: Eerdmans, 1995.

______. "James and the Gentiles (Acts 15.13-21)." Pages 154–84 in *History, Literature, and Society in the Book of Acts*. Edited by Ben Witherington. Cambridge: Cambridge University Press, 1996.

Bauer, Walter. *A Greek-English Lexicon of the New Testament and Other Early Christian Literature*. 2nd ed. Chicago: University of Chicago Press, 1979.

Beale, G.K., and D.A. Carson, eds. *Commentary on the New Testament Use of the Old Testament*. Grand Rapids: Baker Academic, 2007.

Beetham, Christopher A. *Echoes of Scripture in the Letter of Paul to the Colossians*. Leiden: Brill, 2008.

Ben Zvi, Ehud. *Signs of Jonah: Reading and Rereading in Ancient Yehud*. JSOTSup 367. London: Sheffield Academic Press, 2003.

Block, Daniel I. *The Book of Ezekiel: Chapters 1–24*. NICOT. Grand Rapids: Eerdmans, 1997.

Bloom, Harold. *The Anxiety of Influence: A Theory of Poetry*. New York: Oxford University Press, 1997.

Bock, Darrell L. "Luke, Gospel of." Pages 540–52 in *Dictionary of Jesus and the Gospels*. Edited by Joel B. Green, Scot McKnight, and I. Howard Marshall. Downers Grove, IL: IVP Academic, 1992.

______. *Acts*. BECNT. Grand Rapids: Baker Academic, 2007.

Bolyki, János. *Jézus asztalközösségei*. Budapest: Református Teológiai Akadémia, 1993.

Bowker, J.W. "Speeches in Acts: A Study in Proem and Yelammenedu Form." *NTS* 14 (1968): 96–111.

Brawley, Robert L. *Text to Text Pours Forth Speech: Voices of Scripture in Luke-Acts*. Bloomington: Indiana University Press, 1995.

Brodie, Thomas L. *The Birthing of the New Testament: The Intertextual Development of the New Testament Writings*. Sheffield: Sheffield Phoenix, 2006.

Brown, Raymond E. *The Birth of the Messiah: A Commentary on the Infancy Narratives in the Gospels of Matthew and Luke*. Updated ed. ABRL. New York: Doubleday, 1999.

Buttrick, David G. *Homiletic: Moves and Structures*. Philadelphia: Fortress Press, 1987.

Callan, Terrance. "The Background of the Apostolic Decree (Acts 15:20,29, 21:25)." *CBQ* 55 (1993): 284–97.

Calvin, John. *Commentary on Jonah, Micah, Nahum*. Translated by John Owen. Grand Rapids: Christian Classics Ethereal Library, n.d.

______. *Ezekiel 1: Chapters 1-12*. Tranlsated by David Foxgrover. Rev. ed. COTC 18. Grand Rapids: Eerdmans, 1994.

Christensen, Duane L. *Deuteronomy 1,1–21,9*. 2nd ed. WBC 6A. Nashville: Thomas Nelson, 2001.

Conzelmann, Hans. *Acts of the Apostles: A Commentary on the Acts of the Apostles*. Translated by James Limburg, A. Thomas Kraabel, and Donald H. Juel. Hermeneia. Philadelphia: Fortress, 1987.

Craigie, Peter C. *The Book of Deuteronomy*. NICOT. London: Hodder and Stoughton, 1976.

Craigie, Peter C., and Marvin Tate. *Psalms 1–50*. WBC 19. Nashville: Thomas Nelson, 2004.

Denaux, Adelbert. "The Theme of Divine Visits and Human (In)Hospitality in Luke-Acts: Its Old Testament and Graeco-Roman Antecedents." Pages 255–79 in *The Unity of Luke-Acts*. Edited by Joseph Verheyden. BETL 142. Leuven: Leuven University Press, 1999.

Déri, Balázs, Pál Kelemen, József Krupp, and Ábel Tamás, eds. *Metafilológia*. Filológia 2. Budapest: Ráció Kiadó, 2012.

Dunne, John Anthony. "David's Tent as Temple in Amos 9:11–15: Understanding the Epilogue of Amos and Considering Implications for the Unity of the Book." *WTJ* 73 (2011): 363–74.

Dunn, James D.G. *The Acts of the Apostles*. Valley Forge, PA: Trinity Press International, 1996.

Eco, Umberto. "Borges and My Anxiety of Influence." Pages 118–35 in *On Literature*. San Diego: Harcourt, 2005.

Elliger, Karl and Willhelm Rudulph, eds. *Biblia Hebraica Stuttgartensia*. Stuttgart: Deutsche Bibelgesellschaft, 1990.

Emadi, Samuel. "Intertextuality in New Testament Scholarship: Significance, Criteria, and the Art of Intertextual Reading." *CBR* 14 (2015): 8–23.

Ephros, Abraham. "Nineveh and Sodom Juxtaposed: Contrasts and Parallels." *JBQ* 30 (2002): 242–46.

Esler, Philip Francis. *Community and Gospel in Luke-Acts: The Social and Political Motivations of Lucan Theology*. Cambridge: Cambridge University Press, 1989.

Eynde, Sabine van den. "Crying to God: Prayer and Plot in the Book of Judith." *Bib* 85 (2004): 217–31.

Fields, Weston W. *Sodom and Gomorrah: History and Motif in Biblical Narrative*. JSOTSup 231. Sheffield: Sheffield Academic Press, 1997.

Fischer, Alexander Achilles, and Ernst Würthwein. *Der Text des Alten Testaments: Neubearbeitung der Einführung in die Biblia Hebraica von Ernst Würthwein*. Stuttgart: Deutsche Bibelgesellschaft, 2009.

Fitzmyer, Joseph A. *The Gospel According to Luke I-IX: Introduction, Translation, and Notes*. AB 28A. Garden City, NY: Doubleday, 1982.

______. *The Acts of the Apostles*. AB 31. New Haven: Yale University Press, 1998.

Frye, Northrop. *Anatomy of Criticism: Four Essays*. 15th ed. Princeton: Princeton University Press, 2000.

Garrett, Susan R. "Exodus from Bondage: Luke 9:31 and Acts 12:1-24." *CBQ* 52 (1990): 656–80.

Garroway, Joshua D. "'Apostolic Irresistibility' and the Interrupted Speeches in Acts." *CBQ* 74 (2012): 738–52.

Gendy, Atef Mehanny. "Style, Content and Culture: Distinctive Characteristics in the Missionary Speeches in Acts." *SMT* 99 (2011): 247–65.

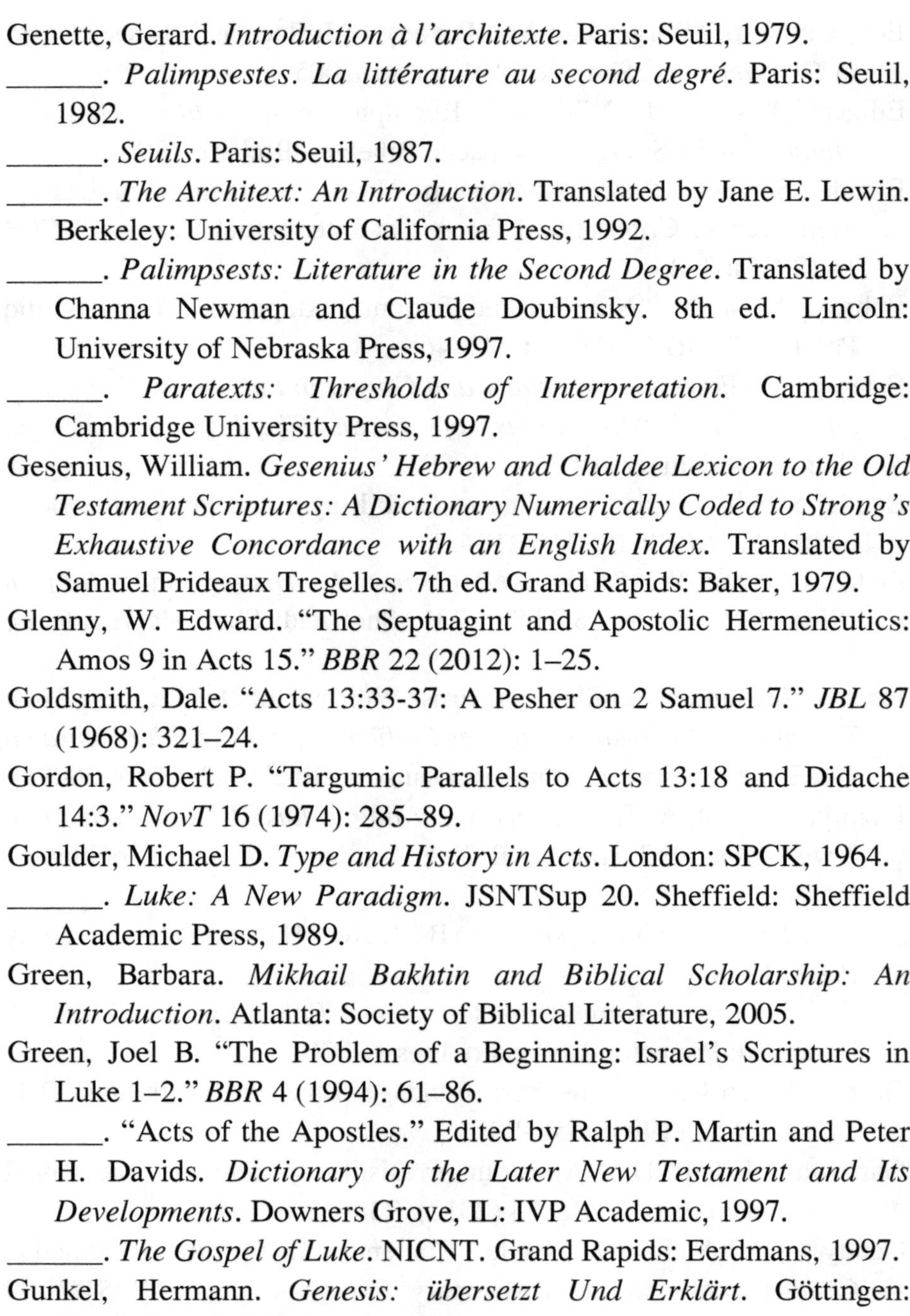

Genette, Gerard. *Introduction à l'architexte*. Paris: Seuil, 1979.

______. *Palimpsestes. La littérature au second degré*. Paris: Seuil, 1982.

______. *Seuils*. Paris: Seuil, 1987.

______. *The Architext: An Introduction*. Translated by Jane E. Lewin. Berkeley: University of California Press, 1992.

______. *Palimpsests: Literature in the Second Degree*. Translated by Channa Newman and Claude Doubinsky. 8th ed. Lincoln: University of Nebraska Press, 1997.

______. *Paratexts: Thresholds of Interpretation*. Cambridge: Cambridge University Press, 1997.

Gesenius, William. *Gesenius' Hebrew and Chaldee Lexicon to the Old Testament Scriptures: A Dictionary Numerically Coded to Strong's Exhaustive Concordance with an English Index*. Translated by Samuel Prideaux Tregelles. 7th ed. Grand Rapids: Baker, 1979.

Glenny, W. Edward. "The Septuagint and Apostolic Hermeneutics: Amos 9 in Acts 15." *BBR* 22 (2012): 1–25.

Goldsmith, Dale. "Acts 13:33-37: A Pesher on 2 Samuel 7." *JBL* 87 (1968): 321–24.

Gordon, Robert P. "Targumic Parallels to Acts 13:18 and Didache 14:3." *NovT* 16 (1974): 285–89.

Goulder, Michael D. *Type and History in Acts*. London: SPCK, 1964.

______. *Luke: A New Paradigm*. JSNTSup 20. Sheffield: Sheffield Academic Press, 1989.

Green, Barbara. *Mikhail Bakhtin and Biblical Scholarship: An Introduction*. Atlanta: Society of Biblical Literature, 2005.

Green, Joel B. "The Problem of a Beginning: Israel's Scriptures in Luke 1–2." *BBR* 4 (1994): 61–86.

______. "Acts of the Apostles." Edited by Ralph P. Martin and Peter H. Davids. *Dictionary of the Later New Testament and Its Developments*. Downers Grove, IL: IVP Academic, 1997.

______. *The Gospel of Luke*. NICNT. Grand Rapids: Eerdmans, 1997.

Gunkel, Hermann. *Genesis: übersetzt Und Erklärt*. Göttingen: Vandenhoeck & Ruprecht, 1901.

Habel, Norman C. “Form and Significance of the Call Narratives.” *ZAW* 77 (1965): 297–323.

Haenchen, Ernst. *The Acts of the Apostles: A Commentary*. Translated by Bernard Noble and Gerald Shinn. Revised and updated by R. McL. Wilson. Oxford: Basil Blackwell, 1971.

Hanula, Gergely. “A „szent nyelvek” fordítása mint nyelvészeti kérdés, különös tekintettel az Újszövetségre.” PhD diss., Eötvös Loránd Tudományegyetem, Bölcsészettudományi Kar, 2015.

Hays, Richard B. *Echoes of Scripture in the Letters of Paul*. New Haven: Yale University Press, 1989.

Hays, Richard B., Stefan Alkier, and Leroy A. Huizenga, eds. *Reading the Bible Intertextually*. Waco, TX: Baylor University Press, 2009.

Hegedus, Timothy M. “Jerome’s Commentary on Jonah: Translation with Introduction and Critical Notes.” MA thesis, Wilfrid Laurier University, 1991.

Hibbard, James Todd and Hyun Chul Paul Kim, eds. *Formation and Intertextuality in Isaiah 24–27*. AIL 17. Atlanta: Society of Biblical Literature, 2013.

Holladay, Carl R., trans. *Historians*. Vol. 1 of *Fragments from Hellenistic Jewish Authors* Edited by Harold W. Attridge. Chico, CA: Scholars, 1983.

Hollander, John. *The Figure of Echo: A Mode of Allusion in Milton and After*. Berkeley: University of California Press, 1981.

Huizenga, Leroy A. “The Akedah in Matthew.” PhD diss., Duke University, 2006.

Huizenga, Leroy Andrew. *The New Isaac: Tradition and Intertextuality in the Gospel of Matthew*. NovTSup 131. Leiden: Brill, 2012.

Huwiler, Elizabeth F. “Patterns and Problems in Psalm 132.” Pages 199–215 in *The Listening Heart: Essays in Wisdom and the Psalms in Honour of Roland E. Murphy*. Edited by Kenneth G. Hoglund, Elizabeth F. Huwiler, Jonathan T. Glass, and Roger W. Lee. JSOTSup 58. Sheffield: JSOT Press, 1987.

Jauss, Hans Robert. *Toward an Aesthetic of Reception*. THL 2. Minneapolis: University of Minnesota Press, 1982.

______. *Aesthetic Experience and Literary Hermeneutics*. THL 3. Minneapolis: University of Minnesota Press, 1982.

______. "The Book Jonah—A Paradigm of the 'Hermeneutics of Strangeness.'" *JLS* 1 (1985): 1–19.

Jefford, Clayton N. "An Ancient Witness to the Apostolic Decree of Acts 15." *Proceedings* 10 (1990): 204–13.

Jervell, Jacob. "The Future of the Past: Luke's Vision of Salvation History and Its Bearing on His Writing of History." Pages 104–26 in *History, Literature, and Society in the Book of Acts*. Edited by Ben Witherington. Cambridge: Cambridge University Press, 1996.

Johnson, Luke Timothy. *Septuagintal Midrash in the Speeches of Acts*. Milwaukee: Marquette University Press, 2002.

______. *The Acts of the Apostles*. SP 5. Collegeville, MN: Liturgical Press, 2006.

Josephus, Flavius. *Josephus: Complete Works*. Translated by William Whiston. London: Pickering & Inglis LTD., 1969.

Juza, Ryan P. "Intertextuality and Tradition in 2 Peter 3:7–13." *BBR* 24 (2014): 227–45.

Kim, Hyun Chul Paul. "Jonah Read Intertextually." *JBL* 126 (2007): 497–528.

Kristeva, Julia. *Sèméiotikè: recherches pour une sémanalyse*. Paris: Éditions du Seuil, 1969.

______. *The Kristeva Reader*. Edited by Toril Moi. New York: Columbia University Press, 1986.

Lenski, R.C.H. *The Interpretation of the Acts of the Apostles 15–28*. Minneapolis: Augsburg Fortress, 2008.

Litwak, Kenneth D. *Echoes of Scripture in Luke-Acts: Telling the History of God's People Intertextually*. London: T&T Clark, 2005.

Malina, Bruce J. "The Received View and What It Cannot Do: III John and Hospitality." *Semeia* 35 (1986): 171–94.

Manning, Gary T. *Echoes of a Prophet: The Use of Ezekiel in the Gospel of John and in Literature of the Second Temple Period*. LNTS 270. London: T&T Clark, 2004.

Marguerat, Daniel. *Les actes des apôtres (1–12)*. Vol. Va. Commentaire Du Nouveau Testament. Genéve: Labor et Fides, 2015.

Marshall, I. Howard. "Acts." *Commentary on the New Testament Use of the Old Testament*. Edited by D.A. Carson and G.K. Beale. Grand Rapids: Baker Academic, 2007.

Mathews, Kenneth. *Genesis 11:27–50:26*. NAC 1B. Nashville: Holman Reference, 2005.

Mauro, Philip. *The Hope of Israel: What Is It?* Swengel, PA: Reiner, 1970.

McWhirter, Jocelyn. *The Bridegroom Messiah and the People of God: Marriage in the Fourth Gospel*. SNTSMS 138. Cambridge: Cambridge University Press, 2006.

Menken, Maarten J.J., and Steve Moyise, eds. *The Minor Prophets in the New Testament*. LNTS 377. London: T&T Clark, 2009.

Merrill, Eugene H. "Paul's Use of 'About 450 Years' in Acts 13–20." *BSac* 138.551 (1981): 246–57.

Metzger, Bruce M., and Bart D. Ehrman. *The Text of the New Testament: Its Transmission, Corruption, and Restoration*. 4th ed. New York: Oxford University Press, 2005.

Motyer, J. Alec. *The Prophecy of Isaiah: An Introduction and Commentary*. Downers Grove, IL: InterVarsity, 1993.

Moyise, Steve, and Maarten J.J. Menken, eds. *Deuteronomy in the New Testament: The New Testament and the Scriptures of Israel*. LNTS 358. London: T&T Clark, 2007.

Niehaus, Jeffrey. "Amos." Pages 315–494 in *Minor Prophets: Hosea, Joel and Amos*. Edited by Thomas Edward McComiskey. Exegetical and Expository Commentary. Vol. 1. Grand Rapids: Baker, 1992.

Novick, Tzvi. "Eschatological Ignorance and the Hafṭarah on Acts 13:27." *NovT* 54 (2012): 168–75.

Ovid. *Metamorphoses*. Translated by David Raeburn. London: Penguin Classics, 2004.

Pervo, Richard I. "Direct Speech in Acts and the Question of Genre." *JSNT* 28 (2006): 285–307.

Petersen, David L. "Hebrew Bible Form Criticism." *RSR* 18 (1992): 29–33.

Peterson, David. "The Motif of Fulfilment and the Purpose of Luke-Acts." Pages 83–104 in *The Book of Acts in Its Ancient Literary Setting*. Edited by Bruce W. Winter and Andrew D. Clark. Vol. 1 of *The Book of Acts in its First Century Setting*. Edited by Bruce W. Winter. Grand Rapids: Eerdmans, 1993.

Phinney, D. Nathan. "The Prophetic Objection in Ezekiel IV 14 and Its Relation to Ezekiel's Call." *VT* 55 (2005): 75–88.

Pietersma, Albert and Benjamin G. Wright, eds. *A New English Translation of the Septuagint*. New York: Oxford University Press, 2007.

Powell, Mark Allan. "Echoes of Jonah in the New Testament." *WW* 27 (2007): 157–64.

Rahlfs, Alfred, ed. *Septuaginta*. Stuttgart: Deutsche Bibelgesellschaft, 1979.

Richard, Earl J. "The Old Testament in Acts: Wilcox's Semitisms in Retrospect." *CBQ* 42 (1980): 330–41.

Richard, Earl J. "The Creative Use of Amos by the Author of Acts." *NovT* 24 (1982): 37–53.

Riffaterre, Michael. *Text Production*. New York: Columbia University Press, 1983.

Robertson, O. Palmer. *The Books of Nahum, Habakkuk, and Zephaniah*. 2nd edition. Grand Rapids: Eerdmans, 1990.

Rosner, Brian S. "Acts and Biblical History." Pages 65–82 in *The Book of Acts in Its Ancient Literary Setting*. Vol. 1 of *The Book of Acts in its First Century Setting*. Edited by Bruce W. Winter and Andrew D. Clark. Grand Rapids: Eerdmans, 1993.

Sasson, Jack. *Jonah: A New Translation with Introduction, Commentary, and Interpretations*. AB 24B. New York: Doubleday, 1990.

Schaff, Philip, ed. *Jerome: The Principal Works of St. Jerome*. Translated by W.H. Freemantle. Vol. 6. Nicene and Post-Nicene Fathers Series II. Grand Rapids: Chistian Classics Ethereal Library, n.d.

Schniedewind, William M. *Society and the Promise to David: The Reception History of 2 Samuel 7:1–17*. New York: Oxford University Press, 1999.

Shelton, John. "The Healing of Naaman (2 Kgs 5.1–19) as a Central Component for the Healing of the Centurion's Slave (Luke 7.1–10)." Pages 65–87 in *The Elijah-Elisha Narrative in the Composition of Luke*. Edited by John S. Kloppenborg and Joseph Verheyden. London: T&T Clark, 2014.

Shepherd, William H., Jr., *The Narrative Function of the Holy Spirit as a Character in Luke-Acts*. Atlanta: Society of Biblical Literature, 1994.

Simon, Uriel. *Jonah: The Traditional Hebrew Text with the New JPS Translation*. Translated by Lenn Schramm. JPSBC. Philadelphia: Jewish Publication Society, 1999.

Soards, Marion L. *The Speeches in Acts: Their Content, Context, and Concerns*. Louisville: Westminster John Knox, 1994.

Spero, Shubert. "'But Abraham Stood yet Before the Lord.'" *JBQ* 36 (2008): 12–14.

Stone, Timothy J. "Following the Church Fathers: An Intertextual Path from Psalm 107 to Isaiah, Jonah and Matthew 8:23–27." *JTI* 7 (2013): 37–55.

Strauss, Mark L. *The Davidic Messiah in Luke-Acts: The Promise and Its Fulfillment in Lukan Christology*. JSNTSup 110. Sheffield: Sheffield Academic Press, 1995.

Strom, Mark R. "An Old Testament Background to Acts 12.20–23." *NTS* 32 (1986): 289–92.

Stuart, Douglas. *Hosea-Jonah*. WBC 31. Nashville: Thomas Nelson Publishers, 1987.

Talbert, Charles H. *Reading Acts: A Literary and Theological Commentary on the Acts of the Apostles*. Macon, GA: Smyth & Helwys, 2005.

Tannehill, Robert C. *The Acts of the Apostles*. Vol. 2 of *The Narrative Unity of Luke-Acts: A Literary Interpretation*. Philadelphia: Fortress, 1989.

Tigay, Jeffrey H. *Deuteronomy*. JPSTC. Philadelphia: The Jewish Publication Society, 1996.

Tucker, W. Dennis. *Jonah: A Handbook on the Hebrew Text*. BHHB. Waco, TX: Baylor University Press, 2006.

Van de Sandt, Huub. "An Explanation of Acts 15.6-21 in the Light of Deuteronomy 4.29-35 (LXX)." *JSNT* 46 (1992): 73–97.

VanGemeren, Willem A. *Psalms*. Edited by Tremper Longman III and David E. Garland. Rev. ed. EBC 5. Grand Rapids: Zondervan, 2008.

Verheyden, Jozef. "The Birthing of the New Testament: The Intertextual Development of the New Testament Writings." *Bib* 87 (2006): 439–42.

Wall, Robert W. "Peter, 'Son' of Jonah: The Conversion of Cornelius in the Context of Canon." *JSNT* 29 (1987): 79–90.

———. "The Function of LXX Habakkuk 1:5 in the Book of Acts." *BBR* 10 (2000): 247–58.

Wedderburn, A.J.M. "The 'Apostolic Decree': Tradition and Redaction." *NovT* 35 (1993): 362–89.

Wenham, Gordon J. *Genesis 16–50*. WBC 2. Dallas: Word, 2015.

Wifstrand, Albert. *Epochs and Styles: Selected Writings on the New Testament, Greek Language and Greek Culture in the Post-Classical Era*. Edited by Lars Rydbeck and Stanley E. Porter. Translated by Denis Searby. WUNT 179. Tübingen: Mohr Siebeck, 2005.

Williams, C.S.C. *A Commentary on the Acts of the Apostles*. 2nd rev. ed. BNTC. London: Adam & Charles Black, 1964.

Witherington, Ben. *The Acts of the Apostles: A Socio-Rhetorical Commentary*. Grand Rapids: Eerdmans, 1997.

Zimmerli, Walther. *Ezekiel: A Commentary on the Book of the Prophet Ezekiel*. Translated by Klaus Baltzer. Vol. 1. Hermeneia. Philadelphia: Fortress, 1979.

Бахтин, Михаил Михайлович. *Проблемы поэтики Достоевского*. Москва - Augsburg: Werden-Verlag, 2002.

Гроссман, Леонид Петрович. *Поэтика Достоевского*. Москва: Государственная академия художественных наук, 1925.

Primary Sources

OLD TESTAMENT

APOCRYPHA AND SEPTUAGINT

MODERN AUTHORS

SUBJECTS

www.ingramcontent.com/pod-product-compliance
Lightning Source LLC
Chambersburg PA
CBHW070027100426
42740CB00013B/2615
* 9 7 8 1 9 4 2 6 9 7 6 2 6 *